MW00851929

US BATTLE TANKS 1917–1945

A16

US BATTLE TANKS 1917–1945

STEVEN J. ZALOGA

OSPREY PUBLISHING
Bloomsbury Publishing Plc
Kemp House, Chawley Park, Cumnor Hill, Oxford
OX2 9PH, UK
29 Earlsfort Terrace, Dublin 2, Ireland
1385 Broadway, 5th Floor, New York, NY 10018, USA
E-mail: info@ospreypublishing.com
www.ospreypublishing.com

First published in Great Britain in 2024

A catalog record for this book is available from the British Library.

ISBN: HB 9781472858825; eBook 9781472858832; ePDF 9781472858849; XML 9781472858856

24 25 26 27 28 10 9 8 7 6 5 4 3 2 1

Artwork by Mike Badrocke, Tony Bryan, Richard Chasemore, Peter Dennis, Howard Gerrard, Terry Hadler, Hugh Johnson, Jim Laurier, Henry Morshead, Steve Noon, Felipe Rodríguez, Peter Sarson, and Johnny Shumate © Osprey Publishing Ltd.

Unless otherwise noted, all photographs in this book are from official US sources including the National Archives and Records Administration II in College Park, Maryland; the Patton Museum formerly at Fort Knox, Kentucky; the US Army Heritage and Education Center in Carlisle, Pennsylvania; the US Ordnance Museum formerly at Aberdeen Proving Ground in Maryland; and the Library of Congress in Washington, DC.

An AUSA title

Cover, page design and layout by Stewart Larking
Index by Alison Worthington
Printed and bound in India by Replika Press Private Ltd

Osprey Publishing supports the Woodland Trust, the UK's leading woodland conservation charity.

To find out more about our authors and books visit **www.ospreypublishing.com**. Here you will find extracts, author interviews, details of forthcoming events, and the option to sign up for our newsletter.

CONTENTS

INTRODUCTION

Prior to World War II, the US Army procured fewer tanks than any of the major armies of Europe. Yet in World War II, the United States manufactured more armored fighting vehicles than any other country. This book examines the early roots of US tanks through their dramatic transformation in World War II.

Until the late 1930s, the US Army shared the popular illusion that the United States could remain outside the turmoil of future European and Asian conflicts. Tanks were widely viewed as useless for traditional American military missions, such as border security on the Mexican frontier or colonial policing in the Philippines. In the late 1930s, as the probability of American involvement in the wars in Europe and Asia increased, so too did US Army interest in expanding its tank force. In 1940, the United States Army began consolidating its scattered infantry tanks and cavalry combat cars into the new Armored Force, planning to quickly create a mighty force of dozens of armored divisions. When the Armored Force was formed, the US Army could barely field a handful of tank battalions. The shocking defeat of France in May–June 1940 also led to the formation of a separate Tank Destroyer command, aimed at creating a force specifically to counter Germany's blitzkrieg tactics.

The scale and speed of American rearmament was strongly accelerated by President Franklin Roosevelt's policy to establish the United States as the "Arsenal of Democracy." Besides arming the rapidly expanding US Army, he intended to use America's considerable industrial resources to reinforce Allied armies with American weapons. Roosevelt proclaimed that the United States would manufacture 44,500 tanks in 1942 and 70,000 by 1943. United States tank production in the 1930s had averaged only 55 tanks annually, and the peak pre-war annual production in 1940 was only 365 tanks. Roosevelt's objectives proved to be overly optimistic. Yet the US industry did manage to increase tank production a hundredfold from only 365 in 1940 to about 35,000 tanks and tank destroyers in 1943. The Lend-Lease program eventually absorbed about 40 percent of US tank and tank destroyer production, with Great Britain being by far the largest recipient. As a result, there was very strong British influence in US tank development and production, especially in the formative period of late 1941–42, when American tank manufacture began to expand.

American tank development was strongly shaped by the policies of the Army Ground Forces (AGF), the branch of the Army responsible for creating and deploying US combat units. The pillars of its weapons policies were "battle-worthiness" and "battle-need." The "battle-worthiness" policy can be traced back to the experiences of the American Expeditionary Force (AEF) in France in 1917–18. In too many cases, equipment purchased for the Army proved to be insufficiently durable in actual combat. Since US units fought 3,000 miles or more away from America's industrial centers, it was essential that equipment be as reliable as possible.

"Battle-need" stemmed from similar roots. US weapons had to be shipped thousands of miles from America's industrial heartland to distant battlefields in Europe and the Southwest Pacific. An exotic panoply of specialized weapons was unacceptable; standardization on a core of standard weapons was essential. In the case of tanks, the need to transport these weapons over vast distances discouraged the US Army from acquiring heavy tanks for most of the war. One of the unexpected deficiencies of the "battle-need" policy was the premise that weapons would only be developed if requested by the fighting arms. The problem with this aspect of the policy was the tyranny of time. When the need for a new weapon had become manifest on the battlefield, it took precious months to undertake development, start production, ship the new weapon to the combat theater, and train the troops to use and maintain it. In the case of tank development, this policy was at the heart of a controversial failure in 1943–44 to field tanks and tank destroyers capable of dealing with new German tanks such as the Panther.

This book looks at American tank development from multiple perspectives. The Army's Ordnance Department was the agency primarily responsible for the engineering development of new tanks and tank destroyers. However, the requirements for the new weapons were strongly shaped by the requirements of the AGF headquarters in Washington, DC. AGF requirements were based on evolving trends such as unit organization and tactical doctrine, as well as feedback from the combat theaters based on recent battlefield experiences. As a result, the engineering aspects of tank development are depicted here in the broader perspective of tactical trends and combat experiences of the US forces in World War II. While this may seem obvious, many histories of US tank development view it entirely from the engineering perspective of the Ordnance Department.

This book is derived from the numerous books that the author has previously written for Osprey Publishing, notably in the New Vanguard and Duel series. The New Vanguard series looks at tank development in detail, while the Duel series examines particular tanks in comparison to their adversaries. For readers interested in more depth than what is presented in this book, these other titles provide far more detail than is possible here in this short survey. They are listed in the "Further Reading" section at the end of this book.

CHAPTER ONE
US TANKS OF WORLD WAR I

ON THE EVE OF THE GREAT WAR

As in many other countries, the earliest American armored combat vehicles were armored trains. These were first used in the Civil War and saw use at the turn of the century in the troubles along the Mexican border. Although well armored and well armed, armored trains obviously were limited in their mobility due to their dependence on rails. A more versatile armored combat vehicle was the armored car. The first American armored cars emerged in the early 1900s, often as private ventures. Major Royal P. Davidson, superintendent of the Northwestern Military and Naval Academy on Lake Geneva in Wisconsin, is most closely associated with the earliest efforts. After arming some small automobiles in 1899–1900, Davidson built the first modern American armored car in 1909 on a Cadillac chassis. Davidson's armored vehicles were demonstrated to the US Army, but none were taken into service.

The outbreak of World War I in Europe in 1914 encouraged US companies to privately develop armored cars for potential export. The Autocar Company in Ardmore, Pennsylvania, manufactured armored machine-gun carriers for Canadian forces in small numbers. The US Congress funded the first US Army armored cars in 1915. In July 1916, the two prototype armored cars were sent to Texas to support Gen. John Pershing's Punitive Expedition into Mexico. They saw little or no combat but were used to patrol the border. Early experiences with these primitive armored cars exposed their tactical shortcomings. The added weight of the armor placed enormous stress on their suspensions and engines. The narrow tires had such high ground pressure that the armored cars were road-bound in most circumstances. Nevertheless, armored car construction continued on a small scale around the United States, funded by local donations for National Guard units.

The first efforts in American tank design can be traced to America's prosperous agricultural tractor industry. Companies such as Holt, Caterpillar, and C. L. Best manufactured a wide range of tractors for industrial and agricultural use. As the war in Europe coagulated into muddy trench warfare, European armies began to buy more and more tractors from the United States. These were used for military tasks such as towing heavy artillery. American tractors were instrumental in early European tank designs since they were at the forefront in track and suspension technology.

Several enterprising American firms tried to drum up European business by offering armored tractors. Edwin Wheelock, general manager of the Pioneer Tractor Company of Winona, Minnesota, supplied the British War Office with plans for a 25-ton armored tractor in April 1915 some months before the first British efforts to develop a tank. Whether this unsolicited proposal had any influence on the British tank program is unrecorded, though Wheelock later claimed that it did. The Automatic Machine Company of Bridgeport, Connecticut, proposed an Automatic Land Cruiser to the British War Office and the French war ministry in July–August 1915. The Oakland Motor Company constructed the "Victoria tank" in December 1915 based on a British requirement. Although not accepted for production, the vehicle appeared at war bond drives around the United States. Numerous American "tanks" appeared after the first British use of tanks in 1916. In most cases, these were simply commercial tractors with sheet-metal structures that were intended for patriotic parades.

The US entry into World War I in April 1917 accelerated US Army interest in tanks. The US Army had very little detailed technical information about French and British tanks. In July 1917, the Army issued two work orders to the Peoria branch of the Holt Company to build technology demonstrators. Both were armed with a single 75mm M1916 pack howitzer, based on the Vickers 2.95-inch mountain gun. These guns were fitted in a ball mount at the front, and there were additional machine guns in barbettes on the side. The tanks were protected by ⅝-inch boiler plate rather than steel armor due to their experimental role.

Vehicle A Model E, later called the Gas-Electric Monitor, was based on the Holt 75 tractor along with a new armored body. It was powered by a Holt 90hp gasoline engine that was linked to a General Electric Company generator that powered two electric motors on either side of the tank. The layout resembled contemporary French tanks such as the Schneider CA 1 rather than British tanks.

ABOVE The Vehicle A Model E, later called the Holt Gas-Electric Monitor, was armed with a 75mm mountain gun in the bow and a water-cooled .30-cal machine gun in sponsons on either side.

RIGHT The strangest American tank of 1917 was the Vehicle B Model E. Photos of this tank are rare, and this one shows it on display in a hangar at Aberdeen Proving Ground in 1925 with its 75mm M1916 pack howitzer seen in the lower left.

BOTTOM The Holt Steam-Driven Three-Wheel Monitor at the Aberdeen Proving Ground, Maryland, in 1918. (Artwork by Felipe Rodríguez © Osprey Publishing)

Vehicle B Model E, later called the Steam-Driven Three-Wheel Monitor, was less conventional. This was based on Holt wheeled agricultural tractors, but with the large 8-foot, sieve-grip tractor wheels in front and the steering wheel at the rear, the reverse of the usual layout. Propulsion was provided by the Doble-Detroit Steam Motors Company, consisting of two steam engines with a combined output of 150hp.

Both of the Holt Monitors were completed in late 1917 and subjected to Army trials at Aberdeen Proving Ground in early 1918. Neither Monitor displayed acceptable mobility or trench-crossing capability. By the time testing was complete, further development was canceled.

In the late summer of 1917, Gen. John J. Pershing, commander of the American Expeditionary Force in France, established a committee of officers to examine the AEF's needs for tank warfare. The report was issued on September 1, 1917 and recommended that a force of 20 infantry divisions would require five heavy and 20 light tanks battalions totaling 375 heavy and 1,500 light tanks.

On September 18, 1917, Pershing telegrammed the War Department that France wished the United States to manufacture 2,000 Renault FT light tanks in addition to the tanks needed by the AEF. Renault sent a representative to Washington in early November along with an initial set of manufacturing drawings. A sample of the Renault FT tank arrived in the United States on November 28, 1917. It was subsequently sent to the Maxwell Plant in Dayton, Ohio, which had been selected to head the program. Due to the scale of the production requirements, the Van Dorn Iron Works of Cleveland and the C. L. Best Company of Dayton were also invited to join the manufacturing effort. Due to the secrecy of the effort, the American-manufactured Renault FT was given the cover name 6-Ton Special Tractor.

The 6-Ton Special Tractor was the Americanized version of the Renault FT. This example is fitted with the early mount for the 37mm gun. None of these tanks reached France before the end of the war.

Engineering work on the 6-Ton Special Tractor began on January 1, 1918. The initial effort was to adapt the manufacturing drawings from their original metric measurements to American manufacturing standards. In addition, Ordnance decided to substitute an American Buda engine rather than trying to reverse-engineer the Renault engine. Contracts were issued to the three Ohio plants for 4,440 tanks at an average cost of $11,500 each.

In February 1918, the War Department informed the AEF headquarters that they could expect to receive 100 American-built 6-Ton tanks in April, a further 300 in May, and 600 per month in subsequent months. This estimate proved wildly optimistic. The original plan had expected that the French engineering drawings would be ready by December 31, 1917, when in fact they were not completed until nine months later in September 1918 due to the numerous changes that were necessary. As a result, the AEF had to turn to the French Army to supply French-manufactured Renault FT tanks for its light tank battalions. The production program ran into numerous hurdles due to the novelty and scale of the tank program.

The first three 6-Ton Special Tractors were completed in July 1918 using soft steel rather than armor plate. By September 1918, 12 had been partially built but without turrets, speedometers, tools, or accessories. The first complete 6-Ton Tractors were finished in October 1918. At the time of the armistice on November 11, 1918, 64 tanks were ready. The first two tanks arrived at the Langres tank school in France on November 20, 1918, a week after the war ended. Eight more arrived in France in December. At the end of the war, the production contracts were curtailed. Eventually, some 952 6-Ton tanks were completed, consisting of 372 gun tanks, 526 machine-gun tanks, and 50 radio-command tanks.

The US Army ordered 15,000 3-Ton Special Tractors from Ford in 1918. Fifteen were shipped to France shortly before the armistice, but the production contract was canceled after the end of the war.

LEFT Ordnance commissioned Ford to build 1,000 Mark I tanks that were similar to the Renault FT but better suited to American mass production. The production contract was canceled after the end of the war, and only a single example was manufactured.

BELOW LEFT The Skeleton Tank was an attempt to achieve the trench-crossing ability of the British rhomboid tanks with the lighter weight of the French Renault FT.

Due to the slow pace of the 6-Ton Tractor program, Ordnance held meetings with Ford Motor Company in March 1918 in the hopes of manufacturing tanks using large automotive facilities. Ford began work on two designs: the small 3-Ton Special Tractor, and the larger Mark I tank. The 3-Ton was a turretless tankette with a two-man crew and a single machine gun. It was powered by two Model T automobile engines that gave it a top speed of up to 8mph. The 3-Ton was expected to cost only $4,000 each, and a contract was issued for 15,000 tanks with production expected to reach 100 per day by early 1919. A test batch of 15 tanks arrived in France shortly before the end of the war. The AEF Tank Corps in France was not at all enthused about the puny tank and recommended that it be converted instead into an artillery tractor. In the event, only the first test batch of 15 tanks was ever completed, and the contracts were canceled after the war.

The Ford Mark I tank was based on the Renault FT configuration, but larger. Ford was awarded a contract for 1,000 tanks, but only a single prototype was completed after the armistice. The contract was canceled along with plans for the Mark II, a Ford-built copy of the Renault FT with a Hudson 60hp motor.

Another alternative to the Renault FT was the "Skeleton Tank" built by the Pioneer Tractor Company starting in June 1918. The idea was to combine the light weight of the Renault FT tank with the trench-crossing ability of the larger British designs. To cut down on costs, much of the structure was made from ordinary iron pipes, and some of the suspension elements were made of wood. Besides cutting down on weight, the Skeleton Tank was designed to be shipped to France as a knocked-down kit to be assembled once it arrived in France. The armored module in the center contained two Beaver 50hp engines and a crew of two. The completed tank weighed 8 tons, and it had a cross-country speed of 5mph. By the time the Skeleton Tank was ready, the war was over.

The largest and most sophisticated tank built in the United States during the war was a collaboration of the US Army Corps of Engineers and the Massachusetts Institute of Technology (MIT). Major Henry Adams of the Corps of Engineers developed a long-range flamethrower that used a steam

War Tank America was built at MIT in 1918 and powered by Doble steam engines. It is seen here on parade in Boston in 1918 before being shipped to France.

boiler to atomize and propel a stream of fuel oil about 90 yards. It was successfully demonstrated in November 1917, leading to a scheme to mount the device in a steam-powered tank as a weapon to attack German pillboxes. War Tank America – also known as the "Steam Tank" – was patterned on British rhomboid tank designs and was powered by a pair of Doble steam engines offering 500hp. It was designed by Prof. E. F. Miller, head of the MIT mechanical engineering department, and built at MIT in Cambridge under the direction of several Army officers. The plan was to mount the Flame Projector, Tractor Type, Mark I in the front of the tank as well as .30-cal machine guns in sponsons on either side. The Army did not have sufficient funds for the project, and it was built at a cost of $60,000 from the donations of Boston bankers. War Tank America weighed some 45 tons and was completed in early 1918. In September 1918, it was dispatched to France and demonstrated to Gen. John Pershing near his headquarters at Chaumont. It arrived too late to take part in any military actions.

In October 1917, Britain shipped a Mark IV tank to the United States for use in war bond drives. Several more followed in 1918, and they became a popular fixture at patriotic events around the United States. In December 1917, France, Britain, and the US joined in the formation of the Joint

TOP The most ambitious US tank program of World War I was the Mark VIII heavy tank, also called the "International" or "Liberty Tank." Here, one of these 38-ton tanks is seen on exhibit in Rock Creek Park, Washington, DC, on February 8, 1921 during an Ordnance exhibition for government officials.

ABOVE An interesting comparison of the three types of tanks manufactured in the United States in 1918–19. From left to right are the Ford 3-Ton Special Tractor, the 6-Ton Special Tractor, and the Mark VIII International heavy tank.

Inter-Allied Tank Committee. The British representatives suggested a joint US–UK–France collaborative effort based on the British Mark VIII heavy tank. France was working on its own future design, the FCM 1, and showed little interest. On January 19, 1918, Britain and the US signed an agreement for a joint assembly effort, with final assembly of the British and American components taking place at a facility near the frontlines at Neuvy-Pailloux, south of Paris. The plan was to manufacture 300 tanks per month, with an eventual objective of 1,500 tanks monthly by the end of 1918. The United States provided the engine, powertrain, and running gear, while British plants provided the armor and armament. The first mild steel hull of the "International Tank" was completed by the North British Locomotive Co. in Glasgow and was shipped to the United States in July 1918 for installation of American components. This prototype was completed on September 29, 1918 and began testing in October 1918. By the time of the armistice, some 100 tank kits had been completed in Britain, along with seven complete tanks. The various US plants had completed about 700 sets of parts by the time of the armistice. The US Army agreed to purchase the 100 kits from Britain. They were shipped to the Rock Island Arsenal, where final assembly of the "Liberty Tank" was completed in January–June 1920.

The Renault FT light tank was the most common type in service with the AEF in 1918, equipping Col. George S. Patton's 304th (1st Provisional) Tank Brigade. Capt. Ranulf Compton, commander of the 327th (345th) Tank Battalion, is seen here between the tanks. The tank on the left is fitted with the riveted omnibus turret with a Puteaux 37mm gun, while the one on the right has the Girod cast turret with an 8mm Hotchkiss machine gun.

AMERICAN TANKS GO TO WAR

The inevitable delays in tank manufacture in the United States made the AEF entirely dependent on tanks obtained from Britain and France. France agreed to provide the Renault FT for light tank battalions, and Britain agreed to provide the Mark V heavy tank. The French Army established a light tank school at Bourg/Langres. The French army agreed to provide enough tanks for two battalions, starting with the loan of 25 Renault FT tanks in March–June 1918 for the training center. The first combat tanks were delivered in three batches between August 21 and September 2, 1918 and consisted of 45 Renault FT tanks with machine guns and 30 tanks with 37mm guns. Led by Lt. Col. George S. Patton Jr., the new 326th (later 344th) and 327th (345th) Battalions were first blooded in the fighting near St. Mihiel on September 12, 1918. Their real trial-by-fire came later in the month during the Meuse–Argonne forest battles which began on September 26 and dragged on through November 1, 1918. Total combat losses were three Renaults in October and 29 in November 1918, from the 214 delivered by France, not counting the 25 training tanks. A total of 213 Renault FT tanks were sent back to the United States after the war.

Col. George S. Patton is seen here consulting with one of his tank company commanders from the 344th Tank Battalion on the afternoon of September 12, 1918, after the first American tank attack in the St. Mihiel salient had run out of steam. The rainy season had already begun, and the ground was "sticky, soggy, awful mud in which the tanks wallowed belly deep." Patton would pay the price for his aggressiveness a few weeks later on September 26, when he was severely wounded while checking on his tanks' progress during the Meuse–Argonne offensive. (Artwork by Steve Noon © Osprey Publishing)

Britain provided 47 Mark V tanks to the 301st Tank Battalion by October 1918 and 12 more after the war. The Mark V and Mark V* first went into combat in the assault on the Hindenburg Line on September 29, 1918. Losses of these tanks were heavy and totaled 33 by the end of the war, though some were later recovered. There are conflicting reports regarding the number of Mark V shipped back to the United States after the war, varying from 28 to 32.

RIGHT Renault FT, 2nd Platoon, Co. C, 344th Tank Battalion, 304th Tank Brigade, AEF, France, 1918. (Artwork by Felipe Rodríguez © Osprey Publishing)

BELOW The 301st Tank Battalion AEF was equipped with the British Mark V heavy tank. This was one of the Mark V sent back to the United States after the war and is seen during training at Camp Meade, Maryland, in the early 1920s.

CHAPTER TWO

US TANKS IN THE INTERWAR YEARS

TANK CORPS DISBANDED

In the aftermath of World War I, the US Army found itself with a substantial tank force including over a thousand light tanks and over a hundred heavy tanks. The "war to end all wars" led to considerable controversy in Army planning. The rising wave of isolationism in the country suggested that there would be no future involvement in high-intensity conflicts in Europe and that the Army would probably return to its usual role as a frontier constabulary on the Mexican border and in the colonies such as the Philippines. Under such circumstances, the need for a separate Tank Corps was viewed as an unaffordable luxury. From the AEF's limited experiences in 1918, tanks were not regarded as a decisive weapon, and many believed that they were not worth the cost or expense. The National Defense Act of 1920 subordinated the Tank Corps to the infantry branch. Most tanks served in companies attached to the regular infantry divisions, with another 15 light tank companies scattered around the country with the National Guard. By the mid-1920s, there were fewer than 500 tanks in service and the remainder in storage. For example, at the end of 1926 there were 320 6-Ton tanks and 72 Mk VIII heavy tanks in Regular Army units, plus 110 6-Ton tanks in the National Guard. The former head of the AEF Tank Corps, Col. S. D. Rockenbach, headed the tank school at Camp Meade with a light and heavy tank battalion. The infantry school at Fort Benning had a single tank battalion for training purposes.

6-Ton M1917 tank, 26th Tank Company, 26th Yankee Division (National Guard), Boston, Massachusetts, 1925. (Artwork by Felipe Rodríguez © Osprey Publishing)

Under these circumstances, tank development was starved for funds, and new tank construction ended for nearly a decade except for prototypes. From 1918 to 1928, the Army spent only $3.5 million on mechanization. Of this, only about $950,000 was spent on tanks and the rest on artillery tractors and artillery self-propelled mounts.

The tanks left over from World War I were far from ideal. Rockenbach viewed the Renault FT and 6-Ton tanks as too small and mechanically unreliable. The Mark VIII Liberty tanks were too slow, too heavy, too long, and too unreliable. The Mark V was widely regarded as the best of the wartime types, but there were too few and they were soon put in storage. Rockenbach wanted a new medium tank that could fulfill the role of both light and heavy tanks. An unstated but widely understood requirement was the need to improve the durability of new tanks. The World War I types were too much like medieval siege engines – useful for a single battle but quickly worn out. The tracks on the heavy tanks had to be replaced after 20 miles of use, and the light tanks had to be rebuilt after 80 miles of operation. The early tanks were so mechanically undependable that the Army used tank carriers to move them any appreciable distance to preserve their meager operating life.

The 6-Ton M1917 formed the bulk of the tank force and so was the subject of modest upgrade efforts through the 1920s. A new French Kegresse suspension with rubber tracks promised to increase mobility and durability. It was unaffordable. A handful of tanks received new engines.

EARLY CHRISTIE TANKS

The lack of funds for modern tank development did not deter at least one engineer from offering the US Army his own designs. J. Walter Christie was a colorful and eccentric automobile designer who had built over a dozen self-propelled artillery mounts for Ordnance in 1918–19. Christie's most

famous innovation was the "convertible" suspension. Christie came up with the idea for a hybrid suspension that utilized large road wheels for road travel; on reaching the battlefield, a set of tracks would be mounted for cross-country travel. As a result, the tank carriers would no longer be needed, saving a great deal of money. Christie's Front Drive Motor Company in Hoboken, New Jersey, received a contract for its M1919 convertible tank in November 1919. It was delivered in February 1921 to Aberdeen Proving Ground (APG) in Maryland for testing. The trials in the wheeled configuration were unimpressive since the large road wheels were rigidly mounted without springs. It was woefully underpowered and barely able to reach 7mph. In April 1921, after two months of disappointing tests, Christie asked for the trials to be suspended so that he could improve the design. Ordnance agreed, and after nearly a year, the tank was returned to APG for further trials. Now called the M1921 convertible tank, Christie had modified the front road wheels with substantial springs for a smoother road ride. The hull had been completely reconfigured, with the turret replaced with a fixed barbette. The 2.24-inch gun was mounted in the bow, and two machine guns placed in ball mounts in the forward part of the superstructure. Although the alterations did improve the automotive performance, the Army felt that the tank was still underpowered, that its maneuverability was poor, and that the tank was mechanically unreliable.

ABOVE The Christie M1919 attempted to adapt one of its self-propelled gun mounts into a tank. It was armed with a 2.24-inch gun in a conventional turret.

BELOW The Christie M1919 tank was completely rebuilt as the M1921 with the turret replaced by a barbette mount. The 2.24-inch gun was repositioned into the bow with .30-cal Browning machine guns on either hull side. It is seen here after getting stuck in a trench during trials at Aberdeen Proving Ground.

Ordnance developed a strong distaste for working with Christie. The designer saw himself as a genius, and his designs beyond reproach. He often refused to make changes requested by Ordnance. He did not have the perseverance or

ABOVE RIGHT Christie worked on a variety of amphibious vehicles in conjunction with Sun Shipbuilding Company of Chester, Pennsylvania. This is his Combined Wheel and Self-propelled Floating Type 75mm Gun Motor Carriage M1922. Christie is seen here on the left speaking to Secretary of the Navy Edwin Denby in hopes of winning a contract from the Marine Corps. Christie's two early amphibious designs were not considered seaworthy by either the Army or Navy.

RIGHT Christie attempted to redeem his previous designs by increasing its freeboard with an enclosed superstructure. This was tested during the US Navy's 1923–24 Fleet Exercise when it was launched toward the Culebra landing site on Puerto Rico from the submarine S-20. It had difficulties in the open sea and was subsequently tested in Chiriquí Lagoon by the 8th Company, 5th Marines.

patience to convert an intriguing design into a functional and reliable machine. The M1921 convertible tank was retired to the APG museum in July 1924, having cost the US Army some $82,000 not counting test costs. Near bankruptcy, Christie sold off his present and future patent rights for vehicle designs to the Army for $100,000 and reorganized his company as the US Wheel Track Layer Corporation in Rahway, New Jersey. Scrambling for cash, he sold the plans for the M1919 tank to the Soviet Union. Chief of Ordnance Maj. Gen. Clarence Williams complained that the Army had paid Christie $839,000 since World War I, netting the inventor a large profit while the Army did not have a single successful vehicle in service based on a Christie design.

ROCK ISLAND ARSENAL TANKS

The Army's tank development in the interwar years was centered at Rock Island Arsenal (RIA) in Illinois. Rockenbach favored the development of a new medium tank, and the program began in 1919. The head of the RIA design section at the time was Maj. Levin Campbell, who would lead Ordnance in World War II. The new design was heavily influenced by the British Medium D tank. The pilot medium tank M1921 was completed at RIA in December 1921 and delivered to APG for trials. It weighed about 22 tons, but its engine proved to be weak and unreliable. The second pilot, the medium tank M1922, entered trials at APG in March 1923. Lessons from these tanks led to the construction of the T1 medium tank that introduced a new 200hp Packard tank engine specially commissioned for tank use. This tank closely resembled the M1921 and was completed in May 1927. The Ordnance Committee recommended standardization as the M1 medium tank, which took place in February 1928. This standardization decision was withdrawn later in 1928 in no small measure due to resistance from the Corps of Engineers, who complained that the tank was too heavy for tactical bridging. Rockenbach had already left his influential tank school post, and support for a medium tank had weakened in favor of a smaller and cheaper light tank.

A pilot of the T1 medium tank was completed in May 1927. A 1928 Ordnance effort to standardize it as the M1 medium tank was thwarted by engineer resistance.

ABOVE The 6-Ton tank was modernized after the war by enlarging the engine compartment and substituting a more powerful Franklin 67hp engine. This version was called the 6-Ton M1917A1, and only a pilot and six series production tanks were rebuilt at the Holabird Depot in 1929–31 due to lack of funds.

RIGHT Harry Knox's T1 light tank series bore a strong resemblance to his T2 medium tank though smaller. Four T1E1 light tanks served with Co. A, 1st Tank Regiment, attached to the Mechanized Force at Fort Eustis in summer 1931.

In September 1923, the Ordnance Department hired an automobile designer, Harry A. Knox, to head its automotive development at RIA. Knox was 48 years old at the time and had been the founder of the Knox Automobile Co. in Springfield, Massachusetts, which manufactured automobiles and trucks prior to World War I. Knox would go on to become the most important American tank designer of the pre-World War II period. Although he is largely forgotten, Knox was responsible for most of the essential features of American tank designs, such as the vertical volute suspension, rubber block track, and a host of other designs.

Knox's first major project was the T1 light tank. It was intended to provide significantly greater durability than the 6-Ton M1917 tank and to serve as the basis for a family of vehicles, including a cargo tractor, mortar carrier, and self-propelled artillery. Trials of the T1 in 1927–28 were successful enough that a test batch of six more vehicles was authorized. Due to the complexity

The T1E2 seen here marked a shift from the French-inspired short 37mm gun to the long Browning 37mm gun.

of the design, RIA solicited bids from the major automobile companies to manufacture the new tank. No American manufacturers wanted to be bothered with such a puny order or to deal with the Army's notoriously bureaucratic procurement process. James Cunningham, Son and Company in Rochester, New York, was the sole bidder and winner of the contract.

To prove their durability compared with the old 6-Ton tanks, the Cunningham T1E1 light tanks conducted a road march from Camp Meade to Gettysburg, averaging 10mph on the 145-mile course. One of the tanks on trials at APG completed over 2,000 miles of tests over two months without serious breakdown. This was an astounding improvement over the 6-Ton tanks and marked a major milestone in American tank development. The successful trials of the Cunningham tanks led to their standardization as the M1 light tank in January 1928. As in the case of the M1 medium tank, standardization was withdrawn shortly afterwards due to several factors described below.

The T1E1 was succeeded by the T1E2 in 1929, with increased armor, increased horsepower, and an improved suspension. Infantry tactics at the time favored tanks firing on the move. The existing short 37mm M1916 gun was not likely to hit its targets and had a slow rate of fire. This led to some interest in a semi-automatic gun, and the T1E2 introduced the Browning 37mm E2 Auto-Gun M1924 that fired from a five-round clip. Infantry complaints about the rough cross-country performance of these tanks led to the design of a spring-hydraulic suspension that was fitted to the T1E3 in 1931.

Comparative technical data: US tanks of the 1920s

	6-Ton M1917	Christie M1921	T1 medium	T1E1 light
Crew	2	2	4	2
Length (feet/inch)	16′5″	18′2″	21′6″	12′8″
Width (feet/inch)	5′9″	8′4″	8′	5′10″
Height (feet/inch)	7′7″	6′10″	9′8″	7′2″
Weight (tons)	7.2	12.6	21.9	7.8
Engine (hp)	42	120	200	110
Max speed (mph)	5	13	14	17
Main gun	37mm M1916 or MG	2.24″ M1920	2.24″ M1920	37mm M1916
Machine guns	0	1	1	1
Max. armor (mm)	15	12	25	10

THE CHRISTIE DISTRACTION

Corps of Engineer concern over the weight of the T1 medium tank led to the start of the new 15-ton T2 medium tank in 1926. Powered by a 312hp Liberty aircraft engine, it had a very peppy performance, with road speeds up to 25mph. Nevertheless, the T2 quickly disappeared due to infantry distaste over front-mounted engine designs, engineer complaints about its weight, and the appearance of a rival Christie tank.

The T2 medium tank of 1929 was armed with a 47mm gun in the turret and 37mm gun in the hull. It had good mobility due to its 312hp Liberty engine. The infantry branch was not enthusiastic about it due to the front-mounted engine.

Christie's "wildcat," the M1928 convertible tank, seen here during US Army tests. Although extremely fast, it was a questionable weapon, being weakly armed and constructed of non-armor steel.

After the failure of his M1919 and M1921 tanks, Christie spent several years trying to perfect his convertible suspension. Patented in April 1928, the new design used identical large road wheels on all stations except the idler and drive sprocket. When the track was removed, the last road-wheel station was powered by a chain drive off the drive sprocket, while the front road wheel steered the vehicle. The suspension used large helical springs, mounted in protected tunnels within the armored hull. This provided a particularly smooth ride compared with the suspensions that dominated tank design at this time. To address the Army's criticism of the sluggish performance of the M1921, Christie used a surplus 300hp Liberty aircraft engine, which he claimed would permit a road speed of 70mph on wheels and 42mph on tracks. The M1928 was not a refined tank, having a bow-mounted machine gun that interfered with the driver. In addition, its flashy performance was due in part to its light weight of 5 tons, made possible by the use of thin sheet steel instead of armor.

Christie's M1928 tank was first displayed to the public on July 4, 1928. It appeared at a fortuitous moment, when a groundswell of younger Army tank enthusiasts was beginning to challenge the lethargy and doctrinal orthodoxy of the past decade. In 1927, Secretary of War Dwight Davis witnessed Britain's Experimental Mechanised Force at Aldershot during an official visit to the UK. On his return, he instructed the US Army to conduct a similar exercise. This began in the summer of 1928 at Camp Meade. The new T1E1 light tanks proved to be reliable performers compared with the decrepit WWI-era tanks. Nevertheless, many younger officers were concerned that they offered insufficient advance over the 6-Ton tank. In contrast, the performance of Christie's "wildcat" tank seemed miraculous and offered the technological promise of an escape from the horrors of static trench warfare and a new dawn of mobile offensive warfare.

On February 19, 1929, Secretary Davis directed Ordnance to purchase the M1928, and funds were approved in the Fiscal Year 1929 (FY29) budget. Disdainful of the Ordnance bureaucracy, Christie provided the M1928 at no cost to the Tank School at Fort Meade for testing but ignored Ordnance's May 1929 request for bids. As a result, the allotted funds reverted to the Treasury, delaying any purchase for at least another year until funding could be re-approved by Congress. Christie belatedly responded in July 1929 that he had spent $382,000 on the project, and so he wanted to sell eight of the tanks at a cost of $82,750 each, which amounted to a development cost of $47,750 each plus the actual manufacturing cost of $35,000 each. This was an impossible sum at the time, particularly after the advent of the Great Depression late in 1929.

Christie had been soliciting bids from foreign governments at the same time as his promotions to the US government. A Polish purchasing mission was offered one tank for $30,000 plus a further $90,000 for manufacturing rights, and Warsaw submitted a down payment. The Soviet Union was also bidding for the tank, and on April 28, 1930 purchased two M1930 tanks at a cost of $30,000 each, plus $100,000 for manufacturing rights.

Changes in Army leadership roiled the negotiations. The new Army Chief of Infantry, General Stephen Fuqua, was very supportive of acquiring the Christie tanks. As a result, the Ordnance Technical Committee on February 13, 1930 recommended the purchase of six M1928 tanks. The $250,000 in the FY31 budget earmarked for the purchase of six to eight Cunningham T1E2 tanks was redirected to the Christie tanks instead. The incoming Chief of Ordnance, Gen. Samuel Hof, was an old Ordnance hand who had been involved in the squabbles with Christie in the early 1920s. Based on a critical report from tank expert Capt. John Christmas, Hof was skeptical of the durability of the Christie tank and wanted to acquire only a single tank for trials before buying any more. In June 1930, the Army Chief of Staff, Gen. Charles Summerall, agreed with Hof. Christie was informed that his May 1930 bid for six tanks plus one configured as a cavalry armored car had been rejected. Instead, he was asked to make an offer for a single tank. Christie responded that would sell a single tank for the exorbitant price of $135,000. He further angered the Army officers involved in the negotiations by claiming that he had "spies" in the Army and government who kept him informed of the inner workings of the negotiations. He also threatened to use his political connections in Congress to pressure the Army into agreeing to a large purchase.

With the end of the fiscal year approaching and the FY31 tank funding about to revert back to the Treasury, Christie acquiesced to a lease deal. A $55,000 contract was signed on June 28, 1930, with Christie promising to deliver a single convertible tank for trials purposes while the Army would provide the Liberty engine and a suitable turret. The contract mandated a September 1930 delivery date. Christie was unable to make the deadline since he was already behind schedule on the delivery of the two Soviet tanks, finally dispatching the two Soviet "commercial tractors" on December 24, 1930. He reneged on the Polish contract in October 1930. The Army learned of Christie's duplicity as well as the much lower price he was offering to foreign buyers, further souring relations. The American M1930 Christie tank was delivered behind schedule to APG on January 19, 1931. The Liberty engine broke down after two days of testing, further delaying the trials. The powertrain was a constant source of problems since the engine was too powerful for the transmission; the Soviets had the same problem.

Egged on by Christie and his many supporters in the Army, Congressman Henry Barbour, the chairman of the House sub-committee on appropriations, held extensive Congressional hearings on the Christie tank in December 1930. Colonel Hiram Cooper, commandant of the Infantry Tank School, strongly praised the Christie tank as did Sereno Brett, a decorated World War I tanker and executive officer of the Experimental Mechanized Force at Camp Meade. Captain Llewellyn Tharp, who had commanded a company of American Mark V tanks in France in 1918, gave extensive testimony why the Christie tank was so much superior to Ordnance's T1E1.

Congressional pressure as well as support for the Christie tank from the infantry and cavalry branches forced Ordnance to purchase a larger batch of Christie tanks. Competitive bids were opened on June 4, 1931, and submissions were received from Christie and Nicholas Straussler from Britain. With Barbour's political support, it was a foregone conclusion that Christie would win the bid. On June 12, 1931, Christie was informed that his firm had won the negotiations and would receive $241,500 in FY32 for seven convertible tanks.

The production series of the T3 medium tank incorporated Christie's convertible wheel/track suspension. It is seen here in the wheeled configuration with the tracks stowed on the mudguards above the wheels.

TOP The cavalry was not happy with the short 37mm gun on their Christie T1 combat cars. As a result, at least one was modified by replacing the gun with a .50-cal heavy machine gun.

MIDDLE When Christie refused to upgrade the T3 convertible tank to infantry specifications, American LaFrance was given the contract to build the T3E2 convertible tank. As can be seen, one of the main changes was to widen the hull to accommodate a four-man crew.

BELOW A T3E1 medium tank named "Tornado" of Co. F, 67th Infantry Regiment (Medium Tank), during First Army maneuvers at Pine Camp, New York, in August 1935.

Christie T3E1 convertible tank, Co. F, 67th Infantry Regiment (Medium Tank). (Artwork by Felipe Rodríguez © Osprey Publishing)

Testing of the new tanks began in December 1931. Of the seven Christie tanks in Army hands, three were designated as T3 medium tanks and allotted to the infantry at Fort Benning. The remaining four were designated as T1 combat cars and sent to the cavalry at Fort Knox. The first tank used a chain drive to power the rear wheel when in road travel, but Christie switched to a gear drive on the remaining six tanks, leading to a change of designation to T3E1 medium tank. The tanks were handcrafted, and different problems cropped up on different tanks. Christie spent far more time on "lawyering and lobbying" and not enough time on quality control at his plant. Furthermore, he resisted Ordnance efforts to make improvements on designs that he regarded as unquestionably flawless.

The infantry wanted at least five tanks to create a normal tank platoon for field experiments. They also wanted several significant improvements, including a wider hull to accommodate a four-man crew. As a result, in October 1932, the Army issued a solicitation for five more tanks designated as T3E2. Christie was unwilling to make such extensive changes and became infuriated when Ordnance sent the bid requests to more than a dozen companies. He believed that he still controlled the patent rights, ignoring the previous Army payment for his patents. Ordnance anticipated legal action and had already been assured by government lawyers that a tank derived from the Christie concepts was within the Army's legal rights. Christie refused to participate in the bidding, and American LaFrance in Elmira, New York, won the contract on December 2, 1932 for $146,000 for five T3E2 tanks.

RIGHT The last of the convertible tanks was the T4, belatedly standardized as the M1 medium tank. This one served with Co. F, 67th Infantry Regiment (Medium Tank), during the Third Army maneuvers at Fort Benning in May 1940.

BELOW RIGHT M1 medium tank, Co. F, 67th Infantry Regiment (Medium Tank), 1940. (Artwork by Felipe Rodríguez © Osprey Publishing)

Christie began a political campaign to get the contract annulled, which dragged on for several years. He had alienated Gen. Hof, and many of Christie's supporters in the Army came to realize that the convertible tanks were poorly made. They quickly became "hangar queens" requiring constant maintenance. The diary of Robert Grow, later commander of the 6th Armored Division, recalled the problems with the new tanks: "Had three Christies running this AM. Took them out for rehearsal. Two promptly broke down. No. 3 Christie broke a crankshaft and camrod and tore the crankshaft open. A mean job. 19th Ordnance is pulling the engine." Ordnance publicized the fact that the Army had to spend more than $38,000 to rectify problems on the Christie tanks in 1932 due to chronic defects.

In the end, the US Army refused to have any further dealings with Christie, and his company went into receivership in 1934. Christie was saved from bankruptcy by a request from Morris Motors in October 1936. British military attachés in the Soviet Union had seen a dazzling display of the BT-5 tanks based on the Christie design in 1936, and there was Army interest in a comparable British Christie tank. Christie still officially owned the prototype M1928 tank and delivered this to the UK as a "farm tractor" plus manufacturing rights for $320,000. This led to the A13 and a subsequent line of British Cruiser tanks such as the Covenanter, Crusader, Centaur, and Cromwell using the Christie suspension.

The American LaFrance T3E2 bore a family resemblance to the Christie design except that the hull had been widened to accept a four-man crew. In many ways, this paralleled the Soviet experience with the BT series that had evolved into the wider A-20, and finally to the T-34 tank of World War II. The new 435hp Curtiss D-12 aircraft engine provided a maximum speed of 58mph on wheels and 35mph on track. The T3E2 suffered the same inherent problem of the Christie design, mating too powerful an engine with too delicate a transmission and final drive.

The next attempt to redeem the Christie design was the T4 convertible tank, designed by Knox's team at RIA. To get around the powertrain problems, a less powerful 268hp Continental engine was used, with a new transmission with controlled differential steering. These tanks proved to be the most successful of the Christie-inspired tanks and also the most numerous, with 19 produced at RIA in 1936–37. Due to the infantry's infatuation with machine guns, three of these were built in the T4E1 configuration, which used a turretless barbette configuration bristling with machine guns. Ordnance recommended standardizing these tanks in February 1936, but this was rejected on the grounds that they were no better armed or armored than the new M2 light tank but cost twice as much. This issue was raised again in 1939, and as a result they were designated as the M1 medium tank. This design

Three of the T4 convertible tanks were constructed in the T4E1 barbette configuration. This is the pilot and is armed with one of the early Browning T2 .50-cal machine guns with barrel cooling fins.

might have evolved into a modern medium tank as occurred in the Soviet Union with the T-34. However, the infantry branch was complacent about the need for greater firepower and improved armor due to its antiquated tank doctrine. The cavalry wanted the T4 but were unable to buy any due to budget constraints. Instead of a Christie-type tank comparable to the T-34, the US Army got the appalling M2 medium tank instead.

KNOX'S LIGHT TANKS

Knox's T1E1 light tank of 1928 represented a major step forward in durability over existing tank types, but the program suffered a series of setbacks in 1928–29. After a short-lived decision to standardize the type as the M1 light tank, the decision was rescinded due in part to infantry criticism of its unorthodox front-mounted engine. Infantry officers were not happy about the driver sitting so far back in the hull, and there were complaints about exhaust fumes leaking into the fighting compartment and fouling the gun sights. The archaic suspension offered a very rough cross-country ride, especially when compared with the Christie tank. Ordnance plans to procure T1E1 tanks with FY30 funding fell through when the money was diverted to the Christie project. The Soviet Union was on the verge of signing a contract with the Cunningham company in February 1930 to purchase 50 of the improved T1E2 tanks, but this deal was abandoned after the Soviet purchasing commission witnessed a demonstration of the impressive Christie tank in April 1930.

Testing of the British Vickers 6-Ton Tank in 1931 led to a complete redesign of the T1 light tank series with a much more modern suspension. This is the T1E4 light tank at Aberdeen Proving Ground in September 1932.

In June 1931, Ordnance tested Britain's new Vickers 6-Ton Tank Type A at APG. This was one of the most modern tanks of the time, and its semi-elliptic leaf-spring suspension and narrow-pitch track offered a much superior ride to the existing Ordnance designs. There was some concern over the fragility of the suspension, so Knox designed a new spring suspension patterned on the Vickers design, receiving a patent in March 1933. To address the infantry concerns over the T1E2 layout, Knox completely redesigned its next iteration, the T1E4, with a more conventional rear-mounted engine. Although the T1 series had been instrumental in creating an effective tank design at RIA, no serial production took place. The T1E6 weighed 10 tons, and in the spring of 1933, the Secretary of War, under engineer pressure, instructed Ordnance to limit future tanks and combat cars to 7.5 tons.

The Mechanized Force at Fort Eustis, Virginia, concluded its maneuvers in the summer of 1931. Douglas MacArthur, the new Army Chief of Staff, rejected pleas by some of the cavalry visionaries such as Adna Chafee for a permanent Mechanized Force, and it was disbanded in October 1931. Instead, MacArthur approved plans by both the cavalry and infantry to undertake mechanization on their own paths. Since the cavalry was not allowed tanks under the 1920 Congressional edict, this obstacle was avoided by designating the cavalry tanks as "combat cars." Due to a shortage of funds, both the infantry and cavalry were obliged to rely on a common RIA light tank design, differing mainly in the turret configuration.

The end of the T1 light tank program and the MacArthur mechanization decision started a new light tank program in June 1933 that would result in the most enduring and successful American light tanks of the interwar years. This program was slow in emerging due to funding cuts stemming from the Great Depression. But it would establish many of the signature technologies of American tanks of World War II, mostly designed by Harry Knox. There were two pilots for this series, both sharing common powertrains and similar hull designs. The powerplant was a Continental radial aircraft engine, and the steering used a controlled differential. The infantry's T2 light tank used Knox's spring suspension inspired by the Vickers design, while the cavalry's T5 combat car used a new Knox invention, a vertical volute spring suspension. While the pilots first used a conventional steel track, Knox designed a novel rubber block track with rubber bushings, later standardized as the T16 track. These two features – vertical volute suspension and the rubber block track – would become characteristic of American light and medium tanks for nearly a decade. In the event, the trials favored the more robust Knox vertical volute suspension over the Vickers-style suspension, and the T2 light tank was suitably altered as the T2E1.

The T2 light tank series eventually emerged in 1936 as the M2A1 light tank. It was armed with .50-cal and .30-cal machine guns in a single turret. It was short-lived, with only nine built due to the infantry's preference for twin-turret versions.

This family of light tanks and combat cars also marked a shift away from the old 37mm M1916 gun to the new Browning .50-cal heavy machine gun as their principal armament. The old French 37mm gun had never been intended for tank fighting, and its armor-piercing round was barely capable of penetrating 15mm (⅝-inch) armor even at 100 yards. The new air-cooled T2 machine gun had been developed at Springfield Armory for the cavalry as their principal anti-tank weapon both for horse transport and vehicle applications. Its projectile had been based on the German WWI 13mm anti-tank rifle projectile, and its armor-piercing round could penetrate 28mm (1.1 inches) of armor at 100 yards and 25mm (1 inch) at 500 yards. Ordnance recommended it for standardization in November 1933 as the .50-cal M2 HB (heavy barrel). Aside from its superior armor penetration compared with the old 37mm gun, its high rate of fire was a substantial advantage. US tank doctrine in the 1930s recommended fire-on-the-move tactics; a machine gun compensated for the inevitable inaccuracy inherent in such a tactic compared with a single-shot, slow-firing gun. The .50-cal was subsequently accepted by the infantry for the same role. After further improvements, both the T2E1 and T5 were accepted for serial production as the M2A1 light tank and M1 combat car. A total of nine M2A1 light tanks and 33 M1 combat cars were manufactured at RIA from the FY36 budget.

The small size of the US Army tank force was due in part to the very modest defense budget of the 1930s, as well as the strategic posture of the Army. Due to America's isolationist foreign policy, it was presumed that the US Army would not become entangled in another major war in Europe. The focus of the Army was homeland defense and policing the colonies and overseas possessions such as the Philippines, missions that did not require a large armored force.

TOP LEFT The infantry switched to twin-turret light tanks in 1936, nicknamed the "Mae West" tanks after the popular actress. This M2A2 Model 1936 shows the early cylindrical turrets, as well as the brush guard added to the hull side to shield the tools. This particular tank originally served with the 43rd Tank Company (National Guard) and became part of the new 191st Tank Battalion at Fort Meade during the September 1940 consolidation. It is seen here on parade in Baltimore, Maryland, in June 1941.

LEFT The M2A2 Model 1937 introduced a new turret design using flat plates instead of the curved plates used on previous versions. This is a tank from the 1st Armored Division during maneuvers at Fort Knox in 1941.

For most of the 1930s, the US Army had a nominal order of battle of two tank regiments, the 66th and 67th Infantry (Light Tanks), and seven organic tank companies attached to infantry divisions. In reality, the only active element of the tank regiments was a single tank company, Company F, 67th Infantry (Light Tanks), at the infantry school at Fort Benning, Georgia. Not counting experimental types, the US Army procured only 321 light tanks from 1930 to 1939, and the cavalry a further 148 combat cars.

RIGHT M2A2 light tank, 29th Tank Company, 29th Division (National Guard), 1939. (Artwork by Felipe Rodríguez © Osprey Publishing)

BELOW RIGHT Modern tanks were in such short supply in the years leading up to World War II that ordinary trucks were sometimes used as substitutes, carrying a large banner on their side. This is the First Army wargame near Winthrop, New York, on August 9, 1940, with an M2A2 Model 1936 light tank of the tank company of the 26th Yankee Division (National Guard) in the foreground.

The M2A1 light tank was not popular in infantry service due to the cramped turret. In the meantime, Ordnance had tested a barbette configuration on one of the T4 pilots as the T4E1, and also a twin-turret design on a T5 pilot as the T2E2. The twin turret was another inspiration from the Vickers 6-Ton "trench sweeper" tank. In the event, the infantry preferred the twin-turret option, and this became the most common configuration for the next several years. The twin turret configuration was standardized as the M2A2 light tank, with the first ten funded in FY36. This initial production batch was sometimes called the M2A2 Model 1935 since production started in 1935. The next production batch of 124 tanks was unofficially called the M2A2 Model 1936 and was produced mainly in FY37. The final production batch of 104 tanks was called M2A2 Model 1937, and they were funded mainly from the FY38 budget. Ordnance decided to shift from curved plate turret construction to the use of flat armor plate, and this occurred in the M2A2 Model 1937 production run. The M2A2 was the most widely produced version of the twin-turreted infantry light tanks, totaling 235. A variety of changes were introduced into the final batch of 73 FY38 infantry tanks, designated as M2A3. Eight of the M2A3 production tanks were powered by Guiberson diesels, designated as M2A3E1.

CAVALRY COMBAT CARS

The M1 combat cars were deployed with the 1st Cavalry (Mecz) and saw their first real display during the Second Army summer maneuvers in 1936. After initial maneuvers at Fort Knox, the 1st Cavalry (Mecz) made a 375-mile road march to Camp Custer, Michigan, a testament to the durability of the new generation of tanks. The cavalry also wanted to begin purchasing the T4 convertible tank, but due to its cost, this plan was abandoned. A new convertible tank, the T6, was designed, but its weight and twin-turret configuration led to its cancellation in November 1935 before a pilot was built. In its place, RIA began to adapt the existing M1 combat car by switching to the convertible configuration as the T7 combat car. Unlike previous convertible tanks which had employed solid rubber rims on their metal wheels, the T7 used a novel type of pneumatic tire to provide a smoother ride. This was designed by Capt. John Christmas, later to be instrumental in the design of the M4 Sherman tank. The pilot of the T7 arrived at APG for trials in August 1938, and a year later it took part in the First Army wargames near Plattsburg, New York. By this time, the existing combat cars had proven durable enough for long road marches, and the Mechanized Cavalry Board recommended a termination of efforts on convertible tanks due to their high cost and complexity.

LEFT M1 combat car, HQ, C Troop, 1st Cavalry Regiment, Fort Knox, 1936. (Artwork by Felipe Rodríguez © Osprey Publishing)

BELOW LEFT M1A1 combat car, E Troop, 13th Cavalry Regiment, Fort Knox, 1938. (Artwork by Felipe Rodríguez © Osprey Publishing)

ABOVE The M1 combat car resembled the infantry's light tanks but used a larger turret with the two machine guns on separate mounts. The original production series used curved plates. This is a combat car of the 1st Cavalry Regiment (Mecz) at Fort Knox in 1936.

ABOVE RIGHT The last attempt to redeem the Christie suspension was the T7 project in 1938. This mounted a new suspension with pneumatic tires to an M1A1 combat car. It was rejected by the cavalry because by this stage, the durability of the basic M1A1 precluded the need for such expensive approaches.

The technical evolution of the M1 combat car continued, mainly aimed at cutting costs and improving service life. Ordnance had been studying the use of the 250hp Guiberson T-1020 radial diesel engine since it promised greater engine life and lower cost. Three combat cars were built as the M1E1 with diesel engines in FY37 and a further seven in FY38. The most visible change in the combat cars was the decision to shift from a cylindrical turret to a polygonal turret. This was primarily due to the cost and complexity of dealing with curved armor steel, and the same process was undertaken with the infantry's light tanks. The combat cars with this feature were designated as M1A1, and they were manufactured in FY38.

RIGHT The M1A1 combat car was essentially similar to the M1, but the turret was constructed of flat armor plates. This vehicle served with C Troop, 1st Cavalry Regiment (Mecz), during the Third Army maneuvers in 1940. The large "2" painted on the bow was for aerial recognition during the wargame.

The M2 combat car introduced a heightened turret and an improved idler wheel. It was redesignated as the M1A1 light tank after the absorption of the cavalry combat cars into the Armored Force in summer 1940. This one served as the command tank of Maj. Gen. George S. Patton, commander of the 2nd Armored Division at this time. He is seen here talking to an umpire during the Third Army maneuvers in Louisiana in 1941.

To further reduce the ground pressure of the combat cars, Harry Knox had developed a trailing idler wheel design. Another improvement was the increase in the turret height to better accommodate the turret crew, called the Improved Cavalry Turret. These new features were incorporated in the FY40 production run as the M2 combat car, and 34 were built.

With war clouds brewing in Europe, the cavalry proposed expanding the 7th Cavalry Brigade (Mecz) into a full mechanized division. To equip this force, the cavalry recommended the procurement of 292 new combat cars with the Improved Cavalry Turret, protectoscope vision ports as developed for the infantry tanks, Guiberson diesel engines, and new pistol ports. This version was designated as the M2A1 combat car. As an offshoot of this project, the cavalry proposed upgrading 88 older M1 combat cars with the Improved Cavalry Turret as the M1A2 combat car. In the event, the Armored Force was created before these plans were realized, and neither the M2A1 nor M1A2 reached the production stage. With the disappearance of the "combat car" designation, the M2 became the M1A1 light tank and the M1 became the M1A2 light tank. The two mechanized cavalry regiments became the core of the new 1st Armored Division.

M1A1 light tank, command tank of Maj. Gen. Patton, 2nd Armored Division, 1941. (Artwork by Jim Laurier © Osprey Publishing)

Comparative technical data, US tanks of the 1930s

	T3 Christie	M2A2 light	M1 combat car	M1 medium	M2A4 light	M2A1 medium
Crew	2	4	4	4	4	5
Length (feet/inch)	18′	13′7″	13′7″	16′1″	14′7″	17′8″
Width (feet/inch)	7′4″	7′10″	7′10″	8′2″	8′4″	8′7″
Height (feet/inch)	7′6″	7′9″	7′5″	7′3″	8′2″	9′
Weight (tons)	11.2	9.5	9.4	13.5	12	42
Engine (hp)	338	250	250	268	250	400
Max speed (mph)	47	45	45	35	34	30
Main gun	37mm M1916	.50-cal M2HB	.50-cal M2HB	.50-cal M2HB	37mm M5	37mm M5
Machine guns	1	2	2	2	4	7
Max. armor (mm)	16	16	16	16	25	38

INCREASING ARMOR AND FIREPOWER

The standard US Army anti-tank weapon up through 1940 was the .50-cal M2 heavy machine gun. This was adequate for most tank fighting since 15–20mm tank armor was still widespread in the mid-1930s and the .50-cal could penetrate this at normal combat ranges. The Spanish Civil War of

LEFT The M2A4 marked the shift in infantry light tanks from machine-gun armament to the 37mm gun. This is an M2A4 of the 67th Armored, 2nd Armored Division, during the Third Army maneuvers in Louisiana in September 1941.

BELOW LEFT M2A4 light tank, Co. H, 66th Armored, 2nd Armored Division, Fort Benning, 1940. (Artwork by Felipe Rodríguez © Osprey Publishing)

1936–39 saw the first large-scale tank-vs.-tank fighting in history. The tanks that took part in this conflict, such as the Soviet T-26 and German PzKpfw I, were lightly armored. However, the dominant technical lesson from the fighting was that contemporary tanks were too thinly armored to face contemporary anti-tank guns such as the German 37mm gun or Soviet 45mm guns, and so European armies began building tanks that were resistant to 37mm guns. In 1938, American studies of the lessons of the Spanish conflict concluded that future US tanks should be armed at least with a 37mm gun, and that the armor basis of the vehicle had to be increased from the existing level of ⅝ inch (16mm), since this could be easily penetrated by a 37mm gun from any realistic combat range. The infantry had already selected a new 37mm anti-tank gun, and so this was selected as the armament for a new version of the M2 light tank series.

ABOVE A mock attack by Co. A, 69th Armored Regiment (Medium), 1st Armored Division in Castor, Louisiana, during the Third Army maneuvers on September 11, 1941, overrunning a towed 75mm anti-tank gun with its M3 half-track prime mover near the general store. The M2A1 medium tank introduced an enlarged turret with vertical sides.

RIGHT An evocative image of the changing of the guard in the US Army's mobile forces. A column from Troop A, 9th Cavalry, being passed by an M2A4 light tank of the 67th Armored, 2nd Armored Division, during the September 1941 maneuvers in Louisiana. The "M" painted on the M2A4 sponson indicates it was serving as a medium tank in the exercise due to the shortage of actual medium tanks.

In December 1938, the infantry branch authorized the construction of the improved M2A4 light tank, fitted with a single large turret with a 37mm gun, and protected with thicker 1-inch (25mm) armor. The modestly improved armor was not adequate to protect the tank against 37mm guns, but incorporation of gun-proof armor would have required a complete redesign of the tank, which the Army could not afford. Other important improvements included the incorporation of radio receivers in all tanks, radio transmitters in command tanks, and a switch from AM to FM radios. The pilot M2A4 was delivered for trials to APG in the spring of 1939. A committee examining the pilot recommended several changes. The committee was concerned that the long tube of the M6 37mm gun might lead to damage when traveling through wooded areas since it projected beyond the bow. So, for an entirely frivolous reason, the M5 37mm gun adopted for tanks was shortened by 5 inches from the towed infantry anti-tank gun, reducing its armor-penetrating capability.

By the time the M2A4 light tank was ready for production in May 1940, war had broken out in Europe. The US government recognized that its isolationist foreign policy was likely to be challenged, and with it, the need for a substantially enlarged and modernized US Army. Rock Island Arsenal was a boutique tank manufacturer hand-building tanks in small batches. As a result, a decision was made to shift tank production from RIA to larger commercial plants to permit a surge in production if war broke out. M2A4 light tank production began at a large railroad manufacturer, American Car & Foundry, in Berwick, Pennsylvania in May 1940. A total of 325 were manufactured in 1940 and four in January–February 1941 for a total of 329. Next, Baldwin Locomotive Works was given a contract for an "educational batch" of 36 tanks since it was presumed it would be building future light tanks. These were manufactured in February–March 1941, bringing total M2A4 light tank production to 365 tanks. In November 1940, Ordnance recommended that the shorter M5 tank gun be replaced by the M6 37mm tank gun, which had the same barrel as the towed infantry tank gun. Although this was approved prior to the end of M2A4 production, this series was only fitted with the M5 gun. Production of the M2A4 was relatively short-lived, as in June 1940 Ordnance recommended that the armor basis be increased from 1 inch to 1.5 inches. This was approved in July 1940, leading to the M3 light tank. The M3 light tank would become the most common US tank at the time of America's entry into World War II.

THE M2 MEDIUM TANK

The T4 medium tank program was short-lived due to the unpopular front-engine configuration. The Ordnance Committee recommended the start of the new T5 medium tank in May 1936. The chassis was an enlarged version of the existing light tank design, using three of the Knox vertical volute bogies per side instead of two. The infantry's obsession with machine guns reached ludicrous levels, with four .30-cal machine guns in barbette mounts around the superstructure, a pair of fixed machine guns in the hull front, a machine gun co-axial to the main 37mm gun, and provisions for two more machine guns on the exterior of the turret for anti-aircraft use. This brought the total to nine .30-cal machine guns! A soft steel pilot of the T5 Phase 1 medium tank reached APG for trials in February 1938.

The most embarrassing example of the infantry branch's infatuation with machine guns was the short-lived M2 medium tank. Aside from the four barbette machine guns, two machine guns in the bow, and the co-axial machine gun in the turret, two more machine guns were fitted to a preposterous mount to the turret sides for anti-aircraft defense. This tank was deployed with the 67th Infantry (Medium Tanks) during the Third Army maneuvers in 1940.

Ordnance officers had been advocating the use of a 75mm gun in medium tanks since the mid-1930s, and previous medium tank designs already had incorporated 47mm or 57mm guns. The decision against the use of a more powerful gun was due to the Chief of Infantry, Maj. Gen. George Lynch, who had declared that a weapon as powerful as a 75mm was "needless." Another odd concept incorporated into this tank was the provision of defector plates on the rear corners, which would permit the aft barbette machine guns to deflect their bullet stream into trenches below the tank.

The Phase I tank was designed to weigh less than 15 tons due to Corps of Engineer pressure, so the armor was a maximum of 1 inch (25mm). With reports from the Spanish Civil War becoming available, the designers at RIA received approval from Ordnance to increase the armor to 1.25 inches (32mm), with a 20-ton limit. This was incorporated into the next Phase 3 pilot; Phase 2 was only a design study. This pilot arrived at APG in November 1938. To provide the T5 with more firepower, the T5E2 was constructed with a 75mm pack howitzer in the right sponson, inspired by the French Char B1 tank. To avoid conflict with the Chief of Infantry's office, the T5E2 was officially labeled as a "gun motor carriage," implying a field artillery weapon. A small turret was included in the design for an optical rangefinder. Although stillborn due to infantry resistance, this would serve as the basis for the later M3 medium tank.

The production version of the T5, the M2 medium tank, retained some features of the Phase 1 such as the symmetric front hull, but used the thicker armor of the Phase 3. Production of 18 M2 tanks was funded in FY39, with production starting at RIA. Although a further 54 tanks were scheduled for FY40, the design had obvious shortcomings. Work on the improved M2A1 began in the summer of 1939. The hull remained much the same, but the armor was increased from 1.25 to 1.5 inches (32–38mm), and a more powerful version of the R-975 radial engine was used, boosting horsepower from 346 to 400hp. The most noticeable change was the turret, which shifted from angled to vertical sides to increase the internal volume. The testing was straightforward, and the M2A1 was substituted for the M2 in the FY40. However, the Army realized that RIA could not cope with the likely increase in medium tank production. Chrysler Corporation was brought in to construct a massive new tank arsenal in Detroit, with the M2A1 as its first product. An August 1940 contract called for the delivery of 1,000 M2A1 tanks by September 15, 1941.

The M2 and M2A1 medium tanks were the most embarrassing and ill-conceived American tanks of the 1930s. Aside from the excessive machine guns, they offered roughly the same level of armor and firepower available on the later light tanks such as the M2A4 in a much larger and clumsier design. The disparity between the size of this tank and its puny main armament was apparent to the testing team at APG. In their June 1940 report, they recommended it be armed with a 75mm gun or howitzer, a type of recommendation usually outside the purview of the testing organizations. Only a fraction of the machine guns could be used at one time. Of the

The T5E2 gun motor carriage was armed with a 75mm pack howitzer in the right sponson. The turret contained an optical range finder and a .30-cal machine gun. This configuration served as the basis for the next step in the evolution of the M2 medium tank family, the M3 medium tank.

five-man crew, the driver operated the two fixed machine guns, the two-man turret crew operated the co-axial machine gun, and the six remaining machine guns were operated by the two-man machine-gun crew inside the hull. The four rotor-mounted guns in the barbette were sighted through a telescopic sight with no periscope, so the machine gunners had poor situational awareness and would have needed direction from the other crew members. The anti-aircraft machine guns stowed on the turret were an even more bizarre idea. Although they could be fired from the turret, the awkward location and mounting made it virtually impossible to hit an enemy aircraft. The alternative was for the two hull gunners to stand up in the two hull roof hatches and employ the machine guns from the simple socket mounts fitted to the roof.

In the wake of the lightning German victory in Poland, on October 17, 1939 the chiefs of infantry and cavalry, Maj. Gen. George Lynch and John Herr, met to discuss the possible organization of the first US armored divisions. Lynch had extremely conservative views of the value of tanks, feeling that they were only useful in supporting the infantry by destroying enemy machine-gun nests. He deferred to the cavalry to lobby for deeper mechanization and suggested that all tanks under 10 tons go to the mechanized cavalry, and that only the tanks over 10 tons, namely the M2 and M2A1 medium tanks, remain with the infantry. The stunning defeat of France in the summer of 1940 swept away the intransigence of the conservative branch chiefs and led to the formation of a new mechanized arm under the leadership of one of the maverick cavalry commanders, Gen. Adna Chaffee.

The formation of the Armored Force on July 10, 1940 sealed the fate of the M2A1 medium tank. Chaffee and his staff had been studying the lessons of the Battle of France and had noted the German use of a 75mm gun on their PzKpfw IV medium tank; likewise, the French Char B1 bis was armed with a 75mm gun. With the Chief of Infantry no longer interfering with tank decisions, Chaffee held a meeting with Ordnance in August 1940 and insisted that medium tanks be armed with a 75mm gun. As a result, the August 15, 1940 contract with Chrysler for 1,000 M2A1 tanks was canceled two weeks later to await a new medium tank design. This was the M3 medium tank, which retained a 37mm gun in the turret but placed a 75mm gun in the hull similar to the French Char B1 configuration. As will be detailed later, this was due to a French effort to have the US manufacture the Char B1 bis in the United States and the provision of a set of engineering drawings. RIA was instructed to build 126 M2A1 medium tanks to satisfy short-term training needs, but production was cut short in August 1941 once Chrysler reached a monthly production rate of 80 new M3 medium tanks. In the event, only six M2A1 tanks were built in 1940 and 88 in 1941 for a total of 94.

Production of US tanks and combat cars 1931–40

Year	1931	1932	1933	1934	1935	1936	1937	1938	1939	1940	Total
Combat Cars											
T1		4									4
M1						33	23	30			86
M1A1, M1E1							3	31			34
M2										34	34
T2, T4, T5, T7	1			2			1				4
Light Tanks											
M2A1				1		9					10
M2A2						10	154	74			238
M2A3								73			73
M2A4										325	325
Medium Tanks											
T3, T3E1			3								3
T3E2				5							5
T4 (M1), T4E1						10	9				19
T5, M2, M2A1								2	18	6	26
Total	1	4	3	8		62	190	210	18	365	861

MARINE CORPS TANKS

Christie attempted to interest the US Marine Corps in several of his amphibious tank designs, but in the event, none were acquired. The Marine Corps formed its first light tank platoon in 1923 using eight 6-Ton M1917 tanks borrowed from the Army. In 1927, the platoon was deployed to the Marine garrison in Tientsin, China. In the early 1930s, the Marines began to search for a very light tank that could be deployed from a small landing craft. The Marmon-Herrington truck company was developing a small artillery tractor for China, and this was modified into a tankette as the CTL-3 (Combat Tank Light). The Marine Corps bought a platoon of five of these in 1937, followed by another platoon of the improved CTL-3A in 1939. In 1940–41, the Marines procured the Marmon-Herrington CTL-6 and CTM-3TBD tanks. These were the last purchases from Marmon-Herrington, in part due to continuing technical problems with the designs as well as innovations in Navy landing craft that permitted heavier tanks. Instead, the Marine Corps decided to purchase the same light tanks as the US Army. In the summer of 1940, the Marine Corps requested the transfer

RIGHT The Marine Expeditionary Force's Tank Platoon at Quantico, Virginia, was equipped with the 6-Ton M1917 tank. The platoon was deployed to Tientsin, China, in 1927 to serve with the garrison there.

BELOW A Marmon-Herrington CTL-3 of the 1st Platoon, 1st Tank Company, of the US Marine Corps in 1938. This could be armed with up to three .30-cal machine guns in the front hull mounts. The Marines sought tanks light enough to be delivered by existing Navy landing craft. Five of these were purchased in 1939.

of 36 of the new M3 light tanks from the Army, receiving the M2A4 light tank instead. These were the only M2A4 known to have seen combat in World War II with US forces, serving with the Marine 1st Tank Battalion on Guadalcanal in August 1942.

Five Marmon-Herrington CTM-3TBD were procured by the Marine Corps concurrently with the turretless CTL-6, the last of the Marmon-Herrington designs to be acquired. Both types were deployed to the Samoa garrisons during the war and never saw combat.

WAR ON THE HORIZON: ORGANIZING THE ARMORED FORCE

On the verge of its entry into World War II in December 1941, the US Army was well underway to a major expansion of its Armored Force. From an equipment standpoint, it had a sound light tank design in the form of the M2A4/M3 light tanks, and a mediocre medium tank in the form of its new M3 medium tank. This later deficiency was rectified when the M3 medium tank evolved into the M4A1 medium tank in early 1942 as is described below. The weakness of US medium tank design was largely due to the peculiarities of pre-war US Army organization. In spite of parsimonious budgets, there was the needless waste of two parallel and duplicative lines of light tanks for the cavalry and infantry branches. Medium tanks were beyond the cavalry's budget, while at the same time the infantry branch neglected medium tanks since its leadership in the late 1930s had an extremely narrow view of the roles and missions of tanks on the modern battlefield.

In spite of these organizational problems, the interwar tank developments provided the new Armored Force with a sound technical foundation. The many innovations of Harry Knox – vertical volute suspension, rubber block tracks, incorporation of aircraft engines into tanks – all helped to shape an American tank tradition that emphasized tank durability. RIA's contribution was not the only component of the success of American tanks in World War II. It was amplified by the 1939 decision to shift from the artisanal construction at RIA to mass industrial production at America's many automotive and railroad factories. This enhanced the durability of the Knox designs due to the quality control process in the American transportation industry. Tank durability is usually overlooked, but it transformed tank warfare and made the

M3 medium tank, Co. D, 2/67th Armored, 2nd Armored Division, 1941. (Artwork by Hugh Johnson © Osprey Publishing)

tank a decisive weapon on the contemporary battlefield. World War I tanks were useful as siege weapons to break an enemy's defensive line, but they were laborious to deploy and not robust enough to last more than a day or two of fighting. World War II American tanks, more so than any other combatant's tanks in World War II, were durable enough to operate for thousands of miles, and months of combat action, without major mechanical breakdowns. This made prolonged mechanized combat a reality.

The Spanish Civil War of 1936–39 was the first major conflict to involve the extensive use of tanks on both sides since World War I. It forced the US Army to reconsider its tank policy. The conflict made it clear that tanks would be an important element in any major war, even in a war involving rag-tag militias such as in Spain. In 1939, the US Army began to shift its infantry doctrine, no longer favoring the use of penny-packets of tanks in company-sized formations for infantry support, but instead shifting to the massed use of tanks with the battalion as the basic tactical unit. As a result, the scattered divisional tank companies were consolidated as the 68th Infantry (Tank), and in January 1940 they were all moved to the infantry school at Fort Benning.

OPPOSITET Tank Battalion (Light) Table of Organization and Equipment March 1, 1942. (© Osprey Publishing)

Armored (tank) battalion (light), TO&E 17–15, March 1, 1942

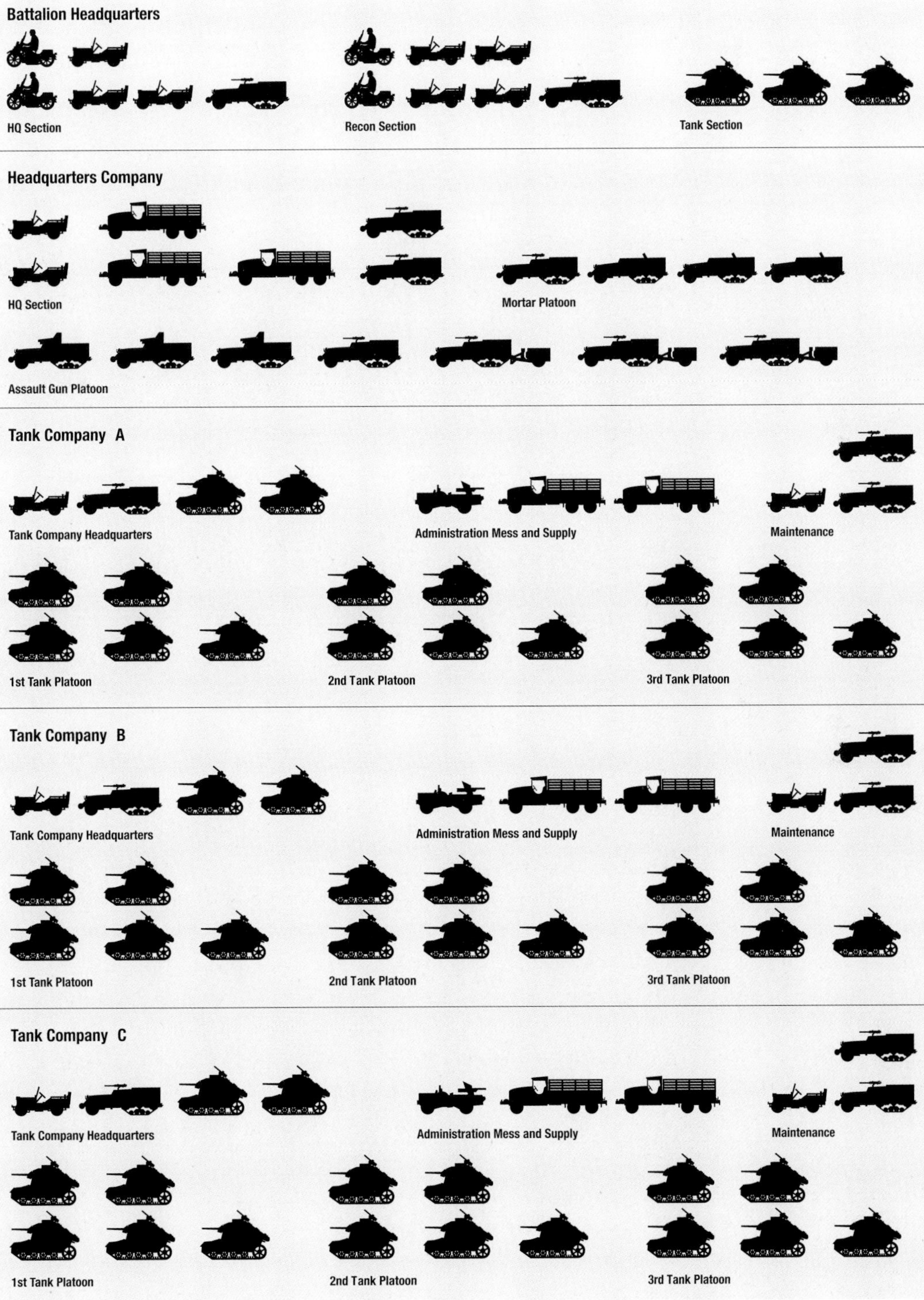

Battalion Headquarters

HQ Section

Recon Section

Tank Section

Headquarters Company

HQ Section

Mortar Platoon

Assault Gun Platoon

Tank Company A

Tank Company Headquarters

Administration Mess and Supply

Maintenance

1st Tank Platoon

2nd Tank Platoon

3rd Tank Platoon

Tank Company B

Tank Company Headquarters

Administration Mess and Supply

Maintenance

1st Tank Platoon

2nd Tank Platoon

3rd Tank Platoon

Tank Company C

Tank Company Headquarters

Administration Mess and Supply

Maintenance

1st Tank Platoon

2nd Tank Platoon

3rd Tank Platoon

When war broke out in Europe in September 1939, the US Army realized that its basic strategic premise that it would not fight again in a major European conflict might no longer be valid. The successful use of massed panzer formations in Poland in 1939 led both the US infantry and the cavalry to begin to experiment with larger armor formations. A Provisional Tank Brigade was created at Fort Benning in January 1940, and new armored units were tested during Army maneuvers in Louisiana that year.

The defeat of the French Army in May–June 1940 was a profound shock to US Army commanders. The French defeat, as well as the 1939–40 experiments, led to a decision on July 10, 1940 to combine the major mechanized elements of the infantry and cavalry into a new combat arm, the Armored Force, headquartered at Fort Knox, Kentucky. The name was chosen as a compromise – the infantry didn't want the cavalry term "mechanized" used, and the cavalry felt the same way about the term "tank," which its officers associated with the infantry. The new force absorbed all of the infantry's tank units, and the cavalry's various mechanized units as well. The initial organization included the first two armored divisions, the 1st based around the cavalry's 1st and 13th Cavalry Regiments, and the 2nd based around the infantry's 67th and 68th Infantry Regiments. A separate 70th GHQ Reserve Tank Battalion was created at Fort George Meade, Maryland, and an Armored Force Board was established to direct the development of new equipment. Command of the Armored Force was handed over to Gen. Adna Chaffee, long one of the most forceful advocates of Army mechanization.

The scale of the Army expansion was daunting: the 1941 scheme was 216 divisions, including 61 armored divisions. In May 1942 this was trimmed back to 187 divisions, with 47 armored divisions. This plan also included 23 armored corps headquarters, each managing two armored divisions and a motorized division with many supporting corps troops. These plans continued to be reduced to more realistic levels, and the total number of armored divisions in Army plans fell to 26 and then 20 armored divisions by the end of 1942. The schemes for a tank destroyer force were equally impressive, with 53 battalions created on paper in December 1941 and a scheme to increase this to 220 battalions.

The French defeat seemed to discredit the idea of scattering the tanks in separate tank battalions attached to the infantry, as the Germans had concentrated nearly all their tanks in the panzer divisions. In contrast, the defeated French had scattered much of their armor among infantry and cavalry formations. US Army tank policy rapidly swung from its previous practice of separate tank battalions to a concentration of the Armored Force. As a result, the primary focus of the new Armored Force was the creation of the new armored divisions. The tactical doctrine of these new formations was heavily

OPPOSITE Tank Battalion (Medium) Table of Organization and Equipment March 1, 1942. (© Osprey Publishing)

Armored (tank) battalion (medium), TO&E 17–25, March 1, 1942

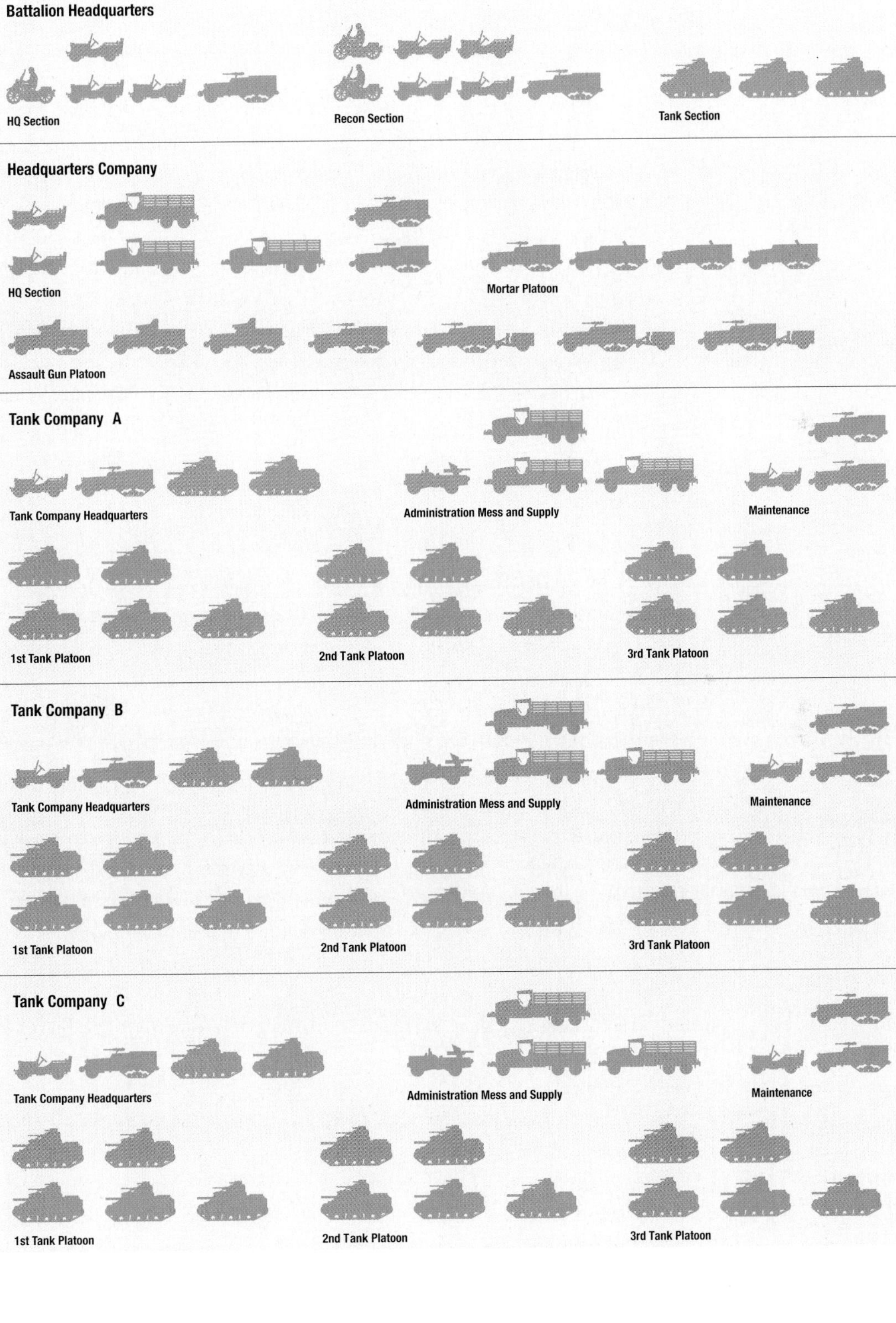

Battalion Headquarters

HQ Section

Recon Section

Tank Section

Headquarters Company

HQ Section

Mortar Platoon

Assault Gun Platoon

Tank Company A

Tank Company Headquarters

Administration Mess and Supply

Maintenance

1st Tank Platoon

2nd Tank Platoon

3rd Tank Platoon

Tank Company B

Tank Company Headquarters

Administration Mess and Supply

Maintenance

1st Tank Platoon

2nd Tank Platoon

3rd Tank Platoon

Tank Company C

Tank Company Headquarters

Administration Mess and Supply

Maintenance

1st Tank Platoon

2nd Tank Platoon

3rd Tank Platoon

shaped by the cavalry, which saw the armored divisions as a modern incarnation of the cavalry force, oriented toward a mobile exploitation role and not an infantry breakthrough role.

Of the armored formations of the major powers, the US armored divisions were most strongly influenced by the German example due to its impressive battlefield record. Nevertheless, the actual organization and doctrine of the US armored division gradually diverged from the German model, both due to institutional biases such as the US tank destroyer concept, as well as different approaches to organization, such as the US pattern of combat commands. The US conception of armored divisions also differed significantly from the British example. British doctrine saw the defeat of enemy armored formations as a principal mission of their armored divisions – a role that was not a preoccupation of the American doctrine. In some respects, US armored division doctrine shared similarities with the tank corps of the Red Army, which also saw the primary mission being exploitation after the breakthrough. This was not the result of direct emulation of the Red Army example, but rather of the similar cavalry tradition that permeated both these two armored forces.

The US armored division was intended primarily for offensive operations and was less suited for defensive missions due to its small infantry component. The armored division could not replace the traditional infantry division but complemented it by offering an alternative with more mobility and firepower. Compared with the 16 armored divisions formed during the war, the US Army eventually deployed 89 infantry divisions.

There were dissenting views, and the Chief of Infantry, Gen. George Lynch, insisted that the infantry still needed tank support to conduct their mission. The War Department approved the formation of new separate tank battalions alongside the new armored divisions, but at first these were very few in number. They were originally called GHQ tank battalions since they were envisioned as separate battalions assigned to the new General Headquarters (GHQ) that had been formed on July 26, 1940. In keeping with the new concept of the use of tank en masse, these battalions were not organic to the infantry divisions but would be assigned at army or corps level to carry out specific missions. This might include some distribution to the infantry division for support, but could also be used for independent missions or to reinforce the new armored divisions. Clearly, the pendulum had swung away from the infantry support mission.

Since the Chief of Infantry was preoccupied with the need to form, train, and equip large numbers of new infantry divisions, decisions on tank formations were dominated by the Armored Force. The decision to rely first on the M3 light tank, and after 1942 on the M4 medium tank, was largely due to the suitability of these designs for Armored Force doctrine. Distracted by

more pressing issues, the Chief of Infantry never paid much attention to the need for a specific infantry support tank akin to British infantry tanks such as the Matilda and Churchill, the Soviet KV and IS heavy tanks, or the German Tiger. As a result, the separate tank battalions were equipped with the same types of tanks and equipment as the battalions of the armored divisions, which tended to place a greater premium on mobility than on armored protection. Infantry support tanks such as the T14 that were developed for British Lend-Lease requirements were not accepted for US Army use.

Armored Force doctrine was tested in the 1940 and 1941 wargames. Here a column of M3 medium tanks of the 1st Armored Division confronts a 37mm anti-tank gun in Castor, Louisiana, on November 11, 1941, during the Third Army wargames as a flight of A-20 bombers flies overhead. As this photo suggests, the wargames were often quite contrived due to the limitations of existing training equipment.

The first of the new infantry tank battalions, the 70th Tank Battalion, was formed at Fort Meade, Maryland, on July 15, 1940 from the troops of the 1st Battalion, 67th Armored Regiment. This was the only separate tank battalion until four more were formed (191st to 194th Tank Battalions) between December 1940 and March 1941 using tank companies from National Guard infantry divisions.

Since the Army planned to use the GHQ tank battalions en masse, there was a need for a higher tactical headquarters to coordinate their operations. During 1941, the Army began the formation of the first tank groups with the activation of the 1st Tank Group (GHQ Reserve) at Fort Knox on February 11 and the 2nd Provisional Tank Group at Camp Bowie

The M5 3-inch gun motor carriage consisted of a Cletrac airfield tractor with a 3-inch M7 gun mounted on the rear. Although standardized, production was never authorized due to complaints about its slipshod design.

on March 1, 1941. The role of the tank group was to serve as a tactical and administrative headquarters for the several tank battalions attached to a corps or army. By July 1942 the number of tank groups had risen to five. The tank groups originally contained as many as five battalions, but it quickly became apparent that this was too many for its limited staff, and so the composition was reduced to two or three. Later, most of the tank groups were renamed as armored groups since they could administer mixed units, including both tank and armored infantry battalions. Ten new tank battalions were formed in June 1941 (751st to 760th Tank Battalions), six as medium tank battalions (751st to 755th) equipped with the new M3 medium tank, and the remainder in the usual light tank configuration, equipped with the M3 light tank. By the end of 1941, the number of GHQ tank battalions had risen to 15. The first of the new tank battalions to enter combat were the 192nd and 194th Tank Battalions, which formed the core of the Provisional Tank Group sent to the Philippines in the autumn of 1941. These units were overwhelmed with the rest of the US Army in the Philippines in April 1942, and their operations had little influence on evolving Army doctrine. In August 1941, the Armored Force received a new commander, Maj. Gen. Jacob Devers, due to Adna Chaffee's terminal illness.

In March 1942, the short-lived General Headquarters evolved into the Headquarters, Army Ground Forces (AGF). The chief of the AGF was Maj. Gen. Lesley McNair, who became the architect of the wartime US Army. He was instrumental in raising, training, and equipping the Army divisions. McNair favored lean, modular combat formations that would be easier to ship overseas. Once in theater, the divisions could be tailored to the local needs by adding additional specialized battalions such as tank, anti-aircraft, engineer, and tank destroyer battalions. The tank group fit neatly into his plans.

The three principal American tank types in early 1942. From left to right: the M3 light tank, M6 heavy tank, and M3 medium tank.

Although the AGF under Gen. McNair and the Armored Force under Gen. Jacob Devers seldom saw eye-to-eye, they both agreed on the need for the tank groups. The Armored Force pushed for the tank group idea since they had plans to deploy tank groups as mini armored divisions, not broken up in penny-packets for infantry support. As it would transpire in 1944–45, the flexibility and potential of the tank groups proved to be illusory, and their drawbacks far outweighed their benefits. The other alternative would have been to deploy the tank battalions as an organic element of each infantry division, but this approach seemed to have been discredited by the 1939–41 blitzkrieg campaigns.

The US Army was slow to appreciate that armored force tactics were evolving in the European war from the tank-heavy focus of the 1939–41 blitzkrieg campaigns to a new combined-arms approach. Both the German and Soviet armies gradually recognized that the infantry needed tank support, and by 1942–43, both armies regularly attached tanks or assault gun units to the infantry for close combat support.

The formation of new tank battalions was slow through 1942, since most of the focus was on creating new armored divisions. Only 14 more battalions were added in 1942, bringing the total to 27 after the loss of two in the Philippines. The separate tank battalions attracted so little attention that in early 1942 Devers remarked that "the tank battalions are now in the category of lost children and that we must take prompt action to bring them into the fold and be in closer touch with their needs and problems." Tank battalions were first committed to action in the Mediterranean theater at the end of 1942. Elements of the 70th and 756th Tank Battalions were deployed to North Africa in November 1942 as part of Operation *Torch*. Four more tank battalions were deployed to North Africa in January–March 1943 (751st, 752nd, 755th, 757th) along with two tank groups (1st and 2nd). Of these units, only the 70th and 751st saw extensive combat.

THE AMERICAN TANK DESTROYER

OPPOSITE TOP The M6 37mm gun motor carriage was an expedient light tank destroyer consisting of the ¾-ton truck with a 37mm anti-tank gun mounted on a pedestal on the rear bed.

OPPOSITE BOTTOM The M3 75mm gun motor carriage was a tank destroyer made up of the M3 half-track mounting an M1897 75mm field gun. This is an early production example with the small shield. This was subsequently replaced by a larger shield to offer the crew more protection from small-arms fire.

The defeat of France in May–June 1940 highlighted the threat of massed panzer attack. At the beginning of the war, each US Army infantry battalion had three 37mm anti-tank guns, each regiment had 18, and each division had 54. As became evident in the 1939–40 campaigns in Europe, cordon defense using infantry anti-tank guns spread thinly along the main line of resistance could not stop the advance of panzer divisions. The concentrated mass of armor would usually overcome the few anti-tank guns in that sector by sheer weight of numbers. To stiffen the anti-tank cordon, in October 1940 the heavy howitzer battalion in each US infantry division was reinforced with an anti-tank gun battery with eight 75mm guns in an expedient anti-tank configuration. Wargames suggested that more was needed, so on July 24, 1941, the War Department ordered the activation of an anti-tank battalion in each division. This battalion included the eight 75mm guns formerly in the artillery battalion, reinforced by two more companies of the new 37mm guns. Beyond these divisional battalions, the Army began to form separate anti-tank battalions under GHQ control. Several of these were used in the Louisiana wargames in the autumn of 1941.

The wargames revealed that organic anti-tank battalions were not the solution, since the divisions tended to deploy them in the main line of resistance, and not maintain them in reserve to respond to armored attack. As a result, when the enemy tanks suddenly appeared, it was difficult to extract the anti-tank guns from their position, move them to the threatened sector, and redeploy them in time to repel the enemy tank attack. Senior Army commanders concluded that what was needed was a vital mass of anti-tank weapons under centralized control that could be dispatched when a panzer threat was identified. The use of separate anti-tank battalions assigned at corps level seemed the best solution. There was some debate as to which combat arm would be responsible for the new weapons. The anti-tank concept was largely the brainchild of the artillery branch, but the War Department decided that it should be managed by a new command that could devote its full attention to the problem.

As a result, the Tank Destroyer Center was established at Fort Hood, Texas, in December 1941, headed by Gen. Andrew D. Bruce. He was an officer from the planning branch of the War Department who had overseen the tank destroyer project since 1940. On December 3, 1941, all anti-tank battalions were removed from the divisions, renamed as tank destroyer battalions, and placed under GHQ control. The change in name of the battalions was supposed to symbolize the change in tactics from defensive to offensive.

NEXT PAGE Tank Destroyer Battalion Table of Organization and Equipment June 8, 1942. (© Osprey Publishing)

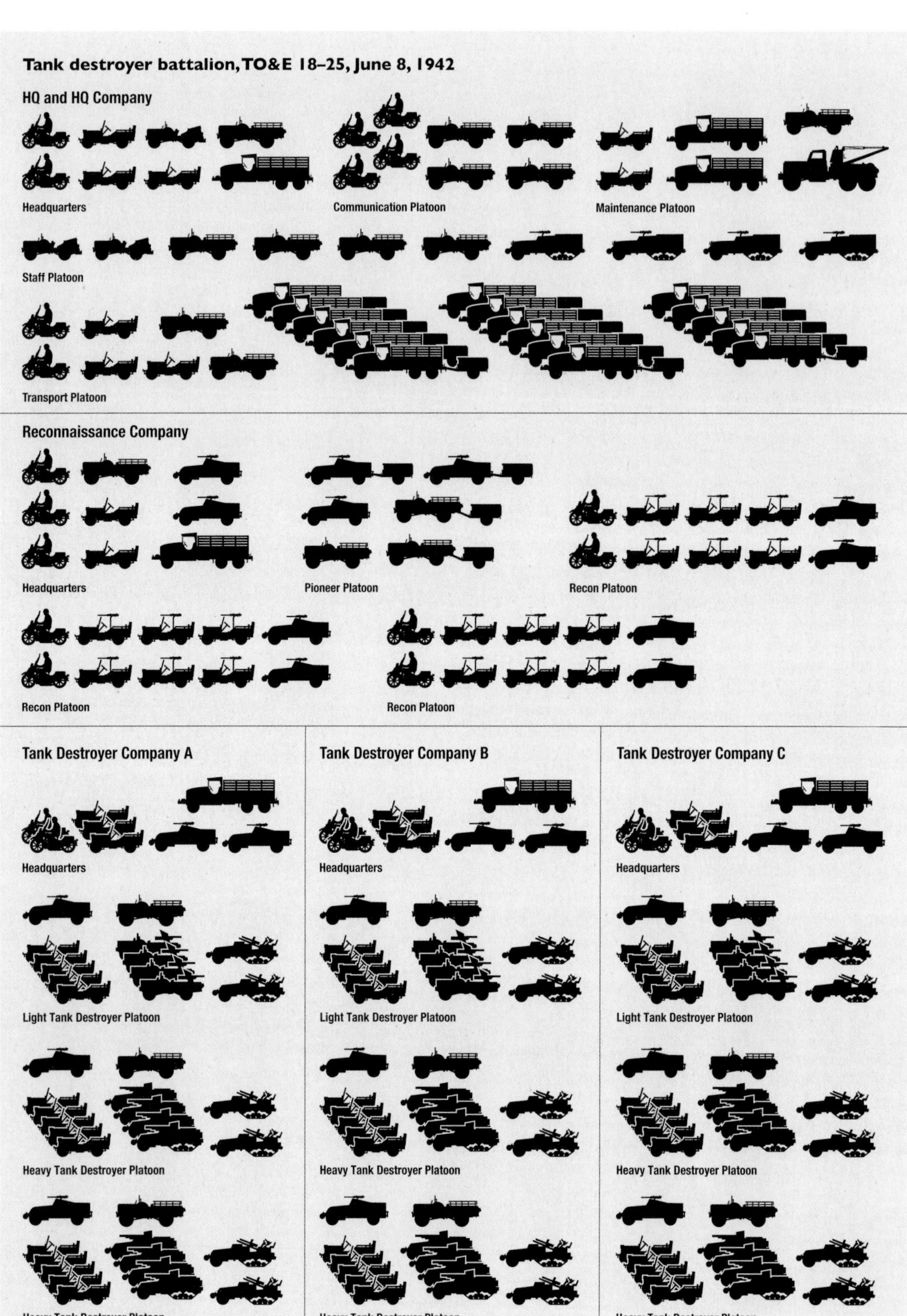

Tank destroyer battalion, TO&E 18–25, June 8, 1942
HQ and HQ Company
Headquarters
Communication Platoon
Maintenance Platoon
Staff Platoon
Transport Platoon
Reconnaissance Company
Headquarters
Pioneer Platoon
Recon Platoon
Recon Platoon
Recon Platoon
Tank Destroyer Company A
Headquarters
Light Tank Destroyer Platoon
Heavy Tank Destroyer Platoon
Heavy Tank Destroyer Platoon
Tank Destroyer Company B
Headquarters
Light Tank Destroyer Platoon
Heavy Tank Destroyer Platoon
Heavy Tank Destroyer Platoon
Tank Destroyer Company C
Headquarters
Light Tank Destroyer Platoon
Heavy Tank Destroyer Platoon
Heavy Tank Destroyer Platoon

Tank destroyer battalion (self-propelled), March 1, 1943

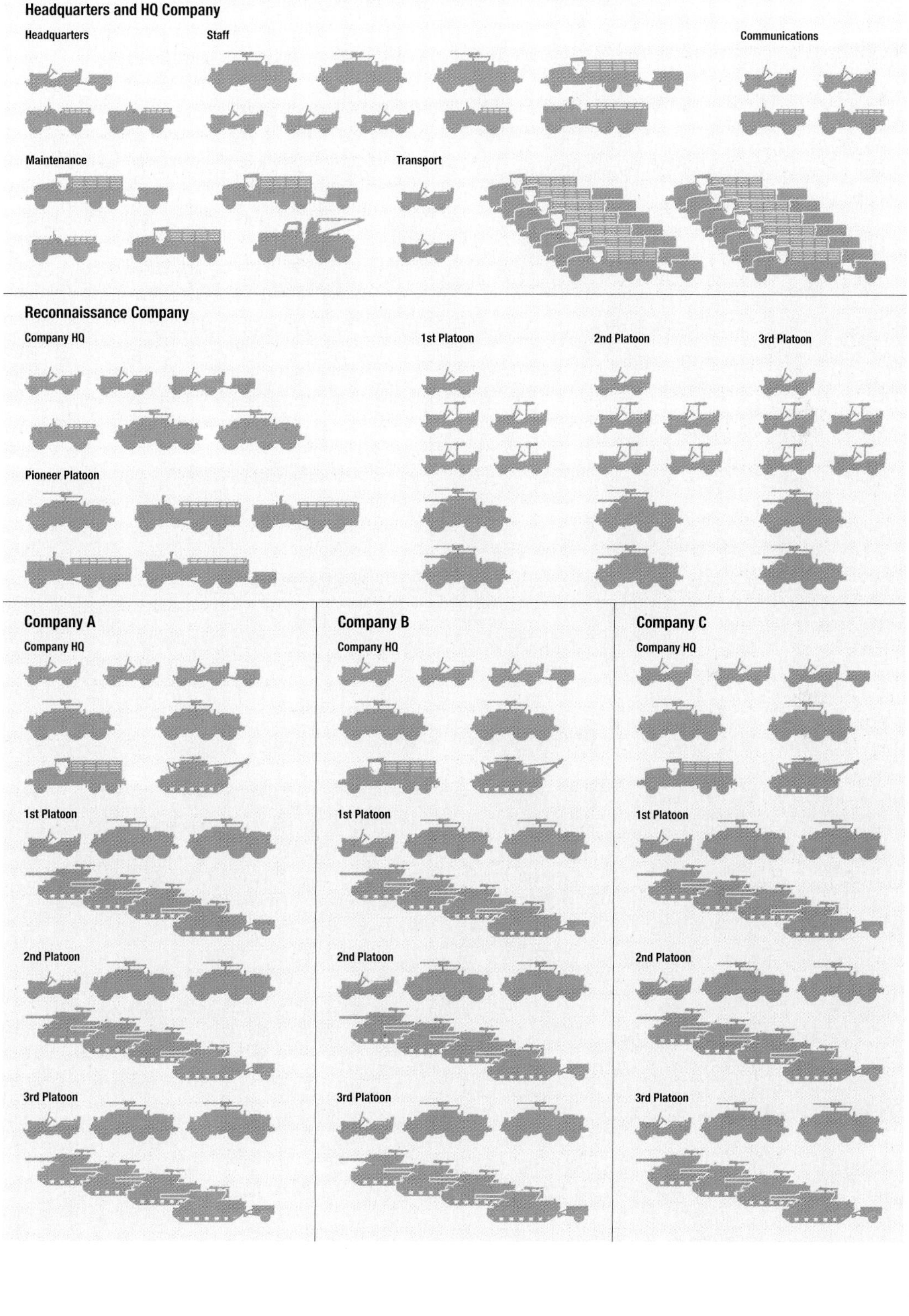

Headquarters and HQ Company

Headquarters

Staff

Communications

Maintenance

Transport

Reconnaissance Company

Company HQ

1st Platoon

2nd Platoon

3rd Platoon

Pioneer Platoon

Company A

Company HQ

1st Platoon

2nd Platoon

3rd Platoon

Company B

Company HQ

1st Platoon

2nd Platoon

3rd Platoon

Company C

Company HQ

1st Platoon

2nd Platoon

3rd Platoon

PREVIOUS PAGE Tank Destroyer Battalion (Self-Propelled) Table of Organization and Equipment, March 1, 1943. (© Osprey Publishing)

Bruce had been pushing for some time for a more dynamic response to the tank threat than the artillery branch's approach that favored towed guns. The new motto of the tank destroyers – "Seek, Strike, Destroy" – emphasized the view that speed and mobility were key. The tank destroyers would remain behind the frontlines in reserve, and when the panzer attack became evident, the tank destroyers would rush to the scene at high speed and destroy it in a fast-moving battle of maneuver.

Tables of organization and equipment were approved on December 24, 1941 for two types of tank destroyer battalions – light and heavy. The light tank destroyer battalion had three companies each, with 12 towed or self-propelled 37mm anti-tank guns, for a total of 36 per battalion. The heavy tank destroyer battalion had three companies each, with four self-propelled 37mm anti-tank guns and eight self-propelled 3-inch anti-tank guns. There was a surge of organization in December 1941 as 53 tank destroyer battalions were created consisting of 26 towed light battalions, two self-propelled light battalions, and 25 heavy battalions. The heavy battalions were often created from existing divisional anti-tank battalions. The large number of towed light battalions was a tacit recognition that better equipment was not yet available.

The issue of what type of weapons were ultimately needed for the tank destroyers was a long-running controversy within the Army, and a source of rancorous debate between Generals McNair and Bruce. McNair was an artilleryman and favored the use of towed guns as a more economical solution

BELOW The M10 3-inch gun motor carriage was based on the chassis of the M4A2 medium tank but with a lightly armored turret and superstructure. This is one of the pilots at Aberdeen Proving Ground in 1942, and the gun is pointing rearward in travel position. The early M10 suffered from a turret imbalance problem, and the first attempt to rectify it was to place steel grousers on the upper rear turret sides.

The crew layout of the M10 3-inch GMC tank destroyer. (Author)

to the tank problem; Bruce felt that towed guns were too slow to deploy, and he favored self-propelled weapons. The Armored Force weighed in and suggested that they use tanks. Bruce retorted that he wanted something faster and lighter than tanks, more akin to "a cruiser than a battleship." The tank destroyer advocates fixed on a legend from the 1940 campaign that the French Army had successfully used anti-tank guns mounted in the rear of trucks to defeat the panzers and saw this as a short-term technical solution to their problem. The first US Army tank destroyers were expedient designs rushed into production to equip the weaponless new battalions. The French 75mm gun was bolted into the back of the M3 half-track, resulting in the M3 75mm gun motor carriage (GMC), while the new 37mm anti-tank gun was placed on a pedestal mount in the rear of the Dodge ¾-ton truck to result in the M6 37mm GMC light tank destroyer.

A more satisfactory Ordnance design appeared in June 1942 as the M10 3-inch GMC, consisting of a 3-inch gun mounted in an open turret on the M4A2 medium tank chassis but with lighter armor than the basic tank version. General Bruce opposed the production of the M10 tank destroyer as being

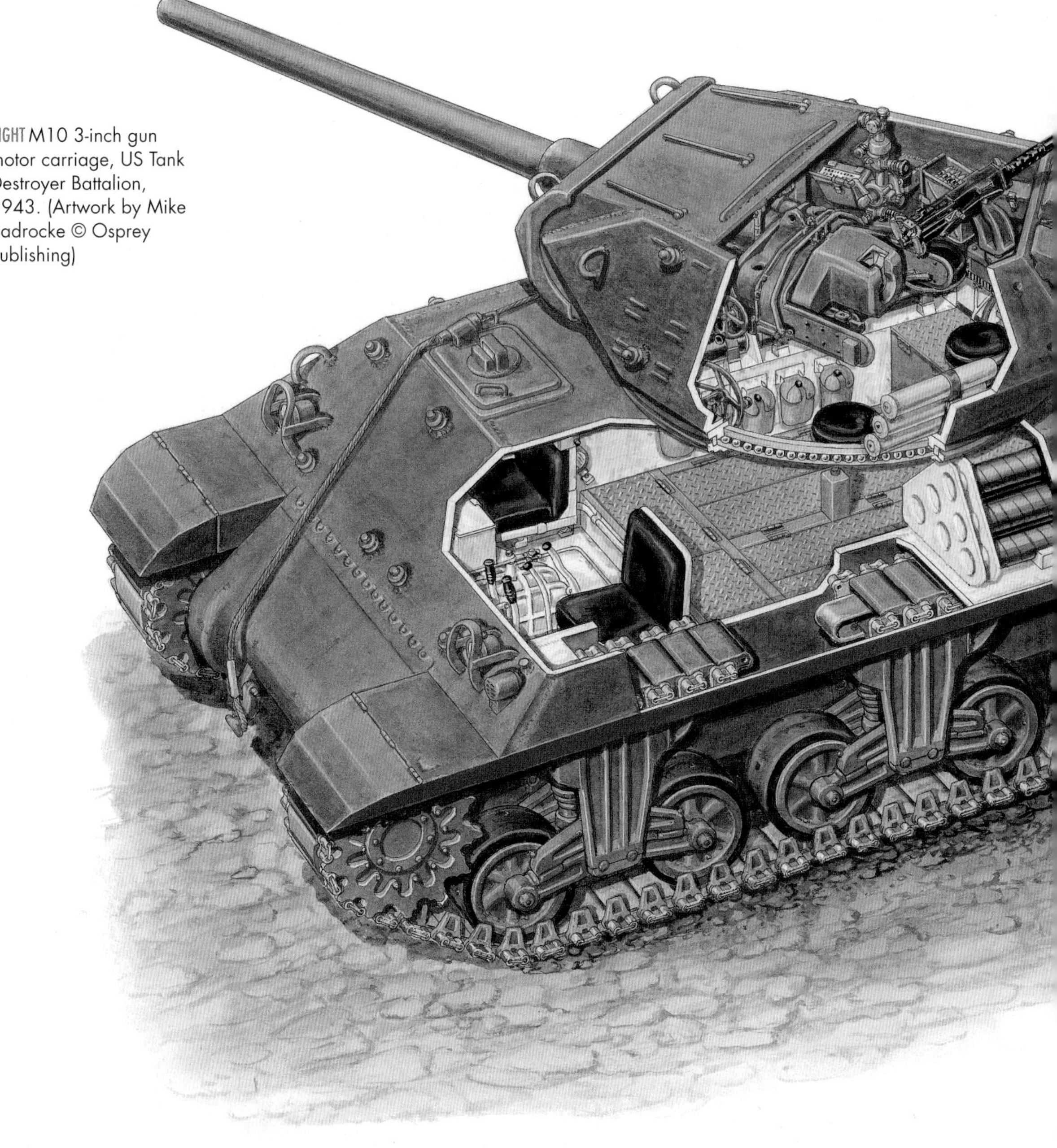

RIGHT M10 3-inch gun motor carriage, US Tank Destroyer Battalion, 1943. (Artwork by Mike Badrocke © Osprey Publishing)

simply another expedient design without the speed and agility he desired in a tank destroyer. He was overruled by the AGF, which wanted an adequate design in production as quickly as possible to equip the many new battalions. From March to August 1942, 27 more tank destroyer battalions had been formed, bringing the total to 80, and there was a desperate need for a modern weapon for these units. The first M10 3-inch GMC was completed in September 1942, and they were quickly put into service.

M10 turret interior. (Artwork by Richard Chasemore © Osprey Publishing)

CHAPTER THREE

US TANKS IN WORLD WAR II

THE TANK DESIGN PROCESS

Tank development in the US Army was undertaken by the Ordnance Department. Interplay between the various Army branches was managed by the Ordnance Committee, with periodic meetings chaired by an Ordnance officer and attended by the infantry, engineer, and other branches. Once a program was approved by the Ordnance Committee, the design was undertaken by a mixture of Army and industry teams. Usually, a small number of pilots were constructed and then subjected to testing to determine whether they were suitable for their intended role. At this stage, a weapon usually had a "T" prefix (Test), such as T26.

There were two principal types of testing: developmental and operational. Developmental testing usually began at the tank factories, which often had a small test range to conduct basic mechanical trials. Once these were completed, the prototypes were shipped to Army facilities, mainly to Aberdeen Proving Ground in Maryland. The development trials were intended to determine whether the design was automotively sound, as well as to test new sub-systems, such as the turret and weapons. During the developmental trials, an additional batch of prototypes were dispatched to the user branches to determine whether the new design satisfied the tactical requirements. Tank tests were primarily conducted by the armor branch at Fort Knox, Kentucky, and tank destroyers to Fort Bliss, Texas.

As a result of the trials, the Ordnance Committee could then approve or disapprove of the new design by recommending its adoption as "standard" Army equipment. As part of this process, the original "T" test designation was changed to a standard "M" number. For example, the experimental T6 medium tank became the M4A1 medium tank once it was standardized. Modification programs on an existing tank design received an "E" experimental suffix during development. For example, the M4E6 was the testbed for mounting the 76mm M1 gun on the M4 medium tank. Standardized variants received an "A" suffix, such as M4A1, M4A2, etc.

Some equipment was adopted for use as a temporary expedient, even if it did not satisfy all requirements. This equipment was considered "limited standard" and often retained its "T" designation since it had not been standardized. Examples include the Marmon-Herrington T14 light tank or the T1E1 mine exploder. When an older tank type was no longer acceptable for frontline use, it was downgraded from standard to limited standard, and eventually to obsolete. In this case, its designation did not change.

THE M3 LIGHT TANK

Although the M2A4 light tank was a substantial improvement over the previous light tanks and combat cars, it had technical and design problems. Work began on the improved M3 light tank in July 1940. The added weight of armor caused mobility problems on the M2A4 and was partly resolved by a shift to the enlarged rear idler that increased the area of ground contact. The long recoil mechanism of the M5 37mm gun in the M20 combination mount projected far outside the M2A4 turret, making it difficult to protect. A modified design was needed, resulting in the M5 37mm gun with a new short-recoil mechanism in the M22 combination mount. Finally, the existing 1-inch (25mm) armor was not deemed adequate to protect the tank from contemporary anti-tank guns. However, a frontal protection of 1.5 inches (38mm) of armor was all the chassis could bear, even though it did not offer proof against 37mm anti-tank guns at normal combat ranges. The M3 light tank entered production at American Car & Foundry in March 1941. This large railroad manufacturer would eventually become the second largest US tank producer during the war. The M3 was the most numerous US tank at the outbreak of the war and would be the principal US type to see combat in the first year of the war. The original production batch of 100 M3 light tanks were fitted with the D37812 riveted turret. The M3 turret underwent continual evolutionary improvement during production, starting with the new D38976 welded turret in April 1941.

The M3 light tank was an adequate if uninspiring design compared with its European contemporaries. The US Army in the 1930s was a backwater in armored vehicle design, and the M3 light tank was an inevitable reflection of

OPPOSITE The second production batch of M3 light tanks switched to the new D38976 welded turret in April 1941. These are some of the 427 M3 light tanks provided to the Brazilian Army in World War II.

LEFT The first hundred M3 light tanks were fitted with the D37812 riveted turret. This example served at the Cavalry Replacement Center at Camp Funston, Kansas, in March 1942, forming part of the cadre of the 9th Armored Division later that year.

this neglect. The M3 light tank was comparable or superior to older European designs of the late 1930s, such as the Soviet T-26S, the Polish 7TP, and the Czech/German PzKpfw 38(t). However, the Spanish Civil War experience had been interpreted very differently in Europe than in the United States, reinforcing a trend to larger, more heavily armored, and better armed tanks. Prior to the outbreak of World War II, most European armies had abandoned the light tank as the basis of their armored forces, favoring medium tanks that were larger and more than 5 tons heavier. In France, this led to the Somua S35 and Char B1 bis, and in Germany to the PzKpfw III and PzKpfw IV. The most radical solution was attempted in the Soviet Union, where the Spanish Civil War lessons inspired the T-34 design, which would replace both their infantry's light tanks and the cavalry's cruiser tanks. While the main influence in tank design in the 1920s and 1930s came from Britain and France, it was Soviet and German innovations that dominated the wartime experience.

Aside from US Army orders, Britain began ordering the American light tanks in late 1940 due to their own shortage of tanks. The first order for light tanks was 100 M2A4 light tanks. The further supply of the M2A4 was halted once the improved M3 light tank became available. The two new American tanks shared a confusing similarity in nomenclature – the M3 light tank and M3 medium tank – and Winston Churchill inspired the practice of renaming American tanks after American Civil War generals. The M3 light tank was

The Stuart saw its combat debut with the British Army in North Africa in November 1941 during Operation *Crusader*. The Stuart tanks had numerous small improvements added by workshops in Egypt, such as additional stowage bins and dust shields.

called the General Stuart, after the Confederate cavalry general J. E. B. Stuart, and the M3 medium tank was named the General Lee, after the legendary Robert E. Lee. None of these names were sanctioned by the US Army, nor were they commonly used by US troops during the war. However, the names did become popular in the United States after the war and are still widely used. They are used here for convenience's sake.

The Stuart tank did not conform to British design or tactical concepts. Although an infantry tank by US standards, it was lightly armored compared with British infantry tanks such as the Matilda. Nor did the Stuart have the range deemed necessary for a cruiser tank, being capable of only about 75 miles on firm ground and about 45 miles in rough desert conditions. However, in technical terms it was closer to the British cruiser tanks than to the infantry tanks, and so was used as such when first issued to units in the Western Desert in 1941. In terms of armament, its 37mm gun was similar to the standard British 2-pdr in anti-armor penetration at usual combat ranges but had the advantage of firing a high-explosive round that was useful in engaging targets other than tanks, such as anti-tank guns and infantry. If the British tankers were a bit wary of the Stuart's unfamiliar features, they were pleased with its automotive reliability compared with existing British cruiser tanks. By 1941, the Stuart was a mature design based on the proven Harry Knox components that had matured during the 1930s.

The first large shipment of Stuart tanks arrived in Egypt in July 1941. By the autumn of 1941, enough Stuarts had arrived to equip the three tank regiments of the famous "Desert Rats," the 7th Armoured Division. These units first saw combat in the November 1941 Operation *Crusader*. British tankers complained about the short range of the Stuart and its cramped turret, but the British problems in the Desert War were more tactical than technical.

The Stuart continued to see combat in the January 1942 fighting. But following Crusader, shipments of the more powerful M3 Lee and Grant medium tanks began to arrive. As a result, the British armored regiments began reorganizing, and gradually shifted to a composition of one squadron of Stuarts and two squadrons of Grants. The role of the Stuart continued to decline during 1942 as more modern equipment became available. When the new M4A1 Sherman medium tank began to arrive in the summer of 1942, the Stuarts were shifted out of the line squadrons, and transferred to reconnaissance. By the time of the El Alamein offensive in the fall of 1942, the Eighth Army was operating 128 Stuarts, about 11 percent of its force.

The United States Army first deployed the M3 light tank overseas in September 1941 to reinforce the US garrison in the Philippines. The two battalions in the Philippines played a significant role in the December 1941–April 1942 fighting up to the last battles on Bataan. The Stuart tank saw combat in British hands in the Asia-Pacific theater. Britain dispatched the 7th Armoured Brigade to Burma, including the 7th Hussars. The Stuart light tanks fought a series of costly rearguard actions, including several tangles with the Japanese 14th Tank Regiment. By the time the survivors of the unit reached British lines in India, only one Stuart remained in action. But the Japanese advance had been brought to a halt short of India.

A dramatic view as a pair of A-20 bombers conduct a mock raid on a tank column of M3 light tanks of the 34th Armored Regiment, 5th Armored Division, at the Desert Training Center in the Mojave Desert near Indio, California, in September 1942. The "M" on the turret indicated that the tanks were serving as substitutes for medium tanks during the exercise due to a shortage of actual medium tanks at the time.

M3 LIGHT TANK EVOLUTION

A major aspect of US tank production in 1941 was the adoption of new manufacturing techniques to increase production. A third turret for the M3 light tank, the D39273, was developed in the spring and summer of 1941. This used formed, rolled homogenous armor instead of face-hardened armor as on the two previous types. The basic thickness increased from 1 inch to 1.25 inches. This turret was readily distinguishable from the earlier flat-side turret by its rounded sides and horseshoe shape. Series production of this version began in October 1941, and by 1 February 1942, 1,360 had been completed. This version first saw combat with British forces in North Africa in spring 1942.

One of the main bottlenecks in US tank production was the reliance on radial aircraft engines, such as the Continental W-670 used on the M3 light tank. These same engines were also in demand for various types of aircraft, so the US Army attempted to find alternatives. Ordnance authorized the production of M3 light tanks powered by a Guiberson T-1020 diesel engine, and the first production of the M3 (Diesel) light tank began in June 1941. In total, 1,285 M3 (Diesel) light tanks were produced, about 22 percent of the M3 production. The diesel tanks were not popular in service, and Ordnance concluded that the problems were due to poor engineering and poor manufacturing inspection of the engine. In addition, the US Army was very

The D39273 was the third turret developed for the M3 light tank characterized by rounded sides and horseshoe shape. Series production of this version began in October 1941. This particular example was a pilot for a welded rather than riveted hull.

M3 light tank, 1st Armored Division, Tunisia, 1942. (Artwork by Jim Laurier © Osprey Publishing)

reluctant to deploy tanks fueled with both diesel and gasoline, preferring gasoline since it was also used in all the support vehicles. As a result, in March 1942 the Adjutant General directed that the diesel tanks were to be retained for stateside training where practical.

A fourth M3 turret type entered development in the summer of 1941. British liaison teams had recommended the use of a periscopic sight for the commander instead of a cupola. The turret was redesigned in early 1942, eliminating the cupola and adding two roof hatches. The new D58101 turret was sometimes called the "streamlined" or "low-profile" turret in the US Army. Production of this final version of the M3 light tank began in February 1942. This was probably the least popular turret configuration. A September 1942 evaluation was scathing: "This turret is practically useless as a fighting compartment. The tank commander and gunner are so cramped that they can operate only at greatly reduced efficiency. The two hatches in the turret are too small for quick ingress and egress to and from the vehicle." The US Army ignored the problems since it was an interim solution on the way to a significantly improved turret.

The final version of the M3 light tank used the D58101 turret. Externally, the turret resembled the D58133 turret of the later M3A1 tank but lacked the turret basket and fire control improvements of the later type.

Ordnance had been developing improved gun fire control systems for the M3 light tank since August 1941 that eventually became merged into an "integrated fighting compartment." A Westinghouse vertical-axis gyrostabilizer allowed the tanks to fire more accurately on the move. An Oilgear power turret traverse was also favored to facilitate turret rotation. A turret basket was needed to prevent the crew from having their legs catching on floor obstructions during fast traverse. The new D58133 turret was externally similar to the D58101 turret, with its main new features being the turret basket and fire controls. This turret switched the position of the turret crew, with the commander shifting to the right and serving as the loader rather than gunner. However, the commander's station was now fitted with a traversable periscope for better surveillance, and the gunner's station also had a periscopic sight, linked to the improved combination gun mount. The M3A1 was also the first version of the M3 series regularly fitted with an internal vehicle intercom system.

There was some doubt about the efficacy of the two sponson machine guns, and these were deleted and the armor opening covered with a small circular plate or deleted entirely on the final production batches. The first M3A1 light tank was completed in May 1942, and production began on a significant scale in July 1942. The last major production change incorporated into the M3/M3A1 light tank series was a welded hull. The pilot version of this configuration appeared in January 1942, and it entered series production in the summer of 1942. Although intended for the M3A1 light tank, this feature also appeared on late M3 light tanks.

The M3A1 light tank introduced the integrated fighting compartment with the new D58133 turret that included a turret basket and improved fire controls. These features are not evident externally. The M3A1 also deleted the sponson-mounted .30-cal machine guns. By this time, the M3/M3A1 production was shifting to an all-welded hull as seen here. Another feature based on British requests was a pair of jettisonable fuel tanks carried on the engine deck that effectively doubled the range of the Stuart.

The British were very unhappy about the M3A1's new features. As a result, the M3 light tank with the previous D58101 turret remained in production for Lend-Lease requirements in parallel to the M3A1 light tank until August 1942, when all M3/M3A1 production finally ceased. Since M3 production continued alongside M3A1 production for several months, the very late production M3 light tanks were fitted with later upgrades in parallel with the M3A1, such as the welded hull. This makes visual distinction between the two difficult. Production of the M3/M3A1 finally ended in August 1942.

IMPROVING THE STUART: THE M3A3 AND M5 LIGHT TANK

As a result of the pressure to reduce Army reliance on aircraft engines for tank propulsion, in the summer of 1941 an M3 light tank was modified with a pair of Cadillac automobile engines connected to a Hydramatic automatic transmission. Further development of the type was authorized in November 1941 as the M4 light tank, with plans to incorporate a new and more spacious welded hull. The M4 light tank was fitted with the same turret as the M3A1 light tank, but because it had a lower drive train, some of the components could be relocated and provide more room for the crew. Trials of the prototype were conducted in April 1942, but it was decided to redesignate the vehicle as the M5 light tank to avoid confusion with the new M4 medium tank. Production of the M5 took place at the Cadillac Motor Car Division and at the Massey Harris Company beginning in April and July 1942, respectively.

While this process was going on, the Army concluded that similar hull improvements could benefit the M3 series still being produced at American Car & Foundry. The new M3A3 light tank hull used a sloped glacis plate like the M5 light tank, but also had sloped side armor. In response to British requests, a bustle was added to the turret rear to enable the radio to be located nearer to the commander. The pilot for the M3A3 was completed in August 1942, and series production began at American Car & Foundry in January 1943.

By the autumn of 1942, the US Army had enough experience with the new M3A3 and M5 light tanks to make a better appreciation of their relative merits. The M5 was generally favored over the M3 series due to the automotive improvements of the new Cadillac engines and the automatic transmission. The only major advantage of the new M3A3 was the new turret bustle, and this was incorporated into the M5 light tank in September 1942 as the M5A1 light tank. As a result, the US Army decided to standardize on the M5 and M5A1 light tanks, and all of the M3A3 production was earmarked for Lend-Lease. When production of the M3A3 concluded in September 1943, American Car & Foundry switched production to the M5A1. At its peak in early 1944, three plants were producing the M5A1. Production halted in June 1944.

The US Army began steps to replace the M3 light tank in March 1941 with the M7 light tank. This was originally a 16-ton design armed with a 37mm gun with enough armor to withstand German 37mm anti-tank gunfire. As the war continued, German anti-tank guns continued to increase in power. Additional armor was added to the M7 design, and its firepower was increased to a 57mm gun and finally to a 75mm gun. In the process, its

The M3A3 light tank introduced a new hull and turret design. It was earmarked nearly exclusively for Lend-Lease and is seen here with the 3rd Company, 1st Battalion, 1st Provisional Tank Group, in Burma on March 4, 1944. This unit was composed of Chinese crews with American advisors and technical support.

LEFT The M5 light tank was a complete redesign of the Stuart. This tank served with the 102nd Cavalry Reconnaissance Squadron (Mecz) and is seen here during training at Chiseldon Camp in England in March 1943.

BELOW The M8 75mm howitzer motor carriage was based on the M5 light tank, but with a larger, open turret and 75mm howitzer. It was used as a light assault gun in light tank battalions. As the light tank battalions were retired, its principal role was to provide fire support in mechanized cavalry units.

RIGHT The T7E2 light tank pilot was armed with the 57mm gun. It was intended to replace the M3/M5 Stuart tank family.

BELOW The T7E2 light tank gradually morphed into the M7 medium tank, with thicker armor and a 75mm gun. This doomed the program since the Army needed a new light tank, not a competitor for the Sherman tank.

weight increased from 16 tons to 28 tons, and its automotive performance suffered accordingly. The Army selected International Harvester Company to manufacture the new tank and funded a new plant in Bettendorf, Iowa. An initial order for 3,000 tanks was awarded in November 1942. Production started in December 1942, but the Armored Force categorically refused to accept the vehicle, arguing with the Ordnance branch that it had failed to meet its design objectives and that the M7 had in reality become a medium tank heavier than the M4 Sherman but inferior in most respects. The Army Ground Forces backed the Armored Force, and M7 tank production ceased. The problem was tactical more than technical. In 1941–42, the US Army still thought that a light tank was viable on the modern battlefield for major missions such as infantry support and tank fighting. Combat in North Africa in 1943 made it clear that this was no longer the case.

COMMERCIAL EXPORT TANKS

American policy on weapons export was based on an April 23, 1923 decision by President Warren Harding's administration to limit the War Department from selling weapons abroad based on the popular myth that "merchants of death" had been responsible for pushing the United States into World War I. The War Department revoked the Harding arms sale policy on January 10, 1930, in the hopes that arms export might encourage the growth of an American arms industry. Very few sales ensued until the approach of war in 1939–40.

In the early 1930s, the Caterpillar Tractor Company in Peoria was approached by several foreign governments for the sale of tractors for military use. Afghanistan requested the design of an armored body that could be fit to the Caterpillar Diesel 40 tractor and ordered nine tractor tanks and three tank bodies. The armor plate was manufactured by the Henry Disston Saw Works near Philadelphia, which also conducted the final assembly. The tanks were armed with a 37mm gun M1916 in the turret and a .30-cal machine gun in a ball mount in the hull front. These were delivered in 1935, and due to publicity, four more were ordered by China in 1936 though never delivered. Several other countries examined the type, including Canada.

BELOW LEFT Several of the Caterpillar-Disston tractor tanks delivered to Afghanistan in 1935 survived well into the 1990s. At some point, they were rearmed with a Soviet 14.5mm KPVT heavy machine gun in place of the original 37mm gun, and with a 12.7mm DShK in place of the .30-cal hull machine gun. This particular example was on display at the Afghan Army Museum in the 1980s. (Wojciech Łuczak)

BELOW Mexico purchased seven of these CTVL-1 light tanks from Marmon-Herrington in April 1938. They are seen here on parade in front of Mexico City's Palace of Fine Arts on September 20, 1940.

RIGHT Some of the Marmon-Herrington CTMS-1TBI light tanks ordered for the KNIL in the Dutch East Indies were diverted to the Dutch Marines on Suriname in the Caribbean in 1942.

BELOW RIGHT The US Army was saddled with Marmon-Herrington tanks originally ordered for China. This photo from the Provisional Tank Company of the 138th Infantry near Fort Glenn, Umnak, Alaska, in 1942 includes a T16 light tank (CTLS-4TAC) on the right and a T14 light tank (CTLS-4TAY) on the left.

In the 1930s, the Marmon-Herrington company was heavily involved in commercial export of various types of military vehicles including trucks, artillery tractors, and light tanks. After developing the CTL-3 tankette for the US Marine Corps, in 1938 they sold the eight CTVL tankettes to the Mexican Army in 1937.

With war clouds brewing in the late 1930s, several countries approached the United States about purchasing US tanks. In the spring of 1940, the French government dispatched a purchasing commission to the United States to acquire military equipment. One of the efforts of the commission was to convince US industry to manufacture French tanks. This included the Char B1 bis battle tank, the Somua S35 cavalry tank, and the Hotchkiss H39 infantry tank. France expressed interest in purchasing 12,000 Char B1 bis tanks manufactured in the United States by a consortium headed by the Baldwin Locomotive Works, with Britain expressing some interest in ordering the tank as well. Engineering plans for these tanks were delivered to the United

The MTLS-1G14 medium tank was the largest of the Marmon-Herrington commercial export tanks and was armed with a pair of 37mm guns. This example was used for test purposes by the US Army at Aberdeen Proving Ground.

States Army, but France capitulated in July 1940 before an actual Char B1 bis tank was shipped to the United States.

After the fall of the Netherlands in May 1940, the Royal Netherlands East Indies Army (KNIL: Koninklijk Nederlans Indisch Leger) sent a purchasing commission to the United States to acquire tanks and trucks to deal with the growing threat of Japanese invasion of the oil-rich territories. Marmon-Herrington offered the commission its new CTL-6, another evolution of the turretless tankettes sold to the US Marine Corps. The KNIL wanted a conventional tank with a turret, and Marmon-Herrington developed the CTLS-4 for this requirement. This light tank was fitted with a small turret with a .30-cal machine gun as well as up to two .30-cal machine guns in the hull front. Curiously enough, two versions were offered: the CTLS-4TAC, with the turret on the right; and the CTLS-4TAY, with the turret on the left. Marmon-Herrington was also working on slightly larger tanks, the CTMS-ITB1 light tank, with a 37mm gun, and the MTLS-1G14 medium tank, with a pair of 37mm guns. The Dutch Purchasing Committee placed an initial $4.7 million order for 320 Marmon-Herrington tanks in June 1940, with deliveries scheduled to take place by March 1942. They enlarged the order several times in 1940 and 1941, finally totaling 628 tanks, including 234 CTLS-4, 194 CTMS-ITB1, and 200 MTLS-1G14, with deliveries to be completed by December 1942.

All of the CTLS-4 light tanks were completed by April 1942. However, the Japanese began invading the oil-rich Dutch East Indies in January 1942, seriously disrupting the tank deliveries. In mid-February 1942, the first 20 Marmon-Herrington CTLS-4 light tanks arrived on Java. They saw combat in March 1942 before the KNIL was overwhelmed. A further 149 CTLS-4 tanks that were en route were diverted to Australia where they were used for training. Marmon-Herrington continued to manufacture the tanks, and the Dutch government-in-exile accepted a total of 89 tanks, including 39 CTLS-4 light tanks, 30 CTMS-1TBI light tanks, and 19 MTLS-1G14 medium tanks. These were shipped to Dutch army garrisons in the Dutch West Indies in the Caribbean.

The Chinese showed interest in the Marmon-Herrington CTLS-4 light tank and placed an order through Lend-Lease for 240 tanks on the proviso that the turret be modified to accommodate a larger .50-cal machine gun. These were manufactured in March–July 1942 before anyone realized that they were still armed with the .30-cal machine gun. The turret was far too small to accommodate a .50-cal machine gun. The Chinese refused to accept delivery.

The United States helped raise three Free French armored divisions with Lend-Lease tanks. This is an M4A4 medium tank with an M8 75mm assault gun behind it during training exercises in Tunisia in 1943.

The loss of the Dutch East Indies and the rejection of the Chinese order left more than 250 assorted tanks at the Indianapolis factory, with more in various stages of construction. In June 1942, the US Army decided to accept most of them for emergency service. On July 23, 1942, the Ordnance Department declared the CTLS-4 as limited standard and designated the CTLS-4TAY as Light Tank T14, and CTLS-4TAC as Light Tank T16. These were formed into improvised tank companies for coastal defense. Of the 253 T14/T16 tanks in US Army service, more than half were dispatched to the Alaskan coast, while the rest were scattered along the Pacific coast and as far away as Bermuda and Newfoundland. They were not well regarded due to their mechanical problems, and they were withdrawn from service in 1943.

Samples of the larger CTMS-ITB1 light tank and MTLS-1G14 medium tank were sent to Aberdeen Proving Ground for evaluation. They were judged to be "thoroughly unreliable, mechanically and structurally unsound, underpowered, and equipped with unsatisfactory armament." Thirty were delivered to armies in Latin America in 1942–43. After attempting to secure interest in the remainder from other Lend-Lease clients during 1943, the remaining Marmon-Herrington export tanks were scrapped in 1944, ending one of the more obscure episodes in US tank history.

LEND-LEASE

Britain's heavy loss of tanks during the Battle of France in May–July 1940 prompted the British government to turn to the United States to purchase tanks. In the summer of 1940, British officials requested the manufacture of the Crusader and Valentine tanks in the USA. This was categorically rejected by Willian Knudsen, chairman of the Office of Production Management, who headed the US military production effort. As a result, the British Purchasing Commission in Washington, DC was obliged to purchase US-designed tanks. Since the obsolete M2A1 medium tank was the only type available, an order for 1,000 was placed in August 1940. This was quickly canceled in favor of the much better M3 medium tank. The order for the M3 medium tanks was gradually increased, along with orders for the M2A4 and M3 light tanks.

While the United States was ostensibly neutral through 1940 and 1941, President Franklin Roosevelt was convinced that the United States would eventually be dragged into the war, and so took steps to prepare for this eventuality. With Britain as the lone defender against Germany and Italy, Roosevelt began surreptitious steps to assist in arming the British forces. This culminated in the March 1941 Lend-Lease Act. The program enabled the

United States to provide Britain with tanks and other equipment at no immediate cost, to be used until returned or destroyed. The program was later extended to the Soviet Union and other allies.

A central tenet of Roosevelt's military policy in 1940–41 was to establish the United States as the "Arsenal of Democracy," with a massive expansion of military production, not only for the US Army, but for Allied armies. Roosevelt set a goal of manufacturing 44,500 tanks in 1942 and 70,000 in 1943.

At a joint meeting of the British Tank Mission and US Tank Committee on March 30, 1942, objectives were set up for the scale of supply of US tanks to Britain. As can be seen in the accompanying chart, the program planned to ship most tanks to Britain and other Lend-Lease recipients in 1942–43.

Proposed US tank procurement program 1942–43

Type	UK	US	Other	Total
1942				
Light tanks	3,500	2,534	4,554	10,588
Medium tanks	5,777	4,100	4,123	14,000
Sub-total 1942	9,277	6,634	8,677	24,588
1943				
Light tanks	1,750	9,734	6,450	17,934
Medium tanks	14,493	14,600	6,085	35,178
Assault tanks	8,500	0	0	8,500
Sub-total 1943	24,743	24,334	12,535	61,612
Total 1942–43	34,020	30,968	21,212	86,200

In the event, actual procurement varied considerably from plans, and British and American officials negotiated from month to month over the allotment of US tanks. The short-term focus of these meetings made it very difficult for Britain to plan its own tank production. After prolonged negotiations, in November 1942 both countries approved the Weeks-Somervell Agreement, named after the two officials responsible for British and American military production, Lt. Gen. Ronald M. Weeks, UK Director General of Military Equipment, and Lt. Gen. Brehon Somervell, Chief of the US Army Service Forces. This agreement established a series of annual protocols that set long-term objectives for weapons supplies under Lend-Lease. Not only did it cover US–UK shipments, but Britain and the US also negotiated the levels of supplies for other countries, most notably the Soviet Union. The accompanying table shows US Lend-Lease deliveries to the UK from March 1941 to July 1945.

It will be noticed that there are some discrepancies between this chart and the later chart that summarizes all US Lend-Lease tank shipments. This is because the UK chart does not include shipments prior to March 1941. In addition, there are some differences in categorization. For example, this chart lists the delivery of 828 3-inch GMC tank destroyers vs. 1,648 on the other chart. This is due to the fact that a portion of the M10 tank destroyers were shipped without armament to the UK, where they were fitted with the 17-pdr gun; hence, they were not counted on this first chart, but they were counted in another tabulation. There are also some omissions, such as the lack of M3 75mm GMC tank destroyers in both lists.

Lend-Lease tank and tank destroyer deliveries to UK 1941–45

Type	Mar 1941–Dec 1942	1943	1944	1945	Total
M3A1 light	1,355	907			2,262
M3A3 light		1,539	506		2,045
M5A1 light		3	1,128	290	1,421
M22 aero		107	153		260
M24 light			203	99	302
M3 medium	2,643	212			2,855
M4, M4A1 (75mm)	268	752	2,018	90	3,128
M4A2 (75mm)	456	4,083	501	8	5,048
M4A4 (75mm)	147	5,385	1,631	5	7,168
M4A1 (76mm)			1,330		1,330
M4A2 (76mm)				20	20
M4 (105mm)			488	105	593
M26 heavy			1	6	7
T48 57mm GMC		30			30
M10 3-inch GMC	143	655	30		828
M18 76mm GMC		2			2
Total	5,012	13,675	7,989	623	27,299

Source: Monthly Progress Reports, Army Service Forces, International Aid (1942–45)

ABOVE An M3 medium tank of Co. D, 67th Armored, 2nd Armored Division, during the Carolina maneuvers on November 5, 1941.

RIGHT M3 medium tank, 2/13th Armored, 1st Armored Division, Tunisia, 1943. (Artwork by Hugh Johnson © Osprey Publishing)

US Lend-Lease: tanks and tank destroyers

	UK	USSR	France	China	Other	Total	% of US prod.
M2A4	36					36	9.6
Marmon-Herrington					30	30	12.5
M3 light	5,532	1,676	238	100	703	8,249	59.7
M5 light	1,391	5	413			1,809	20.3
M22 light	420					420	50.6
M24 light	289	2				291	6.1
M3 medium	2,887	1,386			104	4,377	69.9
M4 (75mm)	15,260	2,007	755		53	18,075	54.1
M4 (76mm)	1,335	2,095				3,430	31.5
M4 (105mm)	593					593	12.6
M26	12	1				13	0.4
T48 57mm	30	650				680	70.6
M10 3-inch	1,648	52	443			2,143	31.9
M18 76mm	2	5				7	0.3
Total	29,435	7,879	1,849	100	890	40,153	40.2%

Source: The United States in World War II Statistics: Lend-Lease, Office of the Chief of Military History, 1952

THE M3 MEDIUM TANK

Recognizing the shortcomings of the M2A1 medium tank, in June 1940 the characteristics for a new medium tank were established. Familiarity with the Char B1 bis design helped influence the design of a future medium tank. As mentioned before, France had provided the US government with extensive documentation on the Char B1 bis as part of an effort to manufacture the French tank in the United States. Ordnance had already mounted a 75mm howitzer in the sponson of the M2 medium tank as the T5E2, which served as a testbed for the later M3 medium tank.

In August 1940, the head of the new Armored Force, Gen. Adna Chaffee, met with Ordnance officers to discuss the M3 medium tank requirements. Chaffee made it clear that he wanted a tank with thicker frontal armor and a 75mm gun in a fully rotating turret. Ordnance officials warned Chaffee about their lack of experience in designing a turret, turret ring, and gun mounting sufficient for a 75mm gun, and given the extreme urgency of the requirement, recommended an interim medium tank with a sponson-mounted 75mm gun supplemented with a turreted 37mm gun. In spite of Armored Force reluctance, the M3 medium tank program pushed ahead at full steam.

The crew layout in the M3 medium tank: a driver, a two-man crew for the 75mm gun in the hull, and a turret crew of three. (Author)

Formal design of the M3 medium tank began in September 1940. The design was heavily based on the previous M2A1 medium tank, but with a completely modified superstructure. The M2 75mm gun was mounted in a right-side sponson, and a small 37mm gun turret was located on the left superstructure roof. The idea was that the 75mm gun would engage the most typical targets, such as enemy fortifications or troops, while the 37mm gun would deal with enemy tanks. The Armored Force remained very unhappy with the M3 design. Following Chaffee's retirement due to illness, the new chief, Maj. Gen. Jacob Devers, insisted that its production run be limited to about 360 tanks to cover the gap until the 75mm gun tank was ready. The first pilot was completed at Rock Island Arsenal on March 13, 1941, and serial production began at the new Chrysler Detroit Tank Arsenal in April 1941.

The urgency for rushing the M3 medium tank into production was increased by the arrival of a British purchasing commission in the United States in 1940. Due to heavy tank losses in France, the British Army wanted to purchase 3,650 cruiser tanks in the United States. British tank officers were not keen on the M3 design after being shown early mockups. Part of the problem was that the US and British armies had fundamentally different views about the tactical role of armored divisions. The US favored the traditional cavalry mission of an exploitation force rampaging through the enemy's rear areas after the breakthrough had been accomplished by the infantry. The

British conception focused on the need to defeat the panzer divisions. The US doctrine implied a tank with a dual-purpose gun with an accent on high-explosive firepower, while the British doctrine favored a cruiser tank with a gun oriented toward anti-tank firepower.

Since the United States refused to manufacture British tank designs, the British purchasing team reached an agreement under which a variant of the M3 medium tank would be built for the British Army with a different turret and other modifications. British doctrine favored placing the tank radio in the turret near the commander, which required a bustle on the tank turret that the American M3 medium tank design lacked. Initially, the British government contracted with four American railroad plants to manufacture a total of 2,085 M3 tanks, and the Montreal branch of the American Locomotive Company (ALCO) for a further 1,157 Ram cruiser tanks based on the M3 chassis. The US government placed parallel contracts for 2,220 M3 medium tanks later in the year with the same plants.

Besides the original Rock Island turret, a British team led by L. E. Carr developed the WF2 cast turret based on British requirements. The Rock Island turret had a fully traversable sub-turret above the turret armed with

A column of M3 medium tanks during the driver training course of the Armored Force School at Fort Knox, Kentucky, in June 1942.

The M3A1 used a cast hull instead of the riveted hull of the original M3 medium tank. This tank served with Co. H, 37th Armored, 4th Armored Division, during the Second Army maneuvers in Tennessee in October 1942.

a .30-cal machine gun, a feature deemed foolish by the British. The British WF2 turret had an enlarged turret bustle at the rear for the radio and had a simple hatch instead of a cupola.

The British variant of the M3 medium tank, called the General Grant I in Britain, was manufactured by Baldwin, Pressed Steel Car (PSC), and Pullman Standard Car Co. Besides the different turret, there were other small differences, such as the addition of a periscope for the driver. Production of the custom-built Grant I tank could not meet the British needs for tanks due to high tank casualties in the desert campaign, so Britain also acquired the American version of the M3 medium tank. This had the original Rock Island-designed turret and was known as the General Lee I in the British Army. In total, about 1,660 tanks were completed with the Grant turret, or a bit more than a quarter of the total M3 production.

As more American plants became involved in tank production, the US Army tried to simplify manufacture. One alternative was to employ a single casting for the hull superstructure instead of the complicated riveted design. The cast hull took about 100 man-hours to complete, while the riveted hull took 1,100 hours. This version was designated as the M3A1, and a total of 300 were manufactured by ALCO starting in February 1942. Further production was not undertaken since the casting plants were shifting to the production of a cast hull and turret for the follow-on M4A1 medium tank. Another alternative in hull construction was the use of welded plate construction instead of riveted construction. The first of the welded-hull versions was the M3A2, which was otherwise identical to the basic M3 medium tank. Production of the M3A2 began at Baldwin in January 1942, but was suspended in March when it was decided to switch to the diesel-powered, welded-hull M3A3. The decision to move to the diesel engine was due to the bottlenecks in engine supplies, since the Continental radial engine used in the M3, M3A1, and M3A2 was also used in aircraft production. The engine selected for the M3A3 was the General Motors Model 6046, which combined two Model 6-71 diesel engines. When mounted in a welded hull, the diesel-powered tank was designated as the M3A3, while those manufactured with a riveted hull were designated as M3A5. Production was undertaken at Baldwin in January–December 1942, with a total of 322 M3A3 and 591 M3A5 tanks being manufactured.

The third engine option for the M3 was the new Chrysler A57 multi-bank engine that was created by combining five bus engines at the base to create a star-shaped engine offering 425hp. Although complex, the A57 used available machine tools so it could be rapidly placed into production. Production of the M3A4 was undertaken from June 1942 to August 1942 at the Detroit Tank Plant, with some 109 tanks completed.

Production of the M3 medium tank series continued even after the production of the M4 medium tank began in February 1942. This was largely due to the heavy demand from Lend-Lease as well as the need for more training tanks by the infant US armored divisions. About 70 percent of the M3 medium tanks were exported, primarily to Britain and the Soviet Union.

CANADIAN COUSIN

One of the offshoots of the M3 medium tank was the Canadian Ram cruiser tank. Development of this tank began in early 1941 as a British-inspired alternative to locally manufacturing the M3 medium tank. The Ram used the same lower chassis and suspension as the M3 medium tank and differed primarily in the use of a cast upper hull and single cast turret. These were designed by William Sheehan of General Steel Castings of Granite City, Illinois, the firm that subsequently manufactured these sub-components. Unlike the M3 medium tank, the Ram had its main armament in a single main turret. A subsidiary machine-gun turret, like that on the M3 medium tank, was mounted on the front left of the hull in British fashion during the early production run.

A Ram II cruiser tank during training in 1943. The Ram was between the Lee/Grant and Sherman in features, being based on the M3 medium tank powertrain and suspension, but using a more modern configuration similar to the Sherman. (Library and Archives Canada)

The original Ram I was armed with the British 2-pdr gun as an expedient until the 6-pdr (57mm) gun was ready for production in Canada. The selection of the 6-pdr gun was due to British cruiser tank requirements that favored this gun. The first Ram I was produced in June 1941 at the Montreal Locomotive Works, a subsidiary of American Locomotive of Schenectady, New York. It was tested at Aberdeen Proving Ground, and the US designation M4A5 medium tank was reserved for it, though never used in practice. In terms of cost, US firms provided 57 percent of the sub-components on the Ram, including the engine, transmission, and main castings. Fifty Ram I were manufactured until production shifted to the Ram II in February 1942. A total of 1,899 Ram II were manufactured through July 1943, when the production lines transitioned to the Grizzly tank, a locally produced version of the M4A1 Sherman medium tank. Although the Ram was extensively used for training Canadian tank units, ultimately the Ram cruiser tanks never saw combat. By 1944, the preference was for the 75mm gun since it was more versatile than the 6-pdr due to its better high-explosive round. Some Ram tanks in Britain were converted to other roles, most notably as the turretless Ram Kangaroo infantry carrier that saw combat in Normandy in 1944.

GRANT/LEE COMBAT DEBUT: BRITISH EIGHTH ARMY

The Grant tank saw its combat debut with British armored units in the desert campaign in the spring of 1942 in the cruiser tank role. Unlike the US Army with its light and medium tanks, the British Army categorized tanks by two principal roles: the cruiser tanks in the armored divisions and armored brigades oriented toward defeating panzers; and infantry tanks oriented toward close support of the infantry. The first Grant tanks arrived in the Middle East in November 1941. The Grants were a welcome addition to the British arsenal due to the serious losses endured during Operation *Crusader* in November 1941, and lingering problems with British tank designs. British cruiser tanks were armed first with the 2-pdr and later the 6-pdr guns. Both of these had excellent anti-armor performance but did not offer high-explosive punch. The Afrika Korps was often able to overcome larger British tank forces with numerically inferior panzer units by skillfully employing anti-tank guns with the panzer force. These guns, such as the PaK 38 50mm anti-tank gun, were small targets and nearly impossible to knock out by tank guns firing armor-piercing shot. Likewise, the 88mm Flak gun, used in an improvised anti-tank role, had greater range than

Britain obtained both types of M3 medium tanks, including the Grant with the British-designed WF2 turret on the left, and the Lee with the Rock Island-designed turret on the right.

A British Grant shortly after being issued to the Royal Scots Greys following its deployment to Egypt in September 1942.

British tank guns, and so could stand off at a distance and still wreak havoc with the British tank forces. The Grant offered an antidote to the anti-tank gun threat since it could fire an effective high-explosive projectile that had a much greater chance of disabling an anti-tank gun even without a direct hit. The Grant's 75mm gun was also effective in the anti-tank role and was supplemented by the 37mm gun in the turret, which offered performance similar to the British 2-pdr tank gun.

The Grant's other significant advantage was its automotive reliability. At the time, British tank regiments in the desert were receiving the new Crusader cruiser tank. This tank suffered from engine reliability problems, which resulted in serious mechanical attrition in combat until technical improvements were made. Overall, the Grant was well received. A tank officer recalled, "it was fairly fast with a possible road speed of about 25mph, well-armoured, and considered capable of out-shooting an enemy tank or anti-tank gun except the 88mm. The Grant crews also found their new tank and armament ideal and we looked forward to meeting the panzers more or less on even terms."

The Grant had its share of problems as well. The configuration of the sponson-mounted gun was far from ideal since it offered only limited traverse. The dual 37mm/75mm armament was a distraction to the commander since it was difficult to concentrate on more than one target at a time. The silhouette of the tank was high, which was both a blessing and a curse. In some conditions, it offered the commander a better vantage point for spotting enemy targets in the flat desert wastes. But as often as not, it simply presented a larger target to the enemy. The location of the 75mm gun made it difficult to take advantage of hull-down positions, using terrain to protect the bulk of the tank.

By March 1942, there were about 340 Grants and Lees in Egypt along with American liaison teams to provide training and maintenance assistance. British units seldom distinguished the Grant and Lee, generally labeling both types as "Grants" regardless of the turrets. At the time of the Gazala battles in May 1942, British units had 167 Grants and Lees with the 1st and 7th Armoured Divisions, with more in Egypt equipping other units or being used for training or reserve. This made it the second most common tank type in the armored divisions, compared with 257 Crusaders and 149 Stuarts. At the time, the Grant represented one of the best tanks in the desert. In spite of the new Grant tanks, the May–June Gazala battles went badly for the Eighth Army. The problems were not technical, but tactical. The Afrika Korps continued to display greater combat effectiveness in spite of technical and numerical shortcomings due to better combined-arms tactics. The performance of the Grant during the battle was good, and its 75mm gun proved an unpleasant surprise for the Germans in numerous encounters. The August 1942 fighting at Alam Halfa again saw the Grant as one of the mainstays of the British armored force, with 164 Grants and Lees among the 713 tanks in the forward-deployed units.

The second battle of El Alamein started on October 23, 1942. Churchill pressured on the US government to speed the shipment of new tanks, especially the new M4A1 Sherman. At the time of the battle, Lend-Lease tanks made up the backbone of the British armored forces, with 270 Shermans and 210 Grants. Britain received priority for the new M4 tanks, and the US 1st Armored Division remained saddled with the older M3 medium tank. The Grant was still a viable battle tank in the autumn 1942 fighting since the Afrika Korps still had a few of the long-barreled PzKpfw III Ausf. L or PzKpfw IV Ausf. G. El Alamein was the high point of the Grant's career in the Desert War. As the Sherman was produced, it became the preferred replacement. The Sherman had all of the advantages of the Grant, including its 75mm gun and its automotive dependability, but none of its vices, such as the awkward gun configuration or excessive silhouette. The Grant remained in service as a battle tank through the end of the Tunisian campaign in May 1943, but in dwindling numbers.

The Lee tank remained in British combat service in 1945 in the Pacific theater. This is "Cossack" from C Squadron, 150 RAC, during the advance by the 19th Indian Division on Fort Dufferin near Mandalay, Burma, on March 10, 1945.

M3 MEDIUM TANK COMBAT DEBUT: US 1ST ARMORED DIVISION

The M3 medium tank was ready for deployment to US Army units in the summer of 1941, and first went to the 1st Armored Division. They took part in the Louisiana maneuvers in August 1941, and later with the 2nd Armored Division during the Carolina maneuvers in November 1941. Attitudes about the new tank varied. The new head of the Armored Force, Maj. Gen. Jacob Devers, was highly critical of the design, strongly favoring a more conventional design with the main gun in the turret. Units of the 1st Armored Division were delighted to receive the new tanks since they had been equipped with M3 light tanks armed only with the 37mm "squirrel rifle." Nevertheless, some tankers recognized its odd configuration, and one complained that it looked like "a damned cathedral coming down the road."

The first large-scale use of US tanks after the disastrous Philippines campaign took place with the Operation *Torch* landings in November 1942 along the French North African coast. Elements of the 1st and 2nd Armored

Divisions landed, but only the Combat Command B (CCB) of the 1st Armored Division saw extensive combat in the November–December 1942 fighting. At the time, the 1st Armored Division had three of its medium tank battalions equipped with the M3 and a single battalion with the new M4 and M4A1 medium tanks.

The first major engagement involving the M3 medium tanks was on the afternoon of November 28, 1942, with the 2/13th Armored Regiment, Combat Command B (CCB), 1st Armored Division, near Djedeida, Tunisia. Most of the fighting in early December was a frustrating series of small skirmishes, with most tank losses due to camouflaged German anti-tank guns. The deputy commander of the CCB ruefully noted, "Our M3 medium tanks were no match for the German Mark IV, and our M3 light tanks were obsolete." When a delegation from the Armored Force headed by Gen. Jacob Devers arrived for an inspection, they were amazed that the CCB was still not equipped with the current armor-piercing ammunition and had been using obsolete ammunition usually reserved for training in the United States. The poor performance of the tanks in the December fighting was partly due to this oversight, but the blame falls more heavily on the inexperience of the US units, and the poor coordination of infantry and armor in many of the operations.

The remainder of the 1st Armored Division was re-equipped with the new M4 and M4A1 medium tanks while in the UK, so that by the time they arrived in Tunisia in December 1942, all the medium tank battalions aside from the decimated 2/13th Armored had Sherman tanks. Nevertheless, when the CCB commander was given the option of detaching the battered but battle-hardened 2/13th Armored, or the inexperienced but well-equipped 2/1st Armored with M4 tanks, he wisely chose to stick with the M3 battalion. On February 17, 1943, the 2/13th Armored engaged elements of the 21.Panzer-Division near Sbeitla and knocked out or disabled about 15 German panzers, temporarily blunting the attack. Although CCB was eventually forced to give up Sbeitla, Rommel later noted that the US forces there had fought "cleverly and hard."

The 2/13th Armored covered the American withdrawal through Kasserine Pass. Due to a shortage of Sherman tanks to make up for losses at Kasserine Pass, M3 medium tanks were still in use during the final fighting for Tunisia. By the end of the Tunisia campaign, the 1st Armored Division had 51 M3 medium tanks and 178 M4 and M4A1 tanks. Besides the 1st Armored Division, the 751st Tank Battalion was the only other US tank unit to use the M3 medium tank in Tunisia. It supported the 34th Division in March 1943 during the advance on Bizerte. The Tunisian campaign was the first and last use of the M3 medium tank in combat by the US Army in the Atlantic theater.

THE M3 AND M5 IN COMBAT IN NORTH AFRICA

While the M3 Stuart light tank was being shifted to the reconnaissance role in the British Army by the summer of 1942, it still remained a central element in the US Army's armored divisions. Under the 1942 configuration, the two tank regiments in each division were each composed of two medium tank battalions and one light tank battalion. In addition, the Army was still fielding separate GHQ tank battalions composed entirely of light tanks. The first extensive American use of the M3 light tank in combat since the Philippines came after Operation *Torch* in November 1942, when the US Army landed in North Africa. There was small-scale fighting with the Vichy French in Morocco shortly after the landings. Far more intense combat awaited the 1st Armored Division in Tunisia against both German and Italian tank forces.

"Bucaneer," an M3 medium tank of Co. B, 752nd Tank Battalion, on exercise near Perham Down on Salisbury Plain in England in December 1942 prior to deployment to Tunisia. This is a late production M3 tank with the long M3 75mm guns and without the side hull doors.

M3 medium tank, Co. D, 2/13th Armored, 1st Armored Division, Tunisia, 1943. (Artwork by Hugh Johnson © Osprey Publishing)

Initial skirmishes in late November 1942 disclosed that the M3 light tank was virtually hopeless in a frontal engagement against contemporary German medium tanks, since the 37mm gun could not penetrate the German tank at any reasonable range. Their only chance was a side or rear shot. In contrast,

The combat debut of the M3 medium tank in US hands was with the 2/13th Armored Regiment, Combat Command B, 1st Armored Division, near Djedeida, Tunisia. This photo of one of the unit's tanks was taken two days before at Souk el Arba.

the PzKpfw III was now armed with a very lethal 50mm gun. An Army assessment reached three conclusions: that the 37mm gun was completely inadequate for tank fighting; that the tank had inadequate vision devices which forced the crew to operate with the hatches open, thereby increasing its vulnerability; and that even in desert conditions the narrow track afforded poor floatation. Although the newer M5 light tank had some powerplant advantages, it suffered from many of the same armor and firepower shortcomings.

The Tunisia experience led to debate among US military leaders in North Africa. In June 1943, Lt. Gen. Omar Bradley, commander of II Corps, and Lt. Gen. George S. Patton, commander of the 1st Armored Corps (Reinforced), issued a directive that light tanks were only to be used for reconnaissance and flank security in view of their weakness in dealing with current German tanks and anti-tank guns. The lessons of the North Africa campaign were already under intense scrutiny by the Armored Force in the United States, and plans were underway to reorganize the armored divisions to consider the inadequacies of the light tanks. Under the new armored division structure, the light tank battalions were abolished. Instead, tank battalions would be organized around three M4 medium tank companies and one company of M5 light tanks. The light tanks were deemed suitable for battalion reconnaissance and flank security, but there was some debate whether it would be wiser to trim the light tank strength back to only a platoon per battalion. The separate GHQ

M5 light tank, Co. C, 70th Tank Battalion (L), Oran, Morocco, January 1943. (Artwork by Jim Laurier © Osprey Publishing)

light tank battalions were mostly reconfigured, though dwindling numbers of light tank battalions were used in the Sicily campaign, in Italy, and even in Northwest Europe. By the time of Operation *Husky*, the invasion of Sicily in July 1943, the M3 and M3A1 light tanks had been retired from frontline US Army service in favor of the M5 light tank.

US HEAVY TANKS

The US Army in World War II showed very little interest in heavy tanks, although several types were developed. This was in part due to the problems associated with transporting such tanks to overseas combat theaters by sea. In addition, the engineers continuously opposed heavy tanks through the war due to the absence of adequate tactical bridging for such oversize and overweight tanks.

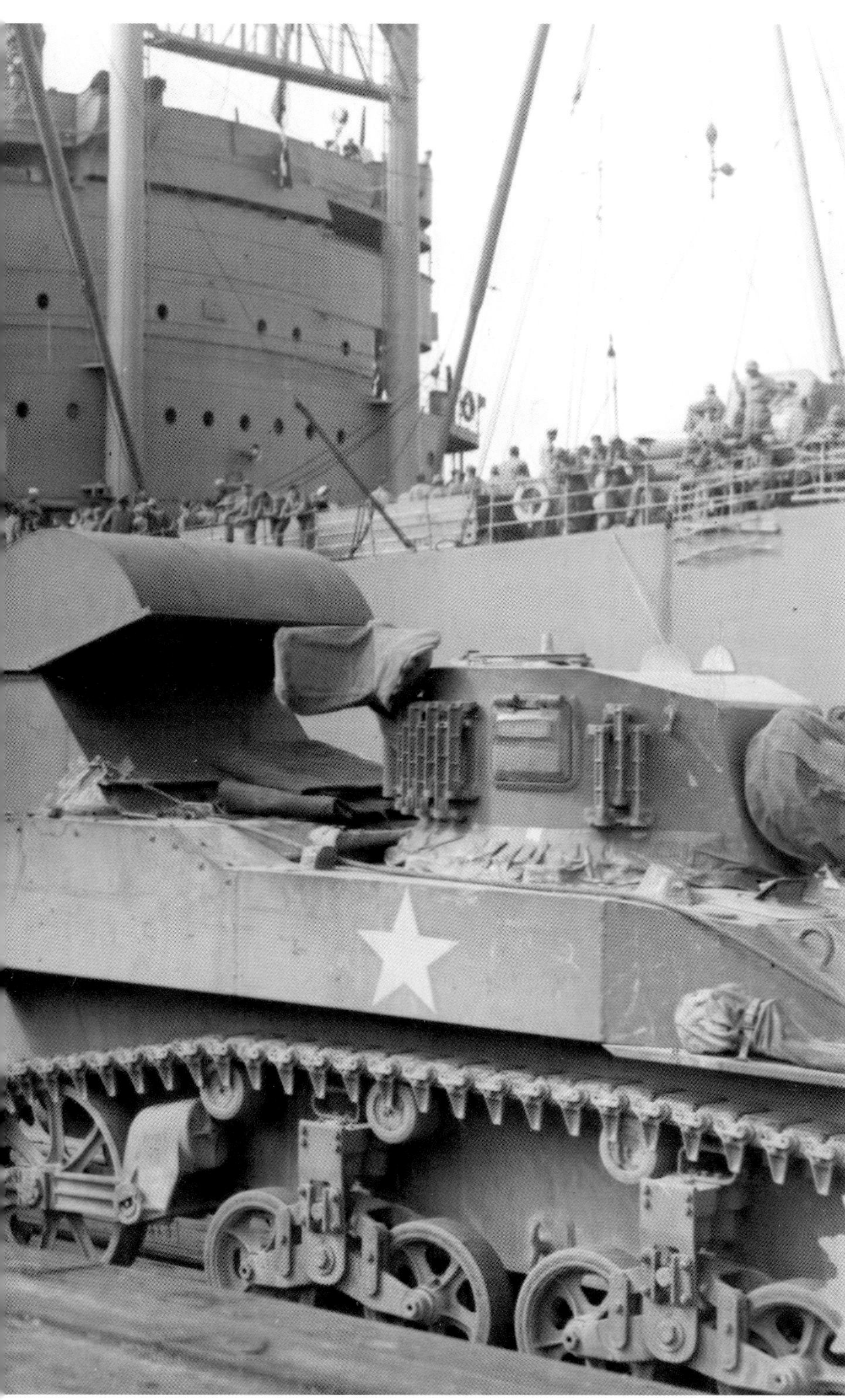

M5 light tanks of the 756th Tank Battalion in Newport News, Virginia, on October 20, 1942 prior to being dispatched to French North Africa for Operation *Torch*. They are fitted with the original style of Project Blue Freeze deep-wading kits to permit amphibious landing.

The development of a 50-ton heavy tank began as early as 1939. Design requirements were finally established in the autumn of 1940 for a tank armed with a 3-inch gun with a secondary 37mm gun in a combination mount in the turret. A T1E1 heavy tank pilot was completed at the Baldwin Locomotive Works in April 1941. A variety of options were developed for the tank, including both cast and welded hulls as well as different engines and transmissions. The T1E2 with a cast hull was standardized on May 26, 1942 as the M6 heavy tank, and the T1E3 with a welded hull as the M6A1 heavy tank. Initial plans approved production of 1,084 heavy tanks, but this was subsequently reduced to 115. The M6 heavy tank had a loaded weight of 63 tons and a road speed of 22mph. Its turret armor and front hull armor was 3 inches (76mm).

The M6 heavy tank met a cold reception at the Armored Forces headquarters. There was no doctrinal role for such a large tank, and the difficulties in transporting it overseas were well appreciated. Operational trials at Fort Knox in early 1943 were scathing about its many technical faults. Ordnance proposed up-arming the tank with a 90mm gun, but the Armored Force was still not interested. Following D-Day, Ordnance proposed a crash program to mount the 105mm T5E1 gun as the M6A2E1 to deal with the Panther and Tiger threat. Ordnance promised to deliver 15 modified tanks in 90 days. AGF was unwilling to support the effort and so Ordnance turned to Eisenhower's US Army in the European Theater of Operations (ETOUSA) headquarters. They responded that the deployment of 15 heavy tanks was impractical and unnecessary. This effectively killed the program. However, Ordnance used the M6 heavy tank chassis as a testbed for the T29 heavy tank program, mounting a T29 tank turret on the M6A2E1-1 in 1945.

A second heavy tank program was started in late 1941 as the T14 assault tank. Lieutenant General Gordon Macready, the head of the British Army mission in Washington, DC, forwarded a British Army request for the production of 8,500 infantry tanks to supplement the troubled Churchill infantry tank. In contrast to the M6 heavy tank, the T14's maximum armor was raised from 3 to 4 inches (76mm to 102mm). The initial armament was the same 75mm gun as in the Sherman tank, but with provisions for the British 6-pdr. The suspension was based on the M6 heavy tank, and it was powered by a Ford V8. At the same time, Britain developed its own heavy assault tank, the A33, patterned on the Cromwell, but with armor up to 4.5 inches. Trials of the T14 were undertaken at Aberdeen Proving Ground from July to December 1943, after which operational trials were conducted at Fort Knox; one of the two pilots was shipped to the UK. The initial test report in February 1944 declared the T14 design as unsatisfactory for a host of technical reasons. However, the program had no future regardless of any

An M6 heavy tank at Fort Knox during operational trials. The M6 was armed with the 3-inch M7 gun, the same weapon on the M10 3-inch tank destroyer.

improvements. The British Army had wanted to obtain the T14 starting in 1943. Since necessary improvements would take months of further development, the T14 would not have been ready for production until 1945. Furthermore, the Churchill infantry tank had become a much more successful design since its rocky start in 1941, and there was no longer a pressing need to replace it. As a result, the requirement was canceled in December 1944.

THE M4 SHERMAN MEDIUM TANK

The development of a derivative of the M3 medium tank with a turret-mounted 75mm gun began in February 1941 under the experimental designation of T6. It used the chassis and powertrain of the M3 medium tank, but it had a new cast turret and hull. The design was also influenced by British

The T14 assault tank was developed in response to a British requirement for a heavy infantry tank. By the time the pilot was ready in 1943, the British requirement had evaporated so no serial production took place.

requirements since the British Army planned to order a significant number of these tanks through Lend-Lease. The turret followed German practices, with a three-man crew: commander, gunner, and loader. The hull crew included a driver on the left side and a co-driver/bow-gunner on the right. To expedite production, two different hull configurations were developed. The welded-hull version was designated as the M4, while the cast-hull version was designated as the M4A1; these types were otherwise identical.

Comparative technical characteristics

	M3 Grant	M4A1 Sherman
Crew	7	5
Dimensions: L x W x H (m)	5.63 x 2.71 x 3.02	5.84 x 2.61 x 2.74
Loaded weight (tonnes)	28.1	30.3
Main gun	75mm M3, 37mm M6	75mm M3
Main gun ammo	65+128	90
Engine (hp)	350	350
Max. speed (km/h)	39	39
Fuel (liters)	662	662
Range (km)	195	195
Ground pressure (kg/cm^2)	0.89	0.96
Armor**		
Mantlet (mm)	76*=>76	76*=>76
Turret front (mm)	76@47=107.5	76@30=87.7
Turret side (mm)	51*=>51	51@5=51.2
Upper hull front (mm)	51@30=58.9	51@~50=79.3
Lower hull front (mm)	51*=>51	51*=>51
Upper hull side (mm)	38@0=38	38@0=38
*curved **armor data provided as: actual thickness in mm @ angle from vertical = effective thickness in mm		

The M4A1 first started production in February 1942 at the Lima Locomotive plant, and M4 production started in July 1942 at the Pressed Steel Car plant. The US Army had planned to equip both the 1st and 2nd Armored Divisions with the M4A1 in the summer of 1942. In the event, the early batches of M4A1 tanks intended for the 1st Armored Division were diverted to the British Army in North Africa after the fall of Tobruk due to Churchill's urgent plea to Roosevelt. The British Army named the M4 medium tank the General Sherman for the Civil War commander.

In British service, the Sherman was more popular than the earlier M3 Lee/Grant medium tanks due to the more practical turret. The battle of El Alamein witnessed the first encounters between the Sherman and the best German tank of the time, the PzKpfw IV Ausf. G. A British report immediately after El Alamein summarized the initial reactions: "First reports from the Western

The T6 pilot at Aberdeen Proving Ground in 1941. The early pilot had a variety of features that differed from the eventual M4A1 medium tank, such as the use of a machine-gun cupola for the commander, the short M2 75mm guns, hull side doors, and two .30-cal machine guns in the hull front.

A comparative view of an M3 medium tank on the left and the T6 pilot on the right.

ABOVE M4 turret interior. (Artwork by Richard Chasemore © Osprey Publishing)

RIGHT M4A4 medium tank, 1943. (Artwork by Peter Sarson © Osprey Publishing)

RIGHT The Sherman underwent continual refinement during production. This is a good example of a typical M4A1 manufactured in spring 1942, the pilot M4A1 from Pacific Car and Foundry. It has the embedded driver visor in front of the driver hatch, the three-piece differential cover, and the early M34 gun rotor mount.

The Sherman's combat debut was during the second battle of El Alamein in September 1942. This is a column from the 9th Lancers of the British 1st Armoured Division.

Desert indicate great satisfaction with Sherman. Position of gun has enabled maximum concealment in hull down position combined with good observation by commander. Have definite evidence of enemy tanks including Mark IV Special [Pz.Kpfw IV Ausf. G] being destroyed at ranges up to two thousand yards."

In contrast, the combat debut of the M4 medium tank in US Army service in North Africa was hardly auspicious. During the Kasserine Pass battles, two companies from 3/1st Armored, 1st Armored Division, were nearly wiped out on February 14, 1943, near Sidi Bou Zid in a one-sided engagement with 10.Panzer-Division supported by Tiger tanks. The following day, 2/1st Armored,

On February 15, 1943, 2/1st Armored, 1st Armored Division, conducted a head-on tank charge near Sidi Bou Zid. About 40 of the battalion's M4 and M4A1 tanks were trapped in the Oued Rouana wadi where they were ambushed by encircling German tanks.

Here's another example of M4A1 evolution, in this case an M4A1 manufactured by Lima Locomotive Works in December 1942. By this stage, the embedded driver visor in front of the driver hatch has been eliminated and the changeover had begun to the one-piece E4186 cast differential housing.

1st Armored Division, conducted a head-on tank charge across open desert against elements of two experienced German panzer divisions situated in well-emplaced defensive positions. The lead tanks were initially taken under fire by camouflaged German anti-tank gun emplacements in the neighboring olive groves, while two panzer battalions enveloped the American battalion. After losing several Sherman tanks to the anti-tank guns, the remaining 40 tanks were trapped in the Oued Rouana wadi where they were gradually shot to bits by the encircling German tanks in a mechanized version of "Custer's Last Stand." The Sherman tank continued to soldier on during the remainder of the Tunisian campaign, alongside diminishing numbers of M3 medium tanks.

1st Armored Division medium tank status in Tunisia

	13 Feb 1943	3 Mar 1943	9 Mar 1943	12 Mar 1943	22 Mar 1943	26 Mar 1943	May 1943
M3 medium tank	20	93	71	77	86	86	51
M4 medium tank	182	100	80	97	125	120	178
Total	202	193	151	174	211	206	229

TACTICAL LESSONS FROM THE EARLY CAMPAIGNS

The US Army learned hard lessons from the Kasserine Pass debacle. The problem was not the new Sherman tank but the inexperience of the tank crews, the unrealistic training, and serious tactical and doctrinal issues. The armored divisions were tank-heavy without enough armored infantry. The 1942-pattern division had six tank battalions but only three armored infantry battalions. Reorganization in 1943 led to a more balanced armored division, with three tank battalions, three armored infantry battalions, and three armored field artillery battalions. The light or medium tank battalions gave way to a standard tank battalion, with three medium tank companies and one light tank company. Infantry commanders began to recommend adding a tank battalion to each infantry division, but this issue had not been settled at the time of D-Day in June 1944.

By the time of Operation *Husky* in July 1943, US armored divisions had retired the M3 in favor of the M4/M4A1 medium tanks. In contrast to the tactical misuse of the 1st Armored Division in Tunisia, the 2nd Armored Division was used in textbook fashion on Sicily. Instead of scattering the division, Gen. George Patton held it in reserve to take advantage of opportunities, eventually using it in a 100-mile dash through Sicily's rough mountains to seize Palermo. The concentrated use of the 2nd Armored Division was a case study in the intended doctrine for armored divisions. Two separate tank battalions took part in combat on Sicily, the 70th (Light) and 753rd (Medium). The Sicily campaign highlighted the difficulties in the use of armor in mountainous terrain, a lesson that would become all too evident in the ensuing year of fighting on the Italian mainland.

From the standpoint of the enemy tank threat, Sicily only reinforced US Army complacency over the adequacy of the Sherman tank. The Italian tank units on Sicily were equipped mostly with obsolete equipment. The panzer units were equipped with the PzKpfw III and PzKpfw IV as in Tunisia, plus an understrength battalion of Tiger tanks. The violent panzer counterattacks against the American beachhead were beaten back by infantry and tanks supported by heavy naval gunfire. The US Army came out of Sicily with no particular fear of dealing with the vaunted Tiger.

There were subsequent combat encounters on the Italian mainland starting with the Salerno landings in September 1943. Although US tankers in Italy thought that the 75mm gun on the PzKpfw IV was superior to that on the Sherman, there was no intense concern about confronting this tank since its turret front and side armor were vulnerable at normal combat ranges. Italy was not well suited to maneuver battles, and the Sherman was deployed

The Tunisian campaign clearly demonstrated the need for improved tank-infantry tactics. Here, an M3 medium tank of the 751st Tank Battalion supports riflemen of the 9th Infantry Division during the capture of Bizerte, Tunisia, on May 7, 1943. (Artwork by Steve Noon © Osprey Publishing)

primarily in separate tank battalions in infantry support roles; tank-vs.-tank fighting was rare. The 1st Armored Division was committed piecemeal to the Italian campaign, most notably during the amphibious landings at Anzio in January 1944. There was extensive tank fighting in the Anzio beachhead, but technical parity between the Sherman and German panzers was still the case. A battalion of the new Panther tank was deployed to Italy in February 1944, but it did not see extensive combat until the fighting on the approaches to Rome in May 1944.

In December 1942, the head of the Armored Force, Maj. Gen. Jacob Devers, led a team to North Africa to hear about combat lessons learned during the fighting. The team included the chief of US Army Ordnance, Gen. G. M. Barnes. Their report noted that "ranking officers of the British Eighth Army as well as members of British tank crews are convinced that the American M4 medium tank (General Sherman) is the best tank on the battlefield. This is the conclusion of the British Eighth Army and our own force on the Tunisian Front."

Tunisia and Sicily showed that more attention had to be paid to tank support of infantry divisions. The tactic of using the separate tank battalions en masse was unsound since the mission was better performed by a true combined-arms unit like the armored division. In addition, the infantry division commanders were unanimous in their need for close tank support. At the same time, combined-arms training of infantry and tank units had been neglected, in part due to the rush to create new divisions, and in part due to the doctrinal neglect of the need for infantry tank support. Infantry commanders frequently had received no training on the best tactics to employ tanks when they were assigned, and often used them for inappropriate missions. In August 1942, prior to the Tunisia operation, McNair came up

This M4A1 named "Major Jim" was the tank of Maj. James Simmerman, executive officer of the 2nd Battalion, 13th Armored, 1st Armored Division. This particular tank was lost covering the withdrawal from Kasserine Pass in late February 1943.

with plans to attach separate tank battalions to armies and corps for combined training. Although this scheme was generally accepted, practical problems meant that little was done. In March 1943, the AGF operations officer, Brig. Gen. John Lentz, argued that the separate tank battalions were a bad idea and that the tank units should be made organic to the infantry divisions. McNair opposed this idea, as he still clung to the idea that the non-divisional battalions would provide a vital mass of firepower and maneuver in the forthcoming campaign in France. McNair issued a directive in April 1943 stressing the need for more combined training by tank and infantry units. But tank battalions were still too few to permit each infantry division to train with a tank battalion, and they were seldom located together at the same base.

In June 1943, Maj. Gen. Walton Walker, commander of IV Armored Corps, returned from a fact-finding mission to Tunisia and urged that separate tank battalions, after receiving basic unit training, be stationed with a corresponding infantry division for further training and remain with that division during entry into combat. On May 11, 1943, Gen. Devers was appointed to head US forces in the new European Theater of Operations (ETO), and Lt. Gen. Alvan Gillem became the Armored Force commander. In July 1943, Gillem visited US units on Sicily and came back convinced that

Operation *Husky* on Sicily in July 1943 was the first clear demonstration of the growing Allied skill in conducting complex amphibious assault operations. Here, M4A1 medium tanks of the 2nd Armored Division come ashore from LSTs on the Gela beachhead using pontoon causeways to facilitate the landing of heavy mechanized equipment without port handling equipment. (Artwork by Steve Noon © Osprey Publishing)

By the time of the Operation *Husky* landings on Sicily in July 1943, the M3 medium tank had been removed from service in combat units in favor of the M4/M4A1 medium tanks. This is "Eternity," an M4A1 produced by the Lima Locomotive Works in September 1942 and serving with Co. E, 2/67th Armored, 2nd Armored Division, on Gela beach on July 10, 1943.

more attention had to be paid to the requirements of tank-infantry cooperation. In spite of McNair's opposition, there was momentum to shift the mission from the massed use of separate tank battalions to support the corps or army, to the dispersed use of the battalions to directly support infantry divisions. The pendulum had swung back again to the traditional role of these units.

In September 1943, the armored division was reorganized with a better balance of tanks, armored infantry, and armored field artillery, ending up with three battalions of each. Since the previous organization of the armored division included two armored regiments with three tank battalions each, this left a surplus of three tank battalions from each of the reorganized divisions. These surplus tank battalions were earmarked as separate tank battalions. In addition to new battalions created in 1943, this expanded the US Army's tank force from 27 to 70 separate tank battalions by the end of 1943.

Lessons from the North African campaign also led to significant organizational changes in the tank battalions. Prior to the 1943 organization, tank battalions were configured either as light or medium tank battalions, equipped solely with light or medium tanks. The North African campaign had made it clear that the M3A1 and M5 light tanks were obsolete and that the medium tank must become the centerpiece of the tank battalion. Although many armor officers recommended abandoning the light tank entirely in favor of medium tanks, AGF was unwilling to do so since there were so many of the new M5A1 light tanks available. The AGF argued that the light tanks could still perform a useful function in the battalion such as scouting and flank

OPPOSITE Tank Battalion Table of Organization and Equipment September 15, 1943. (© Osprey Publishing)

Tank battalion TO&E 17–25 September 15, 1943

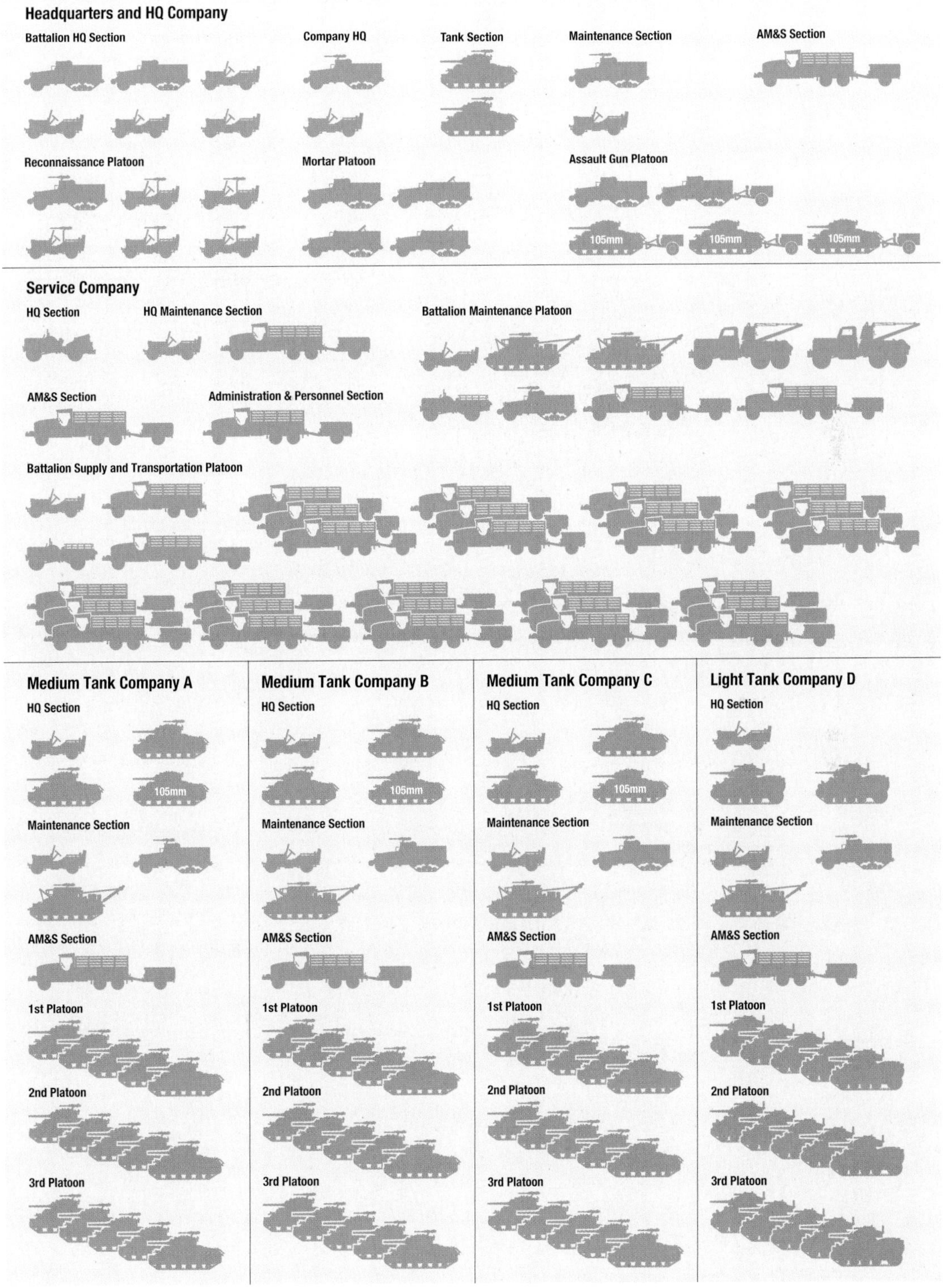

Headquarters and HQ Company

Battalion HQ Section

Company HQ

Tank Section

Maintenance Section

AM&S Section

Reconnaissance Platoon

Mortar Platoon

Assault Gun Platoon

105mm

105mm

105mm

Service Company

HQ Section

HQ Maintenance Section

Battalion Maintenance Platoon

AM&S Section

Administration & Personnel Section

Battalion Supply and Transportation Platoon

Medium Tank Company A

HQ Section

105mm

Maintenance Section

AM&S Section

1st Platoon

2nd Platoon

3rd Platoon

Medium Tank Company B

HQ Section

105mm

Maintenance Section

AM&S Section

1st Platoon

2nd Platoon

3rd Platoon

Medium Tank Company C

HQ Section

105mm

Maintenance Section

AM&S Section

1st Platoon

2nd Platoon

3rd Platoon

Light Tank Company D

HQ Section

Maintenance Section

AM&S Section

1st Platoon

2nd Platoon

3rd Platoon

security. As a result, a new tank battalion organization was developed consisting of three medium tank companies (A, B, C) and one light tank company (D). There were some exceptions to this rule. A few separate tank battalions retained a homogenous light tank organization, though the reasons remain obscure. Both the separate tank battalions and those belonging to the armored divisions followed a common table of organization and equipment (TO&E), with the exception of the rare light tank battalions. The September 1943 changes were the last major reorganization of the separate tank battalions prior to the start of the campaign in the ETO.

The AGF sent out a new directive to corps commanders on October 16, 1943 stressing the need for more combined training of tanks and infantry, but later inspections revealed that little was being done. In April 1944 Gen Gillem organized a conference of senior commanders at Fort Benning to demonstrate proper tank-infantry tactics. Unfortunately, few of the tank battalions committed to combat in France in the summer of 1944 had received proper tank-infantry training due to the belated recognition of this key mission.

The Tunisia battles saw the first extensive use of the tank destroyer battalions. The 601st Tank Destroyer Battalion landed in North Africa at the start of Operation *Torch* in November 1942, still organized as a composite battalion with a mixture of M6 37mm GMC and M3 75mm GMC. Two more battalions followed in December 1942, and four in January 1943. Two of these, the 776th and 805th TD Battalions, were equipped with the new M10 3-inch GMC. The M10 3-inch tank destroyer saw its combat debut with the 805th Tank Destroyer Battalion at El Guettar on March 23, 1943. The fighting at El Guettar was the sole example of the tank destroyer battalions being used according to doctrine as a concentrated force to repulse a massed tank attack. The attack was staged by

Of the various tank destroyers to see service in Tunisia, only the M10 3-inch GMC was deemed acceptable based on combat experience. This example in Oran in March 1943 is fitted with the second style of turret counterweight consisting of wedge-shaped lead slabs.

An M3 75mm tank destroyer of the Anti-Tank Company, 39th Infantry Regiment, 9th Division, in an overwatch position near Kasserine Pass in March 1943.

10.Panzer-Division with about 50 tanks. The 601st and 899th Tank Destroyer Battalions helped beat it off, claiming to have knocked out about 30 German tanks in the process. However, the 601st lost 20 of its 28 M3 75mm GMC, and the 899th lost seven M10 3-inch GMC. There was considerably less tank fighting in the later stage of the campaign, and the tank destroyers were sometimes used as expedient field artillery, a role which they would also adopt in Italy in 1943–44.

The lessons from tank destroyer combat in North Africa were a source of controversy within the Army's senior ranks, with factions seeing the campaign as vindicating their own point of view. A study by the Tank Destroyer School of the actions of one of the battalions in Tunisia concluded that the tank destroyers had "destroyed three times our own losses by outmaneuvering and outshooting a superior force." General Bruce pointed to the battle at El Guettar as a shining example of the potential of tank destroyers. Other officers pointed out that tank destroyers had completely failed to stop the German tank attacks at Sidi Bou Zid and Kasserine Pass, that the one engagement at El Guettar was a Pyrrhic victory with tank destroyer losses as high as panzer losses, and that the tank destroyers in North Africa had little to show even though numbering ten battalions. Major General John Lucas, a special observer for the Army Chief of Staff, concluded that "the Tank Destroyer has, in my opinion, failed to prove its usefulness… I believe that the doctrine of an offensive weapon to

The performance of the tank destroyer battalions in Tunisia was controversial. This group of M3 75mm GMC of the 894th Tank Destroyer Battalion stumbled into an Allied minefield while withdrawing along the Thala road during on the night of February 20, 1943. The M3 75mm GMC subsequently was withdrawn from service in the Mediterranean theater as the far superior M120 3-inch GMC became available.

'slug it out' with the tank is unsound." Lucas supported the deployment of purely defensive anti-tank weapons such as anti-tank guns. Armored Force chief Lt. Gen. Jacob Devers toured North Africa and concluded that "the separate tank destroyer arm is not a practical concept on the battlefield. Defensive anti-tank weapons are essentially artillery. Offensively, the best way to beat the tank is a better tank." Senior commanders in Tunisia, including George Patton and Omar Bradley, were unhappy with the performance of the offensively oriented tank destroyer doctrine, finding them unsuited to actual battlefield conditions.

McNair's AGF headquarters was particularly critical of the emphasis on offensive tactics that seemed to suggest that the tank destroyers would chase around the battlefield looking for enemy tanks. The AGF forced the Tank Destroyer Center to rewrite their basic field manual on tactics, *FM 18-5*, but the issue was so contentious that a year passed before the edition completed in May 1943 was accepted for publication.

The controversial performance of the tank destroyers in Tunisia led to plans to trim back the size of the force. Initial plans in 1941 had called for as many as 220 battalions, reduced to 144 in 1943, and further trimmed back to 106 by the end of 1943. Of the 106 battalions, 61 were deployed to Europe and ten to the Pacific theater, leaving 35 in the United States with little demand for their services. The AGF decided that these were surplus, and in October 1943 began making plans to disband them for their personnel or convert them to other roles such as field artillery, tank, or amphibious tractor battalions. The first five were converted in December 1943, and most of the remainder in March–May 1944.

The most pernicious effect of the North African controversy was that it gave free rein to Gen. McNair to pander to the long-standing prejudices of his fellow artillerymen in favor of towed anti-tank guns. McNair pointed to the successes of British towed anti-tank guns in the fighting in the autumn of 1942 at El Alamein as vindication of the towed anti-tank gun concept. McNair's argument confused a technical issue with a tactical issue. The British anti-tank guns had been effective at El Alamein because the British had been prudent enough to deploy the more powerful 6-pdr (57mm) anti-tank gun in a timely fashion, while the US Army had clung to the obsolete and ineffective 37mm anti-tank gun in its divisional anti-tank companies. The British example did not answer the tactical dilemma of whether it made sense any longer to deploy specialized defensive anti-tank battalions when the US Army was about to embark on a series of campaigns which were primarily offensive in nature.

McNair's assessment of the lessons of the North African campaign were ex-post-facto excuses for policies he had been pursuing before El Alamein. In August 1942, McNair had pushed for the manufacture of a towed version of the 3-inch gun currently used on the M10 3-inch GMC even though it was vigorously opposed by Gen. Bruce. On August 22, 1942, McNair ordered the Tank Destroyer Center to restudy the issue of towed anti-tank guns, noting that they could be unloaded at ports that could not handle heavy tracked vehicles. General Bruce argued that a towed battalion required 300 more men than a self-propelled battalion and required more shipping space since it involved not only the towed gun but its prime mover as well. On January 1, 1943, McNair ordered Bruce to create and test a towed battalion, with the 801st Tank Destroyer Battalion serving as the guinea pig. The trials resulted in

The obvious shortcomings of the M6 37mm tank destroyer led to its withdrawal from combat even before the end of the Tunisian campaign.

a tentative organization, and on March 31, 1943 McNair ordered the conversion of 15 self-propelled battalions into towed battalions. To keep the battalion size down, the reconnaissance platoon was eliminated in towed battalions. In November 1943, McNair ordered that half of all tank destroyer battalions would be converted to towed configuration in time for the forthcoming campaign in France. During the autumn 1943 Louisiana wargames, the newly converted 823rd Tank Destroyer Battalion was attached to several different divisions to show them the uses and limitations of the new formation. As would become evident in the campaign in France, McNair's decision to shift the tank destroyer battalions to a towed configuration made a mediocre combat formation even worse.

If this was not bad enough, Gen. Bruce's action in the technical realm did little to improve the prospects for the successful combat use of the tank destroyer battalions in 1944. Bruce had been pushing for a new self-propelled tank destroyer design since 1941, placing a great deal of emphasis on the need for high speed. Bruce was so adamant on this point that the head of the Special Armored Board, Brig. Gen. W. B. Palmer, complained that his exorbitant expectations would prevent a vehicle from being ready in time to participate in the 1944 campaigns. Bruce finally settled on the new M18 76mm GMC as the answer to his prayers. Its development is detailed below. While the M18 was much faster than the M10, it was also more weakly armored. Its fighting compartment was too small, impairing its combat efficiency compared with the M10 tank destroyer. The firepower of both vehicles was essentially the same, so many officers questioned whether the M18 was justified. General Omar Bradley refused to have the type deployed with his First US Army after trial deployments at Anzio in February 1944 received very mixed reviews. Bruce had let his obsession with high mobility distract him from the primary mission of the tank destroyer force, namely the ability to destroy enemy tanks. When the Ordnance tried to win support for mounting the 90mm gun on the M10 in anticipation of German armor improvements, Bruce objected, arguing that it was not fast enough. As a result, when US Army tank destroyer battalions were deployed in France in 1944, they were still equipped with the same 3-inch tank destroyers available since 1942. Worse yet, many battalions were now armed with the cumbersome new M5 3-inch towed guns.

Fighting in Italy in 1943–44 had few tactical or technical influences on US tank development. Due to the terrain, US tanks were used primarily in an infantry support role. The opposing German forces were equipped much the same as in Tunisia and Sicily, so there were few new technical lessons to be learned. Although the new Panther tank was first deployed to the Anzio sector in February 1944, it was not used in combat in significant numbers until May 1944.

IMPROVING THE TANK DESTROYER

In 1941, the Tank Destroyer Board began to examine some 200 different design proposals for its 3-inch gun tank destroyer. It took nearly three years for this program to reach fruition due to rapidly evolving changes on the European battlefield. General Bruce was unhappy with the Army's selection of various expedient tank destroyers such as the truck-based M6 37mm GMC and the half-track-based M3 75mm GMC. Bruce fastened on to the idea of using a Christie-type suspension as part of his effort to field a very fast tank destroyer. The first of these projects was the short-lived 37mm GMC T42. This quickly vanished due to the obvious inadequacies of the 37mm gun. In April 1942, the Buick Motor Car Division of General Motors Corporation was given a contract for the 57mm GMC T49. The Christie suspension idea was unceremoniously dropped as archaic and wasteful of space, and a torsion bar suspension was substituted. The first T49 pilot was completed in July 1942, but tests showed that problems with the transmission limited the speed of the vehicle to 38mph instead of the desired 55mph.

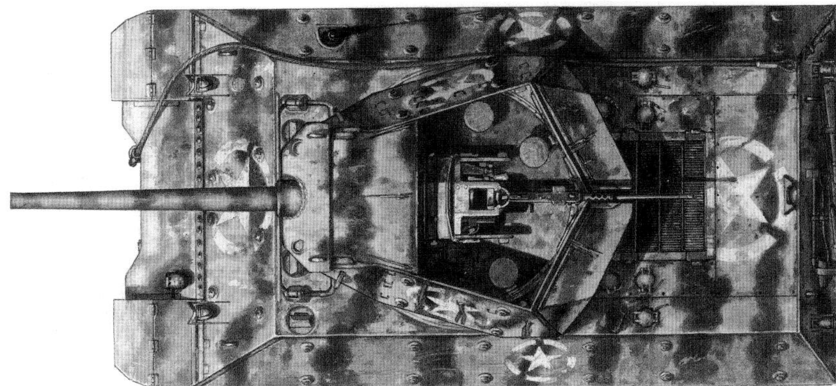

M10 3-inch GMC, 894th Tank Destroyer Battalion, Italy, 1944. (Artwork by Peter Sarson © Osprey Publishing)

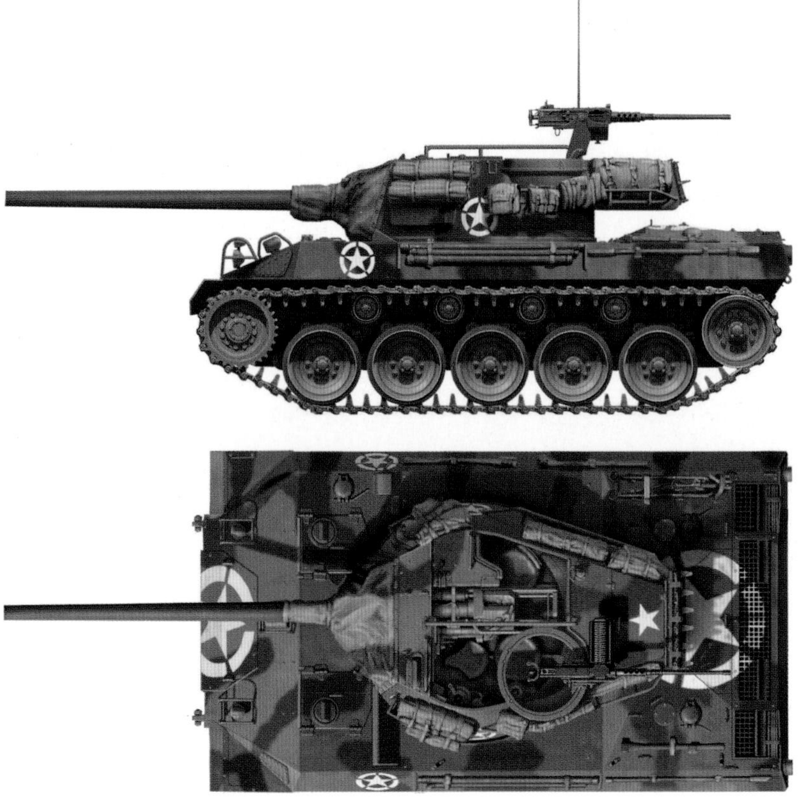

T70 76mm GMC, 894th Tank Destroyer Battalion, Anzio, 1944. (Artwork by Jim Laurier © Osprey Publishing)

After experimenting with light and heavy tank destroyers, on April 23, 1942, the Army decided to standardize on a single type of tank destroyer battalion based around the new M10 3-inch GMC design. As a result, in October 1942 the Ordnance Committee recommended that the second pilot of the T49 be fitted with a larger 75mm gun M3. Due to the need for a larger turret and turret ring, as well as the greater weight and size of the 75mm gun, it was fitted in an open-topped turret. This second pilot was designated as the 75mm GMC T67. The design was doomed from the outset in view of the Army preference for a 3-inch gun for tank destroyers. However, the light chassis precluded the use of the 3-inch M7 gun used on the M10 3-inch GMC. Ordnance had begun to develop a new lightweight 3-inch gun, the M1. This used the same projectiles as the M7 3-inch gun, but a different propellant casing. To avoid confusion with ammunition supply, the M1 gun was reclassified as a 76mm gun, though it was in fact in the same 3-inch (76.2mm) caliber as the M7 gun. With the new gun on the horizon, Tank Destroyer Command indicated it would prefer the new 76mm gun M1 on the T67. The pilot was modified to accommodate the 76mm gun, but automotive trials indicated the need for a more powerful engine than the two 165hp Buick 60 engines used on the T67. As a result, the T67 project was closed in January 1943, and Buick was authorized to build pilots of a suitably modified derivative, the T70 76mm GMC.

The first T70 pilot was completed in April 1943 and began tests in June 1943 at the Milford Proving Ground at Camp Hood, Texas, and at Aberdeen Proving Ground. Buick prepared an outstanding design in a very short space of time, and the T70 pilots proved to be relatively mature in terms of their automotive performance. The T70 contained many innovations that earned it special praise. It was the first US armored vehicle to use torsion bar suspension, which proved to be a significant improvement over the previous vertical volute spring suspensions so characteristic of earlier US tank designs.

By the time the T70 had reached maturity, Gen. Bruce had departed the Tank Destroyer Center to take up a divisional command. McNair and the AGF insisted that production start as soon as possible to provide enough time to train the units that would be deployed in Europe for the summer 1944 campaign. As a result, T70 production began in July 1943 even though testing had only started. No matter how good the design, testing inevitably uncovered many small engineering problems, and the T70 was no exception. As a result, the initial production batches of T70 tank destroyers were hobbled by a number of technical problems, especially in the powertrain.

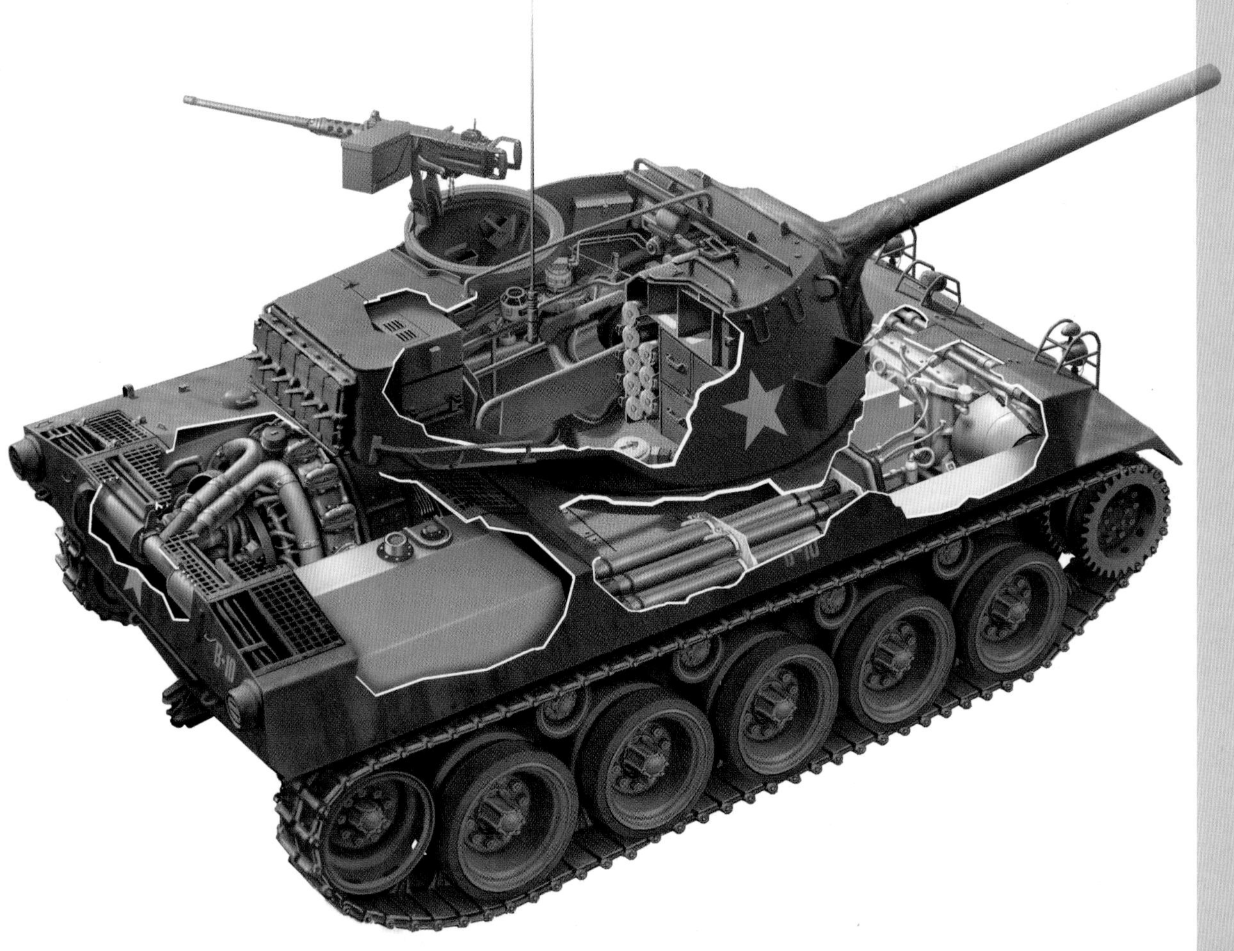

M18 76mm GMC, 704th Tank Destroyer Battalion, France, 1944. (Artwork by Jim Laurier © Osprey Publishing)

In the view of the Tank Destroyer Center, the M18 76mm gun motor carriage represented the ideal tank destroyer due to its exceptional mobility. This view was not entirely shared in the tank destroyer battalions due to the Hellcat's thin armor, cramped fighting compartment, and inability to deal with the Panther tank in a hands-on engagement.

As design flaws were uncovered, changes were made on the production vehicles at Buick. The first serial production vehicles were completed by Buick in July 1943. However, this string of modifications delayed the acceptance of the T70 as standard until March 1944, when it was designated as the M18 76mm GMC. In 1944, the M18 76mm gun motor carriage was viewed by the US Army's Tank Destroyer Center as the ideal tank hunter – fast, hard-hitting, and maneuverable. It was the fastest tracked armored vehicle of World War II, capable of road speeds up to 60mph.

The Tank Destroyer Center wished to deploy the T70 76mm GMC into combat as soon as possible to get feedback about its performance, even before it had been officially accepted as standard equipment. As a result, two T70 vehicles were shipped to the 601st Tank Destroyer Battalion and three to the 894th that were operating in the Anzio beachhead. The new vehicles arrived at the beginning of May 1944, and their crews were quickly trained by Ordnance personnel in time to take part in the breakout operations that began on May 23, 1944. After inspecting the T70 76mm GMC, the 894th Tank Destroyer Battalion commander decided against deploying them alongside the M10 3-inch GMC, feeling that their weak armor would make them too vulnerable. Instead, they were deployed in the battalion's reconnaissance company, where their high speed was felt to be more useful. In general, the battalion was very happy with the M18's excellent automotive performance. Its major automotive drawback was the poor hill-climbing performance on the early vehicles, and its difficulties in mud due to low ground clearance. The battalion found that the M18's high speed "enables the vehicle to cross exposed ground quickly and gain cover without offering a good target. It eliminates wastage of time getting into firing positions." The battalion was also happy with the performance of the 76mm gun, though there was some concern that its construction was not as durable as the M7 3-inch gun in the M10.

The light armor of the M18 bothered the battalion to the extent that "the crews have much less confidence in the T70 than they do in the M10 and this might easily be reflected in the efficiency and determination with which the crew functions in a firefight." The battalion was also concerned about the relatively small interior space of the M18 compared with the M10:

> ... the space inside the T70 is so limited that the crew cannot live in it as they have had to do many times in the M10. Furthermore, the limited space inside the fighting compartment allows only a very small clearance between the base of the [ammunition] round and the back of the turret while loading the piece, making loading more difficult and of necessity much slower than in the M10. Less ammunition can be carried on the T70 and the ammunition is stowed in such a way that only nine rounds are readily available and after firing nine rounds the remainder must be taken from less accessible compartments in the sponsons. Because of the confined space the gunner himself has to get out some of the ammunition on his side of the vehicle.

The battalion concluded in its report that the T70 was an excellent reconnaissance vehicle, "but it is believed to be not as good a weapon for use as a tank destroyer against enemy tanks as is the M10 because of the many limitations pointed out above." In many respects, this evaluation echoed the earlier comments by Gen. Palmer of the Special Armored Vehicles Board, who had warned Bruce and the Tank Destroyer Center about the impact that the focus on speed and mobility would have on other aspects of the vehicle's performance.

UPGRADING THE SHERMAN TANK

There had been a steady stream of small improvements to the Sherman tank during its production run. As mentioned earlier, the M4 series followed the same pattern as the earlier M3 medium tank, with parallel production of several variants using different engines. Besides the M4 and M4A1 powered by a Continental radial engine, the M4A2 was powered by twin GM diesels, the M4A3 by a new Ford V-8, and the M4A4 with the Chrysler multi-bank engine. On January 11, 1943, AGF decided that that preference for US tank units in the future would be the M4A3, M4A1, and M4 in that order. The

The Sherman underwent continual evolution in 1942–43. This illustration shows some of the changing features, starting with the early configuration from the spring of 1942 to 1943, the Quick Fix/Blitz upgrades in the ETO for D-Day, and the late production configuration with the new 47-degree, wet-stowage hull and other improvements. (Author)

diesel-powered M4A2 went almost entirely to Lend-Lease except for a small number used by the US Marine Corps, and training use by the 13th Armored Division. The M4A4 went exclusively to Britain except for small numbers used by the 14th Armored Division for training.

There had been considerable complaints from US tankers in Tunisia about the propensity of the Sherman tank to burn if penetrated by enemy gunfire. This was often attributed to its use of a gasoline engine rather than diesel. However, Ordnance studies of battle experiences concluded that the main culprit was ammunition fires. To remedy this situation, a two-step program was initiated. As a short-term solution, appliqué armor was welded over the hull side to offer better protection to the ammo bins. As a long-term solution, a modernized hull was designed that transferred the ammo bins from the sponson over the tracks to the floor of the hull. This reduced their probability of being hit. In addition, the new ammunition bins were protected by a thin armored cover, and the space between the ammunition tubes was filled with liquid to prevent the ammunition being ignited by spall if the tank was penetrated by enemy gunfire. This new hull design entered production in late 1943, and tanks with this feature were sometimes referred to with a "W" suffix to indicate wet stowage, such as M4A3(W).

Another notable change was the replacement of the older M34 gun mount with the M34A1 combination gun mount. This provided more armored protection for the turret front but was mainly selected since it added a telescopic sight for the gunner. The British Army had been pushing for this upgrade since 1942, arguing that a telescopic sight offered better accuracy than the periscopic gunner's sight then in use.

Many of the US Army tank units in Britain in 1943 had M4 and M4A1 tanks that had been manufactured in 1942 prior to the improvements. A "Quick Fix" program was implemented in 1943 to bring the early Sherman tanks up to current standards in terms of important changes, such as the

The crew layout in the M4A3(W). (Author)

M34A1 gun mount and appliqué armor. These were manufactured as "Blitz kits" in the US and shipped to Britain to be incorporated into the tanks at local depots. Most tanks in the ETO had these upgrades by the time of the D-Day landings in June 1944.

In late 1943, the Army Service Forces dispatched a "New Weapons Board" to the Mediterranean Theater of Operations (MTO) and European Theater of Operations (ETO), with the dual mission of collecting information on the performance of existing US Army weapons as well as informing units deployed overseas of planned improvements in weapons. Their report, published in April 1944, provides some insight into the general attitude within the US Army to the performance of the M4 and M4A1 tanks prior to the Normandy campaign. Overall, the report concluded that "The medium tanks of the M4 series are well liked by the using personnel… The M4 tank is good and well-liked by everyone. However, the fact that the M4 is the outstanding tank of the war to date should not deter us from giving them a better one." In terms of firepower, troops in the MTO felt that the German 75mm gun offered better performance than the Sherman's 75mm gun, and "there is overwhelming demand for 76mm guns in M4 tanks."

The report went on to say:

> Opinion of proper armor thickness was divided. Armored Force troops generally regard the present armor as adequate. They do not want to sacrifice maneuverability, speed, or floatation to gain additional armor protection… Troops were not overly concerned about the hazards of ammunition stowage. There is no interest in further protection of ammunition if it would entail any decrease in the number of rounds

carried. Ready racks in the turret are particularly desired and the tank crews are extremely reluctant to give up ready racks even to increase safety… Tank crews are very little concerned with protection of ammunition and consider accessibility and quantity of primary importance.

Sherman comparative technical data

Type	M4A1	M4A1 (76mm)	M4A3E8 (76mm)
Length (feet)	19.2	24.5	24.7
Width (feet)	8.6	8.6	9.8
Height (feet)	9.0	9.7	9.7
Combat weight (tons)	33.4	35.3	37.7
Main gun	75mm M3	76mm M1A1	76mm M1A2
Elevation	-12 to +25	-10 to +25	-10 +25
Firing rate (rpm)	20	20	20
Co-axial machine gun	.30-cal	.30-cal	.30-cal
Main gun ammo (rounds)	90	71	71
.50-cal HMG ammo	300	600	600
.30-cal LMG ammo	4,750	6,250	6,250
Engine	R-975 C1	R-975 C4	Ford GAA
Horsepower	400	460	500
Fuel stowage (gal)	175	175	168
Range (road, miles)	120	100	100
Max. speed (mph)	24	24	26
Armor thickness (mm)			
Hull front	51	64	64
Hull side	38	38	38
Hull rear	38	38	38
Hull top	19	19	19
Hull bottom	25	25	25
Gun shield	76	90	90
Turret front	76	76	76
Turret side	51	63	63
Turret rear	51	63	63
Turret roof	25	25	25

IMPROVING THE SHERMAN'S FIREPOWER

Ordnance began developing a more powerful 76mm tank gun in 1942. The US Army already had the M7 3-inch gun on the M6 heavy tank and M10 tank destroyer. The M7 was an adaptation of an existing anti-aircraft gun, but its breech was too large to fit comfortably in medium tank turrets. One of the prototypes of the new and more compact T1 76mm guns was placed in an M4A1 tank. The original T1 76mm gun had a length of 57 calibers, but this caused traverse problems when the tank was on a slope due to the excessive weight at the front of the turret caused by the long barrel. The engineers cut 15 inches from the muzzle end of the gun, reducing its length to 52 calibers, which ameliorated the balance problem but decreased the anti-armor penetration of the gun. This was not of immediate concern, since at the time the 75mm gun in the existing M4 tank had proven to be completely adequate on the battlefield. It was standardized as the M1A1 76mm gun in August 1942 though not immediately placed into serial production.

Compared with other tank guns being developed at this time, the M1A1 76mm gun offered mediocre anti-armor performance. The British Army was developing its own 76.2mm tank gun, better known as the 17-pounder. This gun had a barrel length of 55 calibers compared with the 52 calibers of the US 76mm gun. The biggest difference was in the ammunition. The 17-pdr armor-piercing round weighed 37.5lb compared with 24.8lb for the American 76mm round. A more important difference was the propellant load. The 17-pdr round

Ordnance had been working on a Sherman with the new M1 76mm gun since 1942, and a small test batch of M4A1 (76M1) was produced in 1942. AGF resisted putting it into production due to a lack of "battle-need." The Armored Force sent some of the M4A1 (76M1) to the 40th Tank Battalion, 7th Armored Division, at Camp Young at the Desert Training Center, for evaluation, which found that the original Sherman turret was too small for the gun.

contained almost 9lb of propellant compared with only 3.6lb of propellant for the 76mm round. The high chamber pressure of the 17-pdr led to faster barrel erosion, but the British gun designers were willing to trade barrel life for higher anti-armor performance. In contrast, US design practices were far more conservative and favored longer barrel life. While these practices might have been overcome had there been a strong requirement from the Armored Force for superior anti-tank performance, this incentive was lacking. German tank gun development was similar to the British, opting for a high-velocity 75mm KwK 42 gun with an extremely long 70-caliber barrel. Like the British gun, the German weapon had very high chamber pressures of about 48,000psi compared with only 38,000psi on the US 76mm gun, and the German ammunition featured a large 8.1lb propellant charge, ensuring a very high velocity for the projectile. In terms of armor penetration, the US gun could penetrate 116mm of armor at 500 meters, the British 17-pdr 150mm, and the German gun 168mm.

In August 1942, Ordnance recommended that the Army modify existing production contracts so that 1,000 Sherman tanks would be built with the 76mm new gun. In November 1942, the head of the Armored Force, Maj. Gen. Jacob Devers, refused to support the plan, complaining of inadequate testing.

In December 1942, Devers and several other senior officers toured the North African theater to observe trends in tactics and technology. The team visited Britain on the return trip and had the opportunity to discuss future tank requirements with their British colleagues. They were briefed on the next-generation British tank gun, the new 17-pdr, and they witnessed demonstrations of both its towed version and a tank-mounted version. Although the British Army was content with the performance of the 75mm gun on the Sherman tank, they were convinced that the Germans would

Tests showed that it was possible to mount the 90mm Pershing turret on the M4 medium tank. However, no production was authorized since it would not come any sooner than the superior T26E3 tank.

continue to increase the armor thickness on their panzers, and that this would require a continual escalation in gun power to retain parity on the battlefield. Devers changed his earlier opinion about the 76mm gun project and recommended after the trip that "The new high power 76mm gun should be immediately tested in the M4 tank to determine what percentage of these guns should be installed in future tanks… The further perfection of the M4 tank, the best on any front today, should be aggressively continued."

The initial trials of the M4A1 (76M1) found that the internal turret space in the tank was unsatisfactory, and that the design overall was an improvised "quick fix." As a result, the plan to manufacture 1,000 of these tanks was shelved. In view of the strong recommendation from Gen. Devers to accelerate the development of the 76mm Sherman, Ordnance adapted the larger turret from the experimental T23 medium tank to the M4 tank chassis. Two pilots of the M4E6 were authorized on June 17, 1943 and delivered in July 1943. The trials of the two pilots in August were so successful that on August 17, 1943, the Armored Board recommended the M4E6 for production. This went up the chain of command to Headquarters, Armor Command, which on August 21, 1943 recommended that 1,000 M4 tanks be procured.

Tank crewmen show the difference between the 75mm (left) and 76mm round (right) As can be seen, the principal difference was the much larger propellant casing of the 76mm gun, which gave it much higher velocity and greater penetrating power.

In the meantime, Gen. Devers had been reassigned to take command of the European Theater of Operations (ETO). Gen. Alvan Gillem was selected to replace Devers as head of Armored Command. Gillem started his tenure by visiting tank units in North Africa and Sicily to determine what was needed in the future and came back convinced that greater attention had to be paid to tank-infantry cooperation. On his return, Gillem stepped into the dispute over an August 21 letter that had been penned by his subordinates during his absence that pressed for the new 76mm gun. He was troubled by the suggestion that production shift to the 76mm gun, as it was less suitable for infantry fire support against unarmored targets than was the older 75mm gun. The problem was inherent in the shift to high-velocity tank guns. Earlier, low-velocity tank guns, such as the Sherman's M3 75mm gun, could use thin-walled high-explosive projectiles. The thin shell meant that the projectile could contain more high explosive. As velocity increased, the high-explosive shell required thicker walls to withstand the stress of firing. This meant that the shell contained less high explosive. So in the case of the Sherman, the 75mm high-explosive shell contained 1.47lb of explosive, while the 76mm contained only 0.86lb of explosive, or about 60 percent.

A comparison of US tank and tank destroyer ammunition, top to bottom: 75mm APC M61, 76mm APC M62A1, 3-inch APC M62A1, 90mm APC M82 (T33). (First and third artwork by Richard Chasemore, second and fourth artwork by Jim Laurier © Osprey Publishing)

On September 1, 1943, Gillem sent another letter to AGF clarifying the Armored Force's requirements. Gillem was not convinced that the 76mm gun should replace the 75mm gun on the Sherman. Although it clearly had superior armor-piercing capability, it fired a much less effective high-explosive round. To date, the vast majority of tank ammunition expended in combat had been high explosive, so a decrease in this capability seemed a retrograde step. Gillem recommended that the M4 with 76mm gun be deployed in a ratio of either one per every three tanks or one tank platoon per company, or one company per battalion.

In August 1943, the British tank liaison office in the United States suggested equipping US tanks with the 17-pdr, but Ordnance was largely indifferent to the offer, for a variety of reasons. US officers who had seen the gun fired in Britain were surprised by its substantial muzzle flash and the unnerving tendency for flashback at the breech which hinted at design problems. A variety of US guns were in development, including both the 76mm M1A1 and a new 90mm gun, which were believed to be more than adequate to handle the German threat. Furthermore, the British didn't proof-test the 17-pdr in a Sherman turret until late December 1943. A comparative shoot of the US 90mm and British 17-pdr was conducted at Aberdeen Proving Ground in the US on March 25, 1944, followed by a similar trial at Shoeburyness in Britain on May 23, 1944. The British offered to provide 200 guns and ammunition per month to the US within three months of notice. The comparative trials did demonstrate that the 17-pdr had superior anti-armor performance to the American 90mm gun slated for new tank destroyers, to say nothing of the 76mm tank gun. However, by the time that these assessments were made, both the 76mm and 90mm tank guns and ammunition

Ordnance examined the British 17-pdr in 1943–44 but preferred domestic solutions. This is a British Sherman 17-pdr Firefly of Lt. Robert Boscawen, commander of 2 Troop, the Coldstream Guards, 29th Armoured Brigade, guarding one of the Meuse river bridges at Namur on Christmas Day during the Battle of the Bulge.

were already in production in the US, and the 17-pdr would not be available until well after the Normandy landings.

Ordnance resisted the adoption of the British gun for a variety of reasons. The 76mm T4 high-velocity armor-piercing (HVAP) ammunition was completing development, which would boost 76mm gun performance to near the level of the 17-pdr without the need to switch to yet another new gun and ammunition. There was concern that British arsenals could not meet US quantities for either guns or ammunition. But the real problem was that the US Army did not have a realistic appreciation of the future tank threat. Attitudes about the 17-pdr option would change after the Normandy fighting in June 1944. The controversy over future tank guns highlights some problems within the US tank development process that is discussed further on later pages.

Comparative anti-tank gun performance

	US 3-inch	UK 17-pdr
Combat weight (lb)	4,875	4,624
Barrel length (calibers)	L/50	L/55
Ammunition type	M62 APC	APCBC
Initial muzzle velocity (fps)	2,600	2,900
Penetration* (mm)	115	163
*@ 500m, 0 degrees		

BELOW M4A1 (76mm) turret interior. (Artwork by Jim Laurier © Osprey Publishing)

BOTTOM M4A1 (76mm), 3rd Armored Division, France, 1944. (Artwork by Jim Laurier © Osprey Publishing)

The US Army approved the 76mm Sherman as standard on March 30, 1944. It was adopted on three chassis – the M4A1, the M4A2, and the M4A3. Pressed Steel Car Company began delivery of the first M4A1 (76mm) tanks in January 1944, followed by Detroit Tank Arsenal's initial deliveries of the M4A3 (76mm) in March 1944. Fisher's Grand Blanc Tank Arsenal began producing the M4A2 (76mm) in early 1944, but these were intended primarily for export to the Soviet Union under the Lend-Lease program.

HEAVY FIREPOWER

Ordnance had studied the possible use of a 90mm gun as early as 1942 due to reports of the German use of the 88mm gun. There was little user support for such a weapon, with both the Tank Destroyer and Armored Force regarding existing guns as adequate. Nevertheless, Ordnance prudently continued development as a hedge against future threats. After discarding half-baked schemes to mount a 90mm anti-aircraft gun on a Sherman chassis, Ordnance developed the

The M36 90mm gun motor carriage combined a new turret with the 90mm gun to the M10A1 chassis. This is a late production example fitted with a muzzle brake.

T7 90mm gun that was purpose-built for armored vehicle turrets. Although one was mounted in an M10 tank destroyer turret as early as 1942, the associated ammunition was so much larger than the 3-inch ammunition that an enlarged turret was preferred. This resulted in the T71 90mm GMC.

The first pilot of the T71 90mm gun motor carriage was delivered in September 1943. An attempt by Ordnance to rush the design into production was rebuffed by the AGF in September 1943 when it got mixed up in the controversy over 90mm gun tanks. This debate is covered in more detail in the section on the M26 Pershing tank. The Tank Destroyer Board continued to resist the T71 program since it wanted high-speed tank destroyers such as the M18 76mm GMC. General Barnes from Ordnance continued to press the issue and won support from the AFV&W (Armored Fighting Vehicles and Weapons) Section at ETOUSA in London. This created "battle-need," with the officers in the ETO arguing that it would be useful in dealing with Germany's Siegfried Line defenses. As a result, AGF approved production in October 1943. To facilitate production, existing M10A1 chassis were to be upgraded with the new turret and the final batch of M10A1 completed without turrets for this program. Conversions of the 300 turretless M10A1 began at Grand Blanc in April 1944 and were finished in July 1944. The T71 was standardized on June 1, 1944 as the 90mm GMC M36. The first M36 tank destroyers arrived in the ETO in September 1944. After preparation and crew training, they first went into action in October 1944 during the fighting along the German border. Due to the small numbers originally available, it was not possible to equip entire battalions with the M36. As a result, the initial practice was to issue it to existing M10 battalions, usually on a scale of one company at a time. As more became available, entire battalions were reequipped.

A shortage of M10A1 tank destroyers to convert to the M36 obliged Ordnance to convert M4A3 tanks instead, resulting in the M36B1 seen here.

On May 15, 1944, the M36 requirement was increased to 600, and after the tank fighting in Normandy exposed the shortcomings of the M10, the total was increased to 1,400 on July 29, 1944. The large increase caused some difficulties, as only 913 M10A1 tank destroyers could be rounded up from training units and depots of the 1,413 that had been completed. As a result, it was decided to round out the production by mounting the remaining 187 turrets on M4A3 medium tank chassis. This version was later designated as the M36B1, and they were completed at Grand Blanc in October–December 1944. The M36 90mm GMC would prove to be by far the most effective tank destroyer in the 1944–45 campaigns in the European theater.

A NEW HEAVY TANK?

Ordnance had been working on an eventual replacement for the Sherman since 1942 under a program first called the M4X. This was a clean-slate design studying a wide variety of new hull and turret designs as well as new powerplants and armament. The first significant version to reach production was the T23 medium tank. One of the most significant differences from the older Sherman tank was the powertrain layout. On the M4, the transmission was in the front of the tank, which necessitated the use of a drive shaft down the center of the fighting compartment to the rear-mounted engine, forcing the turret to be mounted higher than otherwise might be the case. This led to a higher hull profile, greater hull volume, and more weight. By placing the transmission at the rear of the T23, the turret could be lowered further into the hull. The reduction in the silhouette of the tank made it possible to reduce the internal hull volume and to increase the armor thickness without a drastic increase in the overall weight of the tank. This had the added benefit of making the tank less conspicuous on the battlefield when frontally engaging enemy tanks.

A more controversial innovation was the use of a revolutionary electric transmission. The normal gasoline engine was connected to an electrical generator, which sent a current to the electric traction motors that powered the track. In theory, electric drive promised to transmit more of the power from the engine to the drive sprocket. But in practice, all of these designs proved troublesome and expensive. Furthermore, it added about 1.9 tons to the overall weight of the tank. A pilot was ready in April 1943, and limited production began in November 1943. Although Ordnance strongly advocated fielding the T23E3 in the ETO, local commanders refused. The novel electric transmission promised to be a needless maintenance burden. Instead, the ETOUSA wanted a new tank with more armor and more firepower.

Two alternatives were developed using an improved mechanical powertrain with a fluid torque converter and planetary transmission with manual gear selection. The T25 was fitted with 3-inch (75mm) frontal armor, weighed 36 tons, and was armed with a 90mm gun. The T26 was essentially similar, but with 4-inch (100mm) frontal armor, and so weighed 40 tons. In the autumn of 1943, Lt. Gen. Jacob Devers, commander of ETOUSA, pushed for production of the T26 as an antidote to the German Tiger tank. He requested

The T23 was a new medium tank designed to eventually replace the M4 Sherman. Although Ordnance wanted to start production in late 1943, this was resisted by both the AGF and Armored Force. This is one of the pilots fitted with the new HVSS suspension; others used torsion bar suspension.

that development of the T26E1 be accelerated and that 250 of these be manufactured as quickly as possible so that it would be possible to deploy them on the scale of one per five M4 medium tanks. The War Department forwarded these conflicting recommendations to the AGF for review. The head of AGF, Gen. McNair, flatly turned down the request and his rationale helps illuminate US Army official policy at the time:

> The M4 tank, particularly the M4A3, has been widely hailed as the best tank on the battlefield today. There are indications that the enemy concurs in this view. Apparently, the M4 is an ideal combination of mobility, dependability, speed, protection, and firepower. Other than this particular request – which represents the British view – there has been no call from any theater for a 90mm tank gun. There appears to be no fear on the part of our forces of the German Mark VI (Tiger) tank… There can be no basis for the T26 tank other than the conception of a tank versus tank duel – which is believed unsound and unnecessary. Both British and American battle experience has demonstrated that the antitank gun in suitable numbers and disposed properly is the master of the tank. Any attempt to armor and gun tanks so as to outmatch antitank guns is foredoomed to failure… There is no indication that the 76mm anti-tank gun is inadequate against the German Mark VI (Tiger) tank.

McNair's assessment was both short-sighted and technically incorrect. The idea that the 76mm gun was able to deal with the Tiger was widely held in the US Army in 1943, and quite wrong. The 76mm gun firing the M62 APC (armor-piercing-capped) projectile had a nominal penetration of 109mm at 500 yards, with the armor angled at 20 degrees. The Tiger's gun mantlet was 120mm thick and hull front was 100mm thick. In practice, the 76mm gun could only penetrate the Tiger mantlet at ranges of 100 meters or less and the hull at 400 meters. The Tiger could inflict penetration of the M4 Sherman at ranges more than double these figures. A total of 40 T25E1 and ten T26E1 prototypes were completed at the Grand Blanc tank arsenal from February to May 1944 for continuing trials.

In December 1943, when Dwight Eisenhower took over the senior ETO command from Devers, he refused to support Devers' T26E1 request, as he felt that its only advantage was its heavier armor. He did not feel that such a heavy tank was needed for the armor protection alone, and he failed to appreciate the substantial advantage that its 90mm gun offered since he had been repeatedly informed that the 76mm gun would prove more than adequate against new German tanks. After Normandy, Eisenhower would bitterly charge that he had been deceived on the tank gun issue.

THE PANTHER THREAT

The failure to improve the firepower of the Sherman tank or to adopt a new tank such as the T26 was in large measure due to the US Army's failure to anticipate the future German threat. This was not the Tiger tank threat. The US Army had encountered the Tiger since Tunisia; it had never had a major impact on the battlefield since it was so heavy and expensive that it was only deployed in relatively small numbers in separate tank battalions. The future threat in 1944 was the German Panther tank. This had frontal armor that could not be penetrated by the 3-inch gun on the M10 tank destroyer or the new 76mm gun on the M4A1 (76mm) Sherman tank. Furthermore, it was armed with an excellent 75mm that could kill the Sherman tank at any normal combat range.

The reason for the US Army's failure to anticipate this threat was the AGF's "battle-need" doctrine. This was the AGF policy that insisted that no new tank would be accepted for serial production unless there was a clear demand from the user, namely the Armored Force and tank units in the combat theaters. The AGF dispatched observer teams to the combat theaters to talk to combat commanders about their future weapons needs. Although the "battle-need" policy seemed a very common-sense approach, it had an inherent flaw that caused significant problems in wartime tank development. This policy ignored the tyranny of time. By the time that an observer team visited the frontlines, solicited recommendations, returned to the US, and distributed their findings, the recommendations were often out of date. Furthermore, even if Ordnance took immediate action, it took several months to develop the new weapon or upgrade, several months to manufacture it, and several more months to get it into the hands of the troops.

The clearest example of this problem was the Panther threat in 1944. The US Army first learned about the Panther in the summer of 1943, when the Red Army encountered them during the battle of Kursk. A captured example was put on display in Gorkiy Park in Moscow, which was examined and photographed by Army liaison officers from the Moscow embassy. The Red Army provided Britain and the US with basic technical details about the Panther later in 1943. There was little alarm about this tank in the US since it was mistakenly believed to be another German tank like the Tiger that would be encountered in very small numbers. The US Army had encountered the Tiger in Tunisia in February 1943, in Sicily in July 1943, and sporadically in Italy in 1943 and early 1944. Although a very difficult opponent, it appeared in such small numbers that it did not prove to be a major battlefield concern.

The first worries about the Panther arose in April 1944 at Fort Knox, when intelligence about the organization of new panzer divisions revealed that the Panther was not another heavy tank confined to rare heavy tank battalions. Rather, it was the intended replacement for the standard PzKpfw IV that would be used by all panzer regiments in the panzer divisions. Instead of being a rarity, it might prove to be a widespread threat. Its gun was far more powerful than the 75mm of the M4 Sherman, and it was impervious to standard US tank guns at typical combat ranges, including the new 76mm gun. The US Army first encountered the Panther in small numbers in Italy in May 1944 during the fighting on the approaches to Rome. It was encountered in large numbers by British tank units in Normandy in June 1944, and in small numbers by US tank units in mid-July 1944.

The process of relying on "battle-need" to shape future requirements failed to address future threats. It took months for Ordnance to respond to the demands for better guns and ammunition to deal with the Panther threat. Off-the-shelf solutions, such as newly developed hypervelocity armor-piercing (HVAP) ammunition, provided a short-term solution. Production of HVAP ammunition was ramped up and began to be rushed to Europe.

The British Army, for all of its problems in tank development in World War II, chose another approach for its future tanks. Having seen the steady rise of German tank armor from 1939 to 1943, they anticipated the need for a more powerful tank gun even before the Panther tank threat emerged. On March 9, 1943, the British General Staff established a new policy on tanks which noted:

> Fulfillment of their normal role necessitates that the main armament on the greater proportion of tanks of the medium class should be an effective high-explosive weapon and at the same time as effective a weapon as possible against enemy armour of the type so far encountered during in this war. The smaller proportion of tanks of the medium-class require a first-class anti-tank weapon for the engagement, if necessary, of armour heavier than that against which the dual-purpose weapon referred to above is effective.

In practice, this meant that the British tank force slated for operations in France was based around tanks with a dual-purpose 75mm gun, especially Shermans, while two tanks per troop would be fitted with the new 17-pdr anti-tank gun that was capable of killing the Panther tank.

The AGF "battle-need" policy was reactive rather than proactive. The US Army in World War II did not have an established system to forecast future threats, and so often failed to anticipate future technological requirements. This was especially the case with American tank guns in 1943–44.

The other alternative was a new tank such as the T26E1, which would eventually emerge in 1945 as the M26 Pershing. Could the T26E1 tank have been fielded in Normandy in 1944? This was extremely unlikely, and not merely due to the resistance of the AGF. The design was not mature enough in the autumn of 1943 for there to be much chance of deploying it so quickly. By way of comparison, work on the M4A3E2 assault tank was begun in February 1944, and the first tanks were fielded about eight months later in the early autumn of 1944. The M4A3E2 was only a modification of the M4 tank, not a wholly new design like the T26E1.

Had the US Army better appreciated the threat posed by the Panther prior to D-Day, a more likely course would have been to modify the M4 with a more potent gun. Acceleration of the fielding of 76mm HVAP ammunition would have been one short-term solution, and a 90mm gun on the M4 was not out of the question. Had there been more enthusiasm for a better tank like the T26E1 in the fall of 1943, the first units might have deployed during the Battle of the Bulge in December 1944, rather than during the campaign in Germany three months later. For the M26 to have reached combat in June 1944, its production would have had to have begun by the fall of 1943, while in fact the first prototypes were not completed until February 1944. This could have occurred only if there had been a sense of urgency in the US Army over the need for a new tank that simply did not exist at the time.

AIRBORNE TANKS

The eccentric designer J. Walter Christie had proposed flying tank designs on several occasions. In 1932, he advocated the development of a biplane glider with its tank payload serving as the fuselage. In 1936, he proposed a light-weight tank that could be carried under a bomber and landed after an enemy airfield had been captured. Christie's schemes received no serious Army attention.

The US Army first considered forming special airborne tank units after the successful use of German paratroops at Eben Emael in 1940 and Crete in 1941. The US Army Air Force, the Armored Force, and the Ordnance Department first discussed the technical requirements for an airborne tank in February 1941, and the program was formally initiated in May 1941 as the T9 aero tank. There was no serious consideration given to parachuting the tank since suitable large parachutes did not exist at the time. Instead, the initial scheme was to carry the aircraft under a transport aircraft and air-land the tank once a suitable airfield had been captured by paratrooper or glider infantry.

Christie visionary schemes included the idea of an airborne tank, which he described as the "most revolutionary war invention since the discovery of gunpowder." It is seen here in an illustration prepared in collaboration with the popular magazine *Modern Mechanics and Inventions* in 1932.

Christie offered at least two designs, neither of which was deemed satisfactory. The Marmon-Herrington Company proposed its own design in July 1941, and work on a wooden mockup and pilot vehicle were approved on August 31, 1941. The T9 was designed to be air-landed using the new Douglas C-54 transport aircraft, the military version of the DC-4 airliner. The hull would be suspended under the aircraft, with the turret and crew carried inside. The pilot T9 was completed in April 1942 and sent to Fort Benning for testing. Between the initial design and the pilot, the weight of the tank had crept over the 7.9-ton limit, and a redesign followed which eliminated some features such as the gun stabilizer, turret power traverse, and fixed bow machine guns to save weight. At the end of 1941, the Army planned to acquire about 500 T9 tanks for airborne operations.

Based on the early trials, the design was substantially modified into a more suitable production configuration as the T9E1, with two pilot tanks ready in November 1942. One of the T9E1 pilots was sent to Britain, and in April 1943 the accompanying team reported back that it had been well received and

The M22 aero tank was the only tank developed by the US Army in World War II intended for airborne operations. Although an airborne tank battalion was formed, it was never committed to combat due to the difficulties of transporting even a very small tank. The M22 was more widely used for training as seen here.

that the British preferred the design to their own Tetrarch airborne tank. The team also reported that Britain wanted to obtain T9E1 tanks at "an early date" and that they planned to deliver them into combat using a heretofore secret heavy glider, the Hamilcar. Production was scheduled to begin in November 1942 but was delayed until April 1943 due to lingering technical problems.

Although Ordnance had been generally pleased with the T9E1, the Armored Board at Fort Knox offered a startling different opinion after its own tests. Its September 1943 preliminary report concluded that the "Light Tank T9E1 is not a satisfactory combat vehicle in its present state of development due to the lack of adequate reliability and durability … and cannot be used for landing operations with any degree of success." The Armored Board was particularly unhappy with the transmission and recommended a variety of improvements to the powertrain and turret. Although there were plans to acquire as many as 1,900 T9E1, in the event only 830 tanks were built. Due to the dissatisfaction with the design, the T9E1 was not formally approved until October 5, 1944 as the M22 light tank, and classified only as "limited standard."

In February 1943 the Army Ground Forces ordered the Armored Force to organize an airborne tank battalion and develop suitable training and doctrine in cooperation with the Airborne Command. However, the Airborne Command was skeptical about the need for a battalion-sized formation due to the airlift problem posed by such a large formation, so the first unit was trimmed down to a company. The 151st Airborne Tank Company was activated at Fort Knox on August 15, 1943. Despite the skepticism about the amount of transport capacity that would be available, the 28th Airborne Tank Battalion was organized starting on December 6, 1943.

The Airborne Command had no practical way to deliver the M22 into combat. The US Army Air Force acquired a single British Hamilcar glider for trials, but no effort was made during the war to develop a comparable heavy-lift glider. The method of air-landing the T9A1 with the C-54 was inordinately cumbersome, and in the event, the US airborne divisions conducted no air-landing operations during the war, only paratroop and glider landings. The US Army Air Force began the development of a more satisfactory heavy transport in 1942, the Fairchild C-82 Packet, which had the capacity to carry the M22 intact within its fuselage and unload it through rear clam-shell doors. However, this aircraft did not enter production until September 1945.

The 151st Airborne Tank Company was not available in time for deployment with airborne units on D-Day, and in July 1944 was transferred from Fort Knox to Camp Mackall, North Carolina, where it was quickly forgotten. Due to the lack of interest by Airborne Command, the 28th Airborne Tank Battalion was reorganized as a conventional tank battalion in October

The M22 aero tank was used in combat only once during the war, serving with the British 6th Airborne Armoured Reconnaissance Regiment during Operation *Varsity/Plunder*, the Rhine river crossing, in March 1945. One of the unit's Locust tanks is seen within the hold of the massive Hamilcar glider, used to deliver it into combat.

1944. A total of 25 M22 tanks were ordered for the ETO in April 1944 and delivered in September 1944. A small number were sent to the 6th Army Group in 1944 in Alsace for potential use by the 1st Airborne Task Force. However, the fate of the M22 sent to the ETO remains a mystery, and there is no evidence they saw combat in the hands of US troops.

Of the 830 M22 aero light tanks manufactured, 230 were supplied to Britain under Lend-Lease, where they were called the Locust. A T9E1 pilot was sent to Britain and first flew in a Hamilcar glider on July 13, 1943 to demonstrate the fit. Further evaluation by the AFV School at Lulworth concluded that "this vehicle has shown itself to have a number of weak points both from a mechanical and gunnery point of view … it is just adequate for its intended role." The first 17 production T9E1 were issued to the 6th Airborne Armoured Reconnaissance Regiment in October 1943 to supplement their existing Tetrarch light tanks. Although the original plans for D-Day envisioned the delivery of 17 Locusts and three Tetrarch (3-inch howitzer) by Hamilcar glider, the Locusts were temporarily removed from service due to technical concerns, including the transmission. The improved tanks manufactured during January 1944 dealt with this problem, but they did not arrive in time to be used in Normandy. A small number of British Locusts were used during the Operation *Varsity/ Plunder* Rhine crossing campaign in March 1945.

ABOVE M4A1 medium tank with deep-wading kit and M8 ammunition trailer, Co. A, 741st Tank Battalion, Omaha Beach, D-Day 1944. (Artwork by Felipe Rodríguez © Osprey Publishing)

LEFT M5A1 light tank with deep-wading kit, Co. D, 70th Tank Battalion, France, 1944. (Artwork by Felipe Rodríguez © Osprey Publishing)

SPECIALIST TANKS FOR D-DAY

In 1942, the US Army had begun to develop new technologies to permit tanks to play a role in amphibious landings. Under Project Blue Freeze, special deep-wading kits were designed to permit tanks to be landed into water as deep as their turret while preventing their engine from flooding. This consisted of a variety of water-proofing techniques as well as deep-wading trunks that provided air to the engine and crew while the tank hull was submerged. The Blue Freeze kits were first used during Operation *Torch* landings in French North Africa in November 1942, and subsequently during landings on Sicily in July 1943 and the landings in Italy in 1943–44. These kits were also used in the Pacific, starting with the Kwajalein landing in February 1944, and became the standard method for delivering tanks during amphibious operations.

Some amphibious landings such as Operation *Husky* on Sicily involved landing in the pre-dawn darkness. One possible method for employing tanks in such circumstances was developed by the British Army under the cover name Canal Defence Light (CDL). The British Army encouraged the US Army to manufacture these night-fighting tanks both for amphibious

The T10 Shop Tractor, also called the Leaflet tank, was the US-manufactured version of the British Canal Defence Light. These searchlight tanks were intended to illuminate the beachhead during pre-dawn amphibious landings, or to conduct night attacks.

operations as well as a surprise weapon that might be used in some future operation. In November 1942, the US Army approved the procurement of CDL tanks under the cover name of Project Cassock, with the tanks deceptively named T10 Shop Tractors or Leaflet tanks. The US CDL tank consisted of the M3A1 medium tank chassis with the British-designed searchlight turret. The M3 medium tank was selected for the CDL since it permitted the searchlight turret to be fitted while still retaining the main gun. This was important since these tanks were intended to fight, not simply illuminate the battlefield. A total of 497 T10 Shop Tractors were converted through 1944, and they were deployed in six separate "special" tank battalions. They were trained at Camp Bouse in the remote Arizona desert to preserve the intense secrecy of the project. This was a substantial undertaking, and the six battalions were equivalent to the entire US Marine tank force, or equivalent to the tanks in two armored divisions.

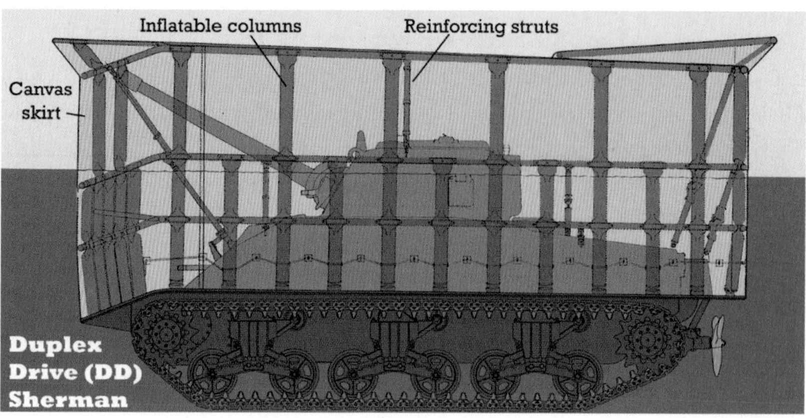

This illustration shows the basic configuration of the DD Sherman tank. (Author)

The Leaflet tanks were deployed to Britain starting in 1943. Early versions of the Operation *Neptune* plan envisioned carrying them ashore on LCTs (Landing Craft, Tank) with their searchlights illuminating the beachhead. Also, they could engage German defenses with their 75mm guns. By the summer of 1943, the plans for the Operation *Neptune* landings in Normandy had shifted from a pre-dawn landing to a daylight landing, removing the need for these secret weapons. Their only combat use came in 1945 when a handful were used for night defense of key Rhine bridges against German frogman attacks.

The failed Dieppe raid in August 1942 highlighted the vulnerability of landing tanks ashore in a heavily defended port. The most useful lesson from this experience was that future Allied landings should avoid conducting amphibious operations against ports heavily defended by coastal gun batteries. This was the reason that Normandy was eventually chosen for the Operation *Neptune* landings. Another lesson suggested that amphibious tanks were a technical solution to the problem of LCT vulnerability, since they could be launched several thousand yards offshore, reducing the vulnerability of the LCTs to German coastal gun batteries. The British Army began improving Nicholas Straussler's amphibious tank concepts. In 1943, DD (Duplex Drive) tanks were created using Valentine infantry tanks. The DD conversion consisted of a canvas screen erected around the upper hull of the tank to create enough buoyancy to float. Propulsion was provided by a duplex drive system that drew power from the tank engine to power propellers under the rear of the tank.

British authorities attempted to interest the US Army in joining this program in the summer of 1943. There was little interest from the US Army since the Blue Freeze deep-wading kits seemed a perfectly adequate means of delivering tanks during amphibious operations. The US Marine Corps rejected the idea since the DD tanks seemed excessively fragile to both high seas and enemy fire. Furthermore, the Marine Corps was starting to procure an amphibious tank based on the LVT amtrac that had much more robust swimming performance.

Although the DD tanks had very mixed results during Operation *Neptune*, they were more successful in the calmer Mediterranean waters during the Operation *Dragoon* landings on the Mediterranean coast of southern France. This is a DD tank of the 191st Tank Battalion on the Plage de la Nartelle near the resort of Sainte-Maxime on August 15, 1944.

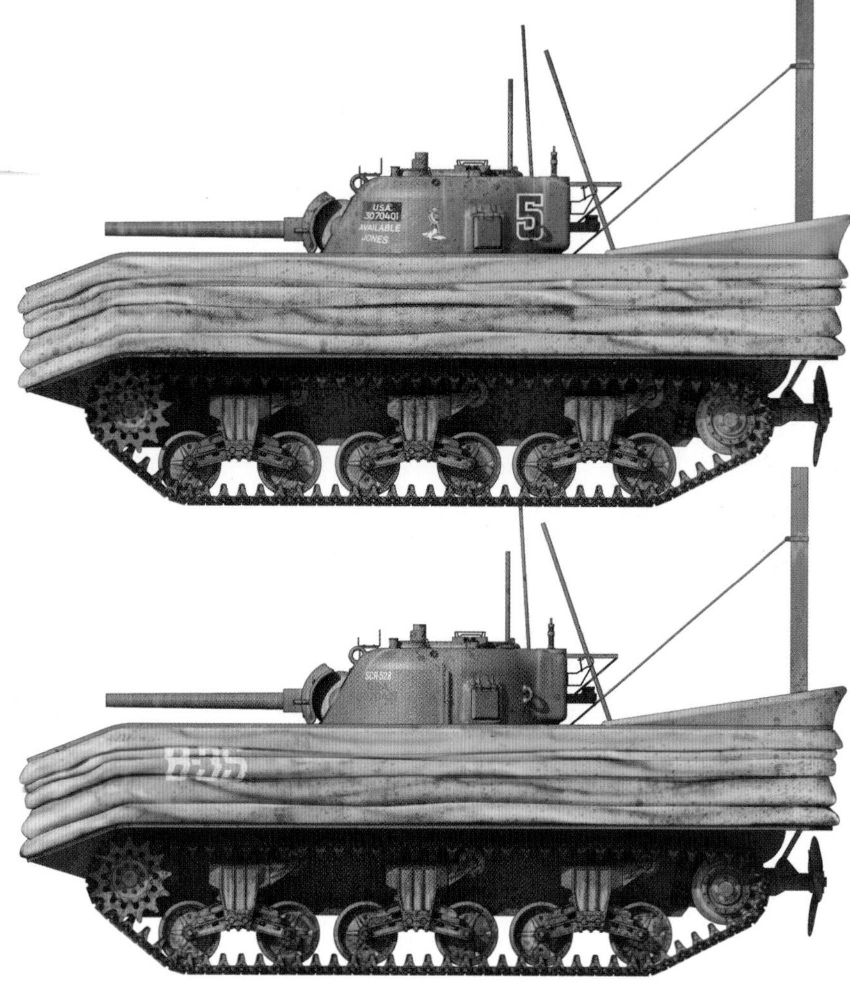

RIGHT M4A1 DD amphibious tank, Co. A, 70th Tank Battalion, Utah Beach. (Artwork by Felipe Rodríguez © Osprey Publishing)

BELOW RIGHT M4A1 DD amphibious tank, Co. B, 741st Tank Battalion, Omaha Beach. (Artwork by Felipe Rodríguez © Osprey Publishing)

COSSAC (Chief of Staff to Supreme Allied Commander) that oversaw the planning of Operation *Neptune* selected the DD tanks as the means to deliver tanks in the opening phase of the future Normandy landings. In November 1943, under British pressure, Lt. Gen. Jacob Devers, the interim commander of ETOUSA, finally relented. Devers received permission from the Army Chief of Staff, Gen. George C. Marshall, to begin construction of DD tanks for the US Army on an expedited basis starting in December 1943. After engineering drawings were finally delivered to the US in January 1944, some 350 DD tanks were completed, with delivery to the UK beginning in March 1944.

Senior US commanders were not happy with the decision to use the DD tanks due to their fragility. Major General Leonard Gerow, commander of the V Corps slated for landing on Omaha Beach, preferred to use deep-wading tanks or light tanks directly landed on the beach from LCMs (Landing Craft Medium). As a compromise, the plan was changed so that, in each tank battalion, two companies would land using DD tanks and one company using deep-wading trunks.

"Cannonball" – an M4 with deep-wading trunks from Co. C, 70th Tank Battalion – fell into a shell hole off Utah Beach. It is fitted with the attachments for the T40 Whiz-Bang rocket launcher; however, the battalion decided against using them during the landings.

A Royal Navy LCT(A)5 landing craft tank in Portland Harbour prior to D-Day, carrying tanks of the 741st Tank Battalion destined for delivery to Omaha Beach. The LCTs carrying the deep-wading tanks carried two M4/M4A1 medium tanks on ramps in the front to permit them to fire at German bunkers on the way into the beach. Each towed an M8 armored ammunition trailer. To the rear is a single M4 dozer tank assigned to assist the engineer gap-breaching teams.

Contrary to the popular myth that the US Army refused to use British "Armoured Funnies" in support of the Neptune landings, US requests for such equipment were not fulfilled due to British shortages. Starting in late 1943, the US Army requested a variety of specialized British equipment, including flamethrower tanks and mine-clearing tanks. None were provided in time for the D-Day landings due to shortages in the British Army that had priority for this equipment.

The most versatile specialized tank used on D-Day was the dozer tank, based on M4 medium tanks. The new design began arriving in the UK in April 1944, and small numbers were issued to the US tank battalions landed in the first waves on D-Day. Other specialized tank equipment was rejected. The M17 Whiz-Bang 7.2-inch demolition rocket launcher was tested for

RIGHT M4 medium tank with M1 dozer and deep-wading kit, Demolition Team 7, 70th Tank Battalion, Utah Beach, D-Day 1944. (Artwork by Felipe Rodríguez © Osprey Publishing)

BELOW RIGHT The most useful innovation for D-Day was the M1 dozer, which allowed the M4 medium tank to perform basic engineer tasks such as pushing aside obstacles and filling anti-tank ditches. This is an M4 dozer tank of the 70th Tank Battalion on Utah Beach supporting Demolition Team-7.

blowing holes in German anti-tank walls but was rejected as ineffective and vulnerable to enemy fire. The Doo-Zit, a specialized frame fitted on the front of a Sherman tank for delivering a large high-explosive charge against German anti-tank walls, was also rejected as too hazardous.

The Operation *Neptune* plan included the use of one tank battalion per regimental combat team in the first wave. The 741st Tank Battalion supporting the 16th Infantry at Omaha Beach suffered a calamity on D-Day when all but five of their DD tanks sank under the rough sea conditions; most of their deep-wading tanks were landed successfully. The 743rd Tank Battalion had greater success, since the US Navy LCT flotilla commander insisted on landing the DD tanks on shore due to the sea conditions. This battalion supported the 116th Infantry on the western side of Omaha Beach. On Utah Beach, the 70th Tank Battalion was more successful in swimming their DD tanks ashore on D-Day due to calmer sea conditions in that sector. The follow-on tank battalions were delivered using the more durable deep-wading technique. Both US Army and US Navy commanders assessed the use of the DD tanks to be a mistake due to the fragility of the system in rough sea conditions. However, DD tanks were used again during the Operation *Dragoon* landings on the Mediterranean coast of southern France on August 15, 1944. Under much more gentle sea conditions, they were used with few technical problems.

LEFT The US Army had planned to use the T40 7.2-inch demolition rocket launcher during Operation *Neptune* to clear beach obstructions. Tests convinced the tank battalions that it was neither safe nor effective.

BELOW Combat Team 8 consisting of elements of the 8th Infantry, 4th Division, supported by M4 tanks of Co. C, 70th Tank Battalion, quickly overwhelmed German coastal defenses on Utah Beach on D-Day, permitting a rapid push out of the beachhead. (Artwork by Howard Gerrard © Osprey Publishing)

The German Panzerfaust anti-tank rocket became an increasing threat to US tanks in 1944–45. Here, a German grenadier of the 352.Infanterie-Division lurks in ambush with a Panzerfaust as an M4 medium tank of Combat Command 3, 3rd Armored Division, passes by during the fighting near Villers-Bocage on June 29, 1944. (Artwork by Johnny Shumate © Osprey Publishing)

US TANKS IN NORMANDY

The brunt of the tank fighting in Normandy in June 1944 was born by the separate tank battalions supporting the infantry. Both the 2nd and 3rd Armored Divisions arrived in Normandy in June, but they were kept in reserve for most of the month until conditions were better suited to their use. By 1944, it was the usual practice to attach one tank battalion and one tank-destroyer battalion to each infantry division. The tank battalions proved to be much more effective in Normandy, since most of the tank-destroyer battalions assigned to the infantry were equipped with the towed 3-inch M5 gun that was ill-suited for use in offensive operations.

The main technical problem facing US tank battalions in Normandy was not the German tank threat, but the problems of tank-infantry cooperation. Most of the panzer divisions in Normandy were in the open farm country to the east where the British and Canadian forces were operating. In the American sector of the front, the only major German mechanized force in June 1944 was the 17.SS-Panzergrenadier Division, which at the time had only a single assault gun battalion. Besides this division, some of the German infantry divisions had a *Sturmgeschütz-Abteilung* (assault gun battalion) with a company of assault guns and a company of *Panzerjäger* (tank destroyers).

The success or failure of the separate tank battalions was closely dependent on the skill of the infantry division's headquarters in the use of tanks. Many infantry divisions had not trained with a separate tank battalion and had a poor appreciation of proper tank tactics. Tank battalions were frequently misused as a result. Most often the problem was the overestimation of their capabilities and the lack of recognition of the vulnerability of the tanks, especially when used in small sub-units of company size or smaller. Division commanders would assign the battalion a mission without proper infantry or artillery support, leading to their speedy decimation. A post-war study of the problem noted:

> … the combat team has become the keystone of all successful operations. The complexity of the new weapons and the limitations of each gives a complete interdependence of them on others to attain efficiency. Nothing is more helpless than a lone tank without artillery or infantry support. Its inherent blindness, its weight and size make it a natural target of all enemy fires. If friendly artillery is not coordinated, a hidden group of anti-tank guns will soon get it. Or if there is no infantry near, as soon as the tank slows down it becomes easy prey to an enemy infantryman with an anti-tank rocket. On the other hand, in operations where the tank-infantry-artillery and engineers are given their proper mission, one for which they have trained together as a team, the strength of each will complement the weakness of the other, thus making the strong concerted effort necessary for success.

Infantry divisions had the most success with tanks when the battalion was assigned for prolonged periods of time, which enabled joint training and an integration of the tank battalion headquarters within the divisional command. Some corps had the sense to semi-permanently attach tank battalions to a specific division and leave it attached for several months. In turn, this allowed the tank battalion to regularly assign specific companies to specific regiments on a long-term basis. Under these circumstances, lessons learned in combat led to more effective tactics, and a level of confidence was built up between the tankers and infantrymen. Throughout the European campaign, both the tank battalion commanders and the infantry division staff pleaded to make the tank battalions an organic part of each division. A General Board report after the war noted that if "the battalion had been an organic unit and trained with the division prior to combat, a better mutual understanding and spirit of cooperation would have always prevailed." However, since there were never enough tank battalions to permanently assign one to each infantry division, this did not occur until after the war.

The problems of tank-infantry coordination had been recognized since the Tunisian campaign in 1943, but remedies were slow in coming. The problems revolved around training, technology, and terrain. Stateside joint training of tank and infantry units was insufficient, and so the Normandy campaign required a hasty improvement. When tank battalions were

ABOVE The bocage hedgerows in Normandy presented a dangerous tactical dilemma. One of the first tactical solutions to allow tanks to pass through the hedgerows was developed by the 121st Engineer Combat Battalion in conjunction with the 747th Tank Battalion. The Sherman tanks were fitted with two lumber prongs on their front differential housing. The tanks would charge into the base of the hedgerow, and then withdraw, leaving two deep tunnels. The engineers pre-packed plastic explosive in ammunition transport tubes, and then packed these into the tunnels. The US troops would withdraw, and the explosives detonated to create a breach. (Artwork by Johnny Shumate © Osprey Publishing)

attached to infantry divisions, typically each infantry regiment received one tank company for support. Ideally, some joint training was undertaken before commitment to combat. As often as not, there was not enough time to do so. Tank battalions complained that the infantry did not appreciate the limitations of tanks in the Normandy terrain and burned through their attached battalion due to poor tactics, expecting another replacement to arrive. The process of linking tank and infantry was time consuming and costly in men and equipment.

On the technical side, communication was a major obstacle. The infantry's AM radios operated in different frequency bands than the tank's FM radios, and so no direct communication was possible. Doctrine expected that the tank companies would communicate to infantry headquarters via FM, and then the messages would be re-transmitted to the infantry platoons or companies on AM channels. Although theoretically possible, this system was not practical in actual combat. Two solutions were improvised in June and July 1944. For small-unit actions, tank companies attached field telephones on the rear of tanks that allowed accompanying infantry to communicate to the tank crew. By mid-July, the First US Army developed a standardized solution that wired the field telephone into the tank's intercom system, significantly improving the method. Some infantry units provided SCR-300 walkie-talkie radios to a select number of tanks during an operation to permit direct radio communication between the tanks and accompanying infantry. SCR-300 radios were still new and in short supply, so this solution was impromptu. The Signal Corps had been aware of this problem since 1943 and had developed a tank-mounted version of the SCR-300, the AN/VRC-3. However, this did not enter service in Normandy until September 1944 and did not become common until late in the year.

Complicating both tactics and technology was the unique terrain in the Calvados region of Normandy where the First US Army was committed. The coastal area was characterized by bocage, a type of hedgerow lining the farm fields to prevent coastal wind erosion. The bocage created an inverted trench system, ideal for the defending German troops. Tanks could not crash through the bocage since the earthen base was so dense and high. New tactics began to emerge in July to overcome the bocage. The first method was dubbed the "Salad Fork." It consisted of a pair of timber prongs fitted to the front of Sherman tanks. The tanks would accelerate across a farm field and plow into the hedgerow opposite. The impact buried the prongs deep in the base of the hedge, and then the tank reversed, leaving two small tunnels. Engineer troops would then pack the tunnels with high explosive and blow a gap through the hedgerow. Although the technique worked, it was time consuming and required excessive amounts of high explosive. By mid-July, a variety of hedgerow cutters were developed in various units. The most famous of these was the Culin device, devised by Sgt. Curtis G. Culin Jr. of the 102nd Cavalry Reconnaissance Squadron. These steel prongs were made from salvaged German beach obstructions. Tests found that tanks fitted with these "Rhino" devices could crash through the hedgerows at high speed.

OPPOSITE The first attempt to develop a bocage cutter was undertaken by the 747th Tank Battalion and 121st Engineer Combat Battalion in mid-July 1944 while supporting the 29th Division.

The first example of a Culin hedgerow cutter was fitted to an M5A1 light tank of the 709th Tank Battalion and demonstrated to senior officers in France prior to Operation *Cobra*.

Several hundred Rhino devices were locally assembled prior to Operation *Cobra* on July 25, 1944. By late July, the First US Army had broken out of the worst of the bocage country into more open terrain south of Saint-Lô. This permitted the commitment of US armored divisions in Normandy, leading to a breakout from Normandy. The armored divisions were better prepared for combined-arms tactics than the separate tank battalions. The 1943 table of organization and equipment included three tank battalions, three armored infantry battalions, and three armored field artillery battalions. Combined-arms tactics were enhanced by the division's three combat command headquarters. These served as the nucleus for adaptive combined-arms tactics since it enabled the division to readily create battle groups of tanks, infantry, and artillery tailored

The Operation *Cobra* breakout began on June 26, 1944, when VII Corps unleashed the 2nd and 3rd Armored Divisions to exploit the gaps created in German defenses by the US infantry divisions the day before. The M4 medium tanks of the 2nd Armored Division seen here were fitted with Culin hedgerow cutters, but the tank units preferred to use roads when possible to speed the advance. (Artwork by Tony Bryan © Osprey Publishing)

M4A1 of the 2nd Armored Division during Operation *Cobra*, July 1944. (Artwork by Richard Chasemore © Osprey Publishing)

to specific missions. A typical combat command could consist of one battalion each of tanks, armored infantry, and armored artillery. Furthermore, the combat commands were usually subdivided into task forces for combined-arms actions at the company level. Operation *Cobra* was the culmination of two months of innovation in training, tactics, and technology that substantially enhanced the combat effectiveness of the US tank units in France.

Although a great deal of ink has been spilled over the threat posed by the Tiger heavy tank, the First US Army had hardly any contact with the Tiger in Normandy. The two Tiger battalions in Normandy were active in the eastern sector against British and Canadian forces. The source of this myth was the tendency of GIs to call any German tank a "Tiger," much as there was a tendency to call any German artillery an "88." During the Operation *Cobra* breakout, US units captured a handful of Tiger II heavy tanks that had been abandoned near Châteaudun. The 3rd Armored Division captured a few derelict Tiger tanks being withdrawn to Germany on a train in late August. The only significant combat encounters were in late August 1944, when Patton's Third US Army leapt the Seine river near Mantes-Gassicourt north of Paris. The German counterattacks included a company of new Tiger II tanks. These had little impact on the fighting, and several were knocked out by M10 3-inch tank destroyers. Further encounters with Tiger tanks did not take place until November 1944 during the Roer fighting and were on a small scale, involving only handfuls of the German heavy tanks.

A column of M4A1 medium tanks confronts PzKpfw IV tanks of the Panzer Lehr Division in the village of St. Gilles, France, on July 26, 1944, during the start of Operation *Cobra*. (Artwork by Richard Chasemore © Osprey Publishing)

Comparative technical characteristics

	M4A3	Panther Ausf. A
Crew	5	5
Dimensions: L x W x H (m)	6.27 x 2.61 x 2.74	8.86 x 3.42 x 2.98
Loaded weight (tonnes)	31.5	44.8
Main gun	75mm M3	75mm KwK 42
Main gun ammo	104	79
Engine (hp)	450	600
Max. speed (km/h)	42	46
Fuel (liters)	635	720
Range (km)	160	200
Ground pressure (kg/cm^2)	1.0	.88
Armor**		
Mantlet (mm)	90*=>90	100*=>100
Turret front (mm)	51@30=58.9	100@5=100.4
Turret side (mm)	51@5=51.2	45@25=49.6
Upper hull front (mm)	51@45=72.1	80@55=139.4
Lower hull front (mm)	51@50=79.3	65@55=113.3
Upper hull side (mm)	38@0=38	40@40=52.2
*curved **armor data provided as: actual thickness in mm @ angle from vertical = effective thickness in mm		

M4A1 (76mm) medium tank, Co. D, 66th Armored, 2nd Armored Division, Operation *Cobra*, 1944. (Artwork by Jim Laurier © Osprey Publishing)

For the US Army, the first significant fighting with the panzers took place in mid-August 1944 around Mortain. As a result of Operation *Cobra*, Patton's Third US Army was able to race down the Atlantic coast past the city of Avranches, breaking into Brittany. Hitler attempted to cut off Patton's spearheads by staging a panzer counterattack toward Avranches codenamed

An M4 medium tank passes by a Panther tank of the Panzer Lehr Division knocked out near the town of La Chapelle-en-Juger during Operation *Cobra* in July 1944.

RIGHT M4A1 (76mm), Sgt. Lafayette Poole, Co. I, 32nd Armored, 3rd Armored Division, France, 1944. (Artwork by Felipe Rodríguez © Osprey Publishing)

BELOW RIGHT M4 medium tank, Lt. Col. Creighton Abrams, 37th Tank Battalion, 4th Armored Division, France, 1944. (Artwork by Felipe Rodríguez © Osprey Publishing)

Operation *Lüttich*. About 250 panzers and 60 assault guns/tank destroyers took part in the attack. The attack quickly floundered after hitting the US 30th Infantry Division around the town of Mortain. Aside from failing in its mission to reach Avranches, the German offensive shifted the best of the panzer forces in Normandy too far west, placing them deeper and deeper into an emerging Allied encirclement trap at Falaise-Argentan. This culminated in the defeat of the German Army in Normandy later in August 1944.

The accompanying chart summarizes US tank and AFV losses in the Normandy fighting. The source of these losses was not recorded. A German assessment in early July 1944 estimated that 42 percent of Allied tank casualties were inflicted by panzers, 11 percent by assault guns and tank destroyers, and about 20 percent by anti-tank guns. These estimates were heavily based on tank fighting in the British sector. Since the US Army encountered far fewer panzers than the British, the primary source of US tank casualties was probably German anti-tank guns, especially the 75mm PaK 40.

"Fury" – an M4 medium tank of Co. F, 66th Armored, 2nd Armored Division, with troops of the 22nd Infantry, 4th Infantry Division, onboard – sets out on a mission in Operation *Cobra* in late July 1944.

US Army AFV losses in Normandy campaign

	Losses to date			Cumulative losses
	6–20 Jun	21 Jun–20 Jul	21 Jul–20 Aug	6 Jun–20 Aug 1944
M5A1 light tank	52	26	201	279
M8 75mm HMC	4	6	18	28
M4 medium tank	187	121	557	865
M4 (105mm) AG	4	3	2	9
M10 3-inch GMC	1	17	28	46
M18 76mm GMC	0	0	6	6
Total	248	173	812	1,233

While the separate tank battalions quickly adapted to battlefield conditions in Normandy, the tank destroyer battalions were at the center of controversy for most of the campaign. At the time of the D-Day landings in Normandy, there were 30 tank destroyer battalions in England, of which 11 were towed and 19 self-propelled. There was very little confidence in the tank destroyer doctrine of massing battalions to deal with the panzer threat. The bocage presented such an obstacle to mobility that it seemed unlikely that battalions held in reserve in the rear could be rushed forward to meet a massed panzer attack. Furthermore, there were few massed panzer attacks in Normandy, yet there was a crying need for armored support by the infantry units that were having a rough time overcoming German defenses in the bocage. Almost from the outset, the battalions were attached to each infantry and armored division. The armored divisions invariably received self-propelled battalions, while infantry divisions received the towed battalions and any leftover self-propelled battalions. The tactics of the self-propelled battalions evolved much along the same lines as the tank battalions described above.

Problems began to emerge almost immediately with the towed gun battalions. The 3-inch gun was so heavy that it proved very difficult to move in the Normandy hedgerows. Once it was moved into position by its half-track, the gun crews had a difficult time placing it into firing position due to the height of the hedgerows. Besides being clumsy to deploy, the 3-inch gun was large and difficult to conceal, and crews were often subjected to small-arms and mortar fire, making their position untenable. During the hedgerow fighting, there were few occasions when the towed guns were used in their intended anti-tank role due to their shortcomings. Most of the fighting for the first two months of the campaign was a close-combat infantry struggle, and the towed battalions had less to offer than the self-propelled battalions in such conditions. As a result, it became standard policy in most battalions of the First Army to leave only two companies for anti-tank defense and leave one company behind the lines in the field artillery role. It was far from ideal in the artillery support role as its ammunition was tailored for anti-armor missions.

In comparison, the self-propelled M10 3-inch GMC was more mobile in the bocage, and its armor gave the crew better protection. Infantry commanders appreciated the psychological boost that the presence of the self-propelled tank destroyers had for their troops. Infantry divisions that received the self-propelled battalions usually committed a company of M10 tank destroyers with each rifle regiment much as was the case with the tank battalions. The M10 was not ideally configured for the close-support role because its open roof left it vulnerable to sniper fire, mortars, and close-range grenade attack. In addition, its armor was thinner than that of the M4 tank, and so it was more vulnerable to German anti-tank weapons. The lack of a power traverse

An M4 medium tank fitted with a T2 Douglas hedgerow cutter, part of Task Force X, CCA, 3rd Armored Division, passes an abandoned 88mm Flak gun near Lougé-sur-Maire on August 17, 1944. The 3rd Armored Division fought a series of costly engagements with Panzergruppe Eberbach on August 15–17, 1944, part of the larger effort to close the Falaise Gap.

M10 3-inch GMC in action in the summer of 1944. (Artwork by Richard Chasemore © Osprey Publishing)

for the turret was a significant drawback in close combat, as it took nearly 80 seconds to traverse the turret 180 degrees. The infantry preferred tank battalions to tank destroyer battalions for other reasons as well. A tank destroyer battalion had only 36 tank destroyers, while a tank battalion had over 50 medium tanks and 17 light tanks, as well as six 105mm assault guns for added firepower. Regardless of these shortcomings, the M10 proved to be a very valuable and versatile vehicle when skillfully employed. A report by the commanding officer of the 5th Tank Destroyer Group in Normandy is illustrative of their successful role in the fighting:

> What is not in the field manuals on tank destroyer use is the effective support which they render to a fighting infantry at the time of actual combat. An infantryman has his fortitude well tested and the mere presence of self-propelled tank destroyers in his immediate vicinity give a tremendous shot of courage to the committed infantryman. For example, at Chambois [during the closing of the Falaise Gap in August 1944], an infantry battalion moved towards the town with utter fearlessness to enemy artillery, mortar, and small arms fire when accompanied by some M10s. However, the M10s were delayed in crossing a stream for about thirty-five minutes. During this time, the infantry battalion continued to their objective which dominated a roadway leading to Chambois. They fought infantry, they bazooka-ed some armored vehicles including three tanks on the road, but on realizing that the M10s weren't firing, they started a retirement. Leading the parade to the rear was a short lad known as "Shorty." Shorty in the lead

> was the first man to see a platoon of M10s who had finally gotten across the stream. Shorty took a good look at the M10s, turned around, and shouted to the other men, "Hell boys, what are we retiring for, here comes the TDs!" The entire company in mass immediately reversed their direction and returned to their excellent positions, and to say they fought for the next few hours with unusual bravery is stating it mildly. The point I am trying to make is that the appearance and the knowledge that self-propelled tank-destroyers were at hand was a major reason that the infantry attained success and victory. Often many men die or suffer to retain or exploit IF the inspiration furnished by the presence of self-propelled tank destroyers is known. The towed guns can be just as brave and thoroughly trained, but they never give much "oomph" to the fighting doughboy when the chips are really down.

The first massed panzer attack occurred on July 11, 1944 when the Panzer Lehr Division staged a counterattack near Le Desert, attempting to drive a wedge through the American sector. It was the first large-scale encounter with the new Panther tank. By coincidence, the road used by the Panzer Lehr Division's Panther tank battalion near Le Desert ran through the sector covered by the 899th Tank Destroyer Battalion. As a result, there were a series of intense, close-range battles between the M10s and Panthers over a two-day period. Although the M10 had a great deal of difficulty penetrating the thick Panther frontal armor, the panzer was far more vulnerable on its flanks, and could be defeated by the 3-inch gun at most combat ranges. Despite the shortcomings of the 3-inch gun, the 899th Tank Destroyer Battalion was credited 12 Panthers, one PzKpfw IV, and one StuG III, and played a central role in blunting the German attack. The tank destroyers took advantage of the hedgerow terrain, and much of the fighting took place at point-blank ranges of under 200 yards. The poor performance of the 3-inch gun against the Panther in frontal engagement came as a shock to the tank destroyer crews, and a major controversy erupted over the lack of an adequate gun for dealing with the new threat.

The inadequate anti-tank capabilities of the M10 revealed by the Normandy tank fighting led to considerable pressure to field the new M36 tank destroyer with the 90mm gun as soon as possible, and on July 6, 1944, Eisenhower's HQ cabled back to the United States asking that all M10 battalions be converted to M36 as soon as possible. Later tank fighting in August, when the Germans launched the panzer counteroffensive near Mortain, only reinforced the Normandy lessons. The First US Army report noted that Mortain "demonstrated the superiority of the self-propelled battalion over the towed unit in conclusive fashion by sustaining fewer losses while destroying more enemy tanks. The mobility of the self-propelled weapon permitted a more flexible and resilient defense, whereas the towed gun, once in position, was unable to maneuver against targets outside its narrow sector of fire or to escape when threatened of being overrun." As a result, in September 1944, Bradley's 12th Army Group requested that, of the 52 tank destroyer battalions committed to the theater, 20 be converted to the promised M36 90mm GMC, 20 retain the existing M10 or M18, and the remaining 12 remain as towed battalions, but completely re-equipped with the forthcoming T5E1 90mm anti-tank gun. In practice, the changes were slow to take effect since the M36 was slow arriving in theater, and the towed 90mm gun never arrived in any significant quantities. The first 40 M36 tank destroyers arrived in France in the first week of September 1944 and were issued to the First US Army. After preparation and crew training, they went into action in October 1944 during the fighting along the German border.

TANK INNOVATIONS IN 1944

The first 120 of the new M4A1(76mm) tanks arrived in Britain in the spring of 1944 to a cold reception. A conference was held at First US Army headquarters on April 20, 1944 to discuss how to distribute them. Few of the tank commanders showed any interest in adopting the new tanks. There were several objections. Many officers complained that the 76mm gun had an inferior high-explosive round to the existing 75mm gun. Furthermore, there was the widespread perception that the 75mm gun was perfectly adequate in the anti-tank role. As a result, the tank battalions would be saddled with a second ammunition type and new maintenance issues for a questionable upgrade in performance.

Consequently, none of the 76mm tanks were committed to the Normandy fighting in June 1944. Opinions began to change in July when British units began encountering the new German Panther tank in large numbers in the fighting around Caen. On July 12, 1944, a special board of officers from Bradley's First US Army was formed to determine which US weapons might be capable of defeating the Panther and Tiger. None of the available US weapons could penetrate the Panther frontally, though the 75mm gun could do so against

The first large-scale tank-vs.-tank battles fought by the US Army in the ETO occurred in September 1944 when Hitler ordered a panzer offensive against Patton's Third US Army in Lorraine. The battle reached its culmination in late September 1944 around the village of Arracourt when the 4th Armored Division overwhelmed the inexperienced panzer brigades with superior training and tactics. (Artwork by Tony Bryan © Osprey Publishing)

Although the original batch of 120 M4A1 (76mm) medium tanks had been spurned by tank units in the ETO in April 1944, encounters with the Panther tank in July 1944 led to a change of heart. These tanks were initially split between the 2nd and 3rd Armored Divisions shortly before Operation *Cobra* on July 25, 1944. This is "Elowee," an M4A1 (76mm) of Co. E, 67th Armored Regiment, 2nd Armored Division, parked near a hedgerow in Champ-du-Boult on August 10, 1944 prior to the attack by Task Force A toward Gathemo later in the morning.

the side and rear depending on range. None of the M4A1 (76mm) tanks were available yet in France, but the M10 3-inch GMC tank destroyer with similar gun performance was found to be incapable of penetrating the Panther glacis at any range but could punch through the Panther mantlet at a range of only 200 yards, instead of the 400 yards promised by Ordnance.

As mentioned previously, Bradley's First US Army did not have any firsthand experience with the Panther until July 11, 1944, when a small battle group of the Panzer Lehr Division staged a local counterattack against US infantry. In that occasion, the panzer attack was beat off with the assistance of M10 3-inch tank destroyers. Encounters with the Panther began to escalate in July as the Wehrmacht poured additional resources into the Saint-Lô sector due to the American advances. The orphaned M4A1 (76mm) tanks were suddenly in high demand. They were split between the 2nd and 3rd Armored Divisions immediately prior to Operation *Cobra*.

The performance of the new 76mm gun was very disappointing when using the available APC ammunition. Although touted as the solution to the German heavy tank problem, it was not able to penetrate the Panther or Tiger frontally except at very close ranges. Ordnance had been developing a more promising HVAP ammunition that consisted of a high-density tungsten carbide core within a lightweight aluminum shell. A shipment of 2,000 rounds of the experimental T4 76mm HVAP ammunition was airlifted to France in August 1944 and began to be distributed on September 11, 1944. It could not penetrate the Panther glacis, but the HVAP punched the Panther mantlet at 800 to 1,000 yards compared with only 100 to 200 for the normal M62 APC. A production order for 20,000 HVAP rounds was issued in the late summer, but production never kept up to demand due to shortages of tungsten carbide. This metal alloy was in high demand for machine tools, limiting the supplies available for ammunition.

Tankers were very enthusiastic about the performance of the new ammunition. Bradley's 12th Army Group decided to issue it on an equal basis to all units equipped with the M4 (76mm) and the M18 76mm GMC tank destroyer. But this usually meant only one round per vehicle per month. By the end of February 1945, each 76mm tank had received, on average, only five rounds of HVAP. By early March 1945, a total of about 18,000 rounds of HVAP had been delivered to the ETO, of which about 7,550 were 76mm rounds (42 percent) and the rest 3-inch ammunition for the M10 tank destroyers.

The number of 76mm Sherman tanks in the ETO increased through the autumn of 1944. The largest confrontation with Panther tanks to date occurred in September 1944, when the Germans launched a panzer offensive against Patton's Third US Army in Lorraine. The attack centered on new panzer brigades that had been hastily formed in the summer of 1944. Of the 340 Panther tanks available on Germany's Westfront, more than half were committed to the Lorraine attack. The new panzer brigades were poorly configured and poorly trained. Instead of being used in mass as Hitler had demanded, they were committed piecemeal in hopes of stymying Patton's advancing forces. The panzer attacks were so disjointed that Patton's Third US Army did not realize it was the target of a panzer offensive. The attacks culminated in a series of tank battles around the town of Arracourt starting on September 19, 1944, which pitted two panzer brigades against the 4th Armored Division. The results were extremely one-sided, with the 75mm Sherman tanks dominating the Panthers and PzKpw IV tanks largely due to the more experienced American tank crews. Technological advantages do not ensure tactical victory. These battles undermine the popular myth that it took five Shermans to defeat a Panther or Tiger. During the Lorraine tank battles, the overall loss ratio of tanks and AFVs was about 2.4:1 in favor of the US Army.

The predominant Sherman variant in the ETO with the 76mm gun was the M4A3 (76mm) that began appearing in France in August 1944. This is an M4A3 (76mm) of the 761st Tank Battalion, one of two segregated African American tank battalions in the ETO. This tank was photographed on November 5, 1944 during the campaign by Patton's Third US Army near Metz.

Pressure from the ETO to field a replacement for the Sherman abated in the autumn of 1944. The rate of tank loss decreased to more moderate levels after the breakout from Normandy in August 1944. The head of the 12th Army Group's armored vehicle section wrote back to Washington, "Probably the problem of the Panther will no longer be with us for the remainder of the war. The German, we believe, has lost most of his armor." The most pressing issue for US tank commanders in the autumn of 1944 was the need to increase tank replacements due to lingering aftereffects of the Normandy losses and insufficient tank reserves in the theater. Tank units were regularly operating at below unit strength, and replacements were not arriving fast enough.

Nor were field commanders particularly insistent on giving priority to more powerful tank guns. The vast majority of ammunition fired by US tanks in the ETO in 1944–45 was high explosive, not anti-armor, since the majority of targets were not panzers. The relative lack of tank-vs.-tank fighting in the autumn of 1944 led many tank commanders to focus on improving tank armor and high-explosive firepower. Observer teams in the ETO reported back a wide range of contradictory recommendations for 1945 tank production. For example, the 6th Armored Division recommended that the Army's 1945 tank program be a mixture of two-thirds of the heavily armored M4A3E2 assault tanks and one-third M4A3 105mm assault guns for the remainder of combat operations in Europe. The 105mm Sherman assault gun was widely viewed as a better replacement for the M4 with 75mm gun. This was basically the same as the M4 with 75mm gun but fitted with a 105mm howitzer. These had been introduced in the summer of 1944 to provide indirect fire support in tank battalions, with a platoon of three in each battalion's headquarters company, and one each in the medium tank companies. The only failing of the M4 105mm assault gun was the lack of power traverse for the turret, a problem that could be readily remedied.

Targets of US Army tanks 1942–45

Target	Average, all theaters	Highest % by theater
Fortifications	21.2	36.4 (SW Pacific)
Buildings	17.3	28.0 (Italy)
Troops	15.5	23.9 (Pacific)
Tanks	14.2	24.4 (North Africa)
Anti-tank guns & artillery	12.8	18.8 (Italy)
Other	10.8	15.6 (North Africa)
Trucks	8.2	12.6 (ETO)

Large-scale encounters with German tanks diminished in the autumn of 1944 due to the heavy casualties suffered in the summer 1944 fighting. The Wehrmacht's panzer strength in the West in September 1944 nearly evaporated, with only 59 tanks and 23 AFVs still operational with Heeresgruppe B (Army Group B). The neighboring Heeresgruppe G had a larger panzer force, but this was largely destroyed in late September 1944 during the battles with Patton's Third US Army that led to the loss of about 340 panzers and AFVs.

In September 1944, the panzer divisions in the West were withdrawn for reconstruction. In late September, Hitler began the first steps to conduct a massive counteroffensive through the Ardennes sometime in late 1944. As a result, he insisted that the panzer divisions be retained in reserve for the Ardennes so as not to repeat the mistakes of the Lorraine panzer offensive, when the panzer brigades were frittered away in piecemeal commitments to deal with local tactical setbacks. This proved impossible due to continued Allied offensives. Operation *Queen*, the First US Army's November offensive toward the Roer, and Operation *Madison*, the Third US Army's November offensive toward the Saar, forced OB West to make limited commitment of panzer units to restrain the American advances. Deployed panzer strength along the Western Front in the autumn of 1944 was very meager as evident from the accompanying chart. Most of the Wehrmacht's panzer strength was kept away from the battlefield in anticipation of the Ardennes offensive.

Operational tanks and AFVs in panzer units in the West: October–December 1944

	PzKpfw IV	Panther	Panzer IV/70	StuG III	Total
1 Oct	22	151	29	13	215
1 Nov	66	130	36	4	236
1 Dec	132	100	60	45	337

TANK DESTROYER IMPROVEMENTS

In January 1944, Bradley's First US Army headquarters staff in England were informed that the M18 76mm GMC tank destroyer would be available for use in time for operations in France. At first, they refused to accept any, stating that they saw no advantage in replacing the M10 with this vehicle and having concerns over the additional logistical burden of a new type. Instead, they indicated they would wait until the M36 90mm GMC became available. In the event, the European theater began receiving some battalions already equipped with the M18.

By the time of the D-Day landings in Normandy in June 1944, of the 19 self-propelled tank destroyer battalions in the ETO, three were equipped with the M18 76mm GMC. All of these belonged to Patton's Third US Army. The M18 battalions were first committed to action in early August when the Third US Army was committed to the exploitation phase of Operation *Cobra*.

The initial production plans for the M18 under the November 1943 program were substantially trimmed back from the original objective of 8,986 to only 2,507. This was due to three principal reasons. To begin with, the AGF's insistence that half of all tank destroyer battalions use towed anti-tank guns dramatically reduced the need for self-propelled tank destroyers. Secondly, the Lend-Lease recipients such as the Soviet Union and Britain showed no interest in the design. Finally, by the time it reached combat in the summer of 1944, it became evident that the 76mm gun was inadequate to deal with the German Panther tank, and the emphasis shifted to rushing the M36 90mm GMC into service as quickly as possible. The M18 proved to be a relatively expensive vehicle to manufacture, with a cost of $55,230, compared with $47,900 for the M10 tank destroyer and $66,900 for an M4A2 (76mm) tank.

During the manufacture of the M18, the publicity department at Buick came up with an advertising campaign highlighting the firm's war production record and decided that "Hellcat" was a more exciting name than Gun Motor Carriage 76mm M18. However, the Hellcat name was purely an invention of Buick and was never officially approved by the Army.

The number of M18 Hellcats in the ETO remained modest through the autumn, finally reaching five battalions in October and nine at the time of the Battle of the Bulge in December 1944. The slow growth in M18 battalions was due to their firepower problems. The 76mm gun on the M18 was no better in anti-tank performance than the 3-inch gun on the M10, so there was little point in converting the M10 battalions, especially when many units preferred the advantages of the M10, such as its more functional fighting compartment.

In view of the Tank Destroyer Center's high hopes for the Hellcat, the M18 76mm GMC design was a disappointment. The primary role of a tank destroyer was its ability to knock out enemy tanks. When it reached service in 1944, the M18 did not have enough firepower to effectively carry out this mission. General Bruce's obsession with speed distorted the design, resulting in superior mobility but mediocre firepower. In the summer of 1944, the M18 was not capable of defeating standard German tanks like the Panther in frontal engagements. Tank destroyer crews were obliged to maneuver to the side or rear of the Panther to effectively engage them. A post-war study by the General Board on tank destroyer employment concluded, "In a very large percent of its employment in this theater, its road speed of sixty miles an hour and its great cross-country speed were never needed." Although the M18 could race forward at high speed on roads, speeds near the forward edge of battle were restricted by the usual constraints of road congestion and slower speeds in cross-country travel. Furthermore, the thin armor and open turret roof of the M18 did not encourage experienced crews to speed forward when in close-combat range, but rather to move forward in a slower and more wary fashion to avoid exposure to enemy sniper, mortar, and artillery fire.

The M18 was a very popular vehicle in the tank destroyer battalion. Most M18 crewmen enjoyed its high road speed and excellent automotive performance. In the muddy conditions typical of the ETO in the autumn of 1944, it was better suited to cross-country travel than most US tanks or tank destroyers. The M18 often proved successful on the battlefield due to good crew training. An early example was the role of the 704th Tank Destroyer Battalion of the 4th Armored Division, which did an exemplary job of defeating German panzer attacks during the Lorraine panzer offensive of September 1944. Except for the Lorraine fighting in September 1944, and the Ardennes fighting in December 1944–January 1945, the M18's anti-tank firepower limitations were not of paramount concern, and they were used as often as not for direct fire support of US infantry units against targets other than the Panther or Tiger tanks.

In the autumn of 1944, the best weapon to defeat the German Panther and Tiger tanks was a new 90mm gun on the M36 tank destroyer. The introduction of the M36 tank destroyer had been expedited by the AFV&W Section of the ETOUSA, a small headquarters staff in London advising senior US commanders on tank issues. The staff had been promoting the adoption of the new 76mm tank gun in anticipation of emerging German threats but had been rebuffed by McNair and the AGF in Washington, DC due to a lack of "battle-need." They next turned their attention to accelerating the adoption of the M36 90mm tank destroyer by bureaucratic subterfuge. Rather than arguing that it was needed to face an emerging German tank threat, a rationale they knew would be rejected by AGF, they instead promoted the M36 as a method to deal with German armored pillboxes along the Siegfried Line. This proved to be more persuasive to AGF, and the M36 90mm tank destroyer began appearing in the ETO in October 1944. Performance against the Panther tank was mediocre due to the limitations of the initial types of anti-tank ammunition when firing against the Panther's tough glacis plate. But as improved ammunition began appearing later in 1944, the M36 90mm tank destroyer became the best American Panther killer in the ETO.

US tank guns 1939–45

Caliber	37mm	75mm	76mm	90mm
Gun type	M5A1	M3	M1	M3
Tube length	L/53	L/40	L/52	L/50
Armor-piercing projectile	M51B1	M61	M62A1	M82
Type	APCBC	APCBC	APCBC	APCBC
Initial muzzle velocity (m/s)	884	617	792	814
Projectile weight (kg)	0.87	6.78	7.0	10.9
Propellant weight (kg)	0.24	0.98	1.64	3.31
Penetration (mm; @500m, 30 degree)	51	62–72	92–96	110–118
Armor-piercing projectile (HVAP)	n/a	n/a	T4 (M93)	T30E16 (M304)
Type			HVAP	HVAP
Initial muzzle velocity (m/s)			1,036	1,020
Projectile weight (kg)			4.3	6.9
Penetration (mm; @500m, 30 degree)			137	194
High-explosive projectile	M63	M48	M42A1	M71
Projectile weight (kg)	0.73	6.7	5.8	10.6
Explosive fill (g)	38	665	390	925

ASSAULT SHERMAN

Another innovation promoted by the AFV&W Section was the M4A3E2 assault tank. This was a version of the M4A3 tank with added armor to make it resistant to German anti-tank guns up to the dreaded 88mm gun. The US Army had never favored the type of infantry tanks found in the British Army, and the jointly developed T14 assault tank had been rejected for US Army service. In January 1944, the AFV&W Section made the case for adopting a heavily armored tank in anticipation of facing the fortified Siegfried Line on the German frontier. AGF accepted this proposal as "battle-need," and Ordnance efficiently responded. The M4A3E2 used a new turret with 6-inch armor in place of the normal Sherman turret's 3-inch thickness. A new final drive casting was fitted on the bow with 5.5 inches of armor. Additional armor plates 1.5 inches thick were welded to the glacis and sides. This increased the tank's weight to 42 tons, yet the existing powertrain and suspension proved to be robust enough. Production was limited to 250 tanks due to its specialized role. The first M4A3E2 tanks were issued to First US Army units in October 1944, a remarkably quick response.

During the Battle of the Bulge, this M4A3E2 assault tank spearheaded the column from the 4th Armored Division that began the relief of encircled Bastogne on December 26, 1944. Named "Cobra King," the tank was commanded by Lt. Charles P. Boggess, who led Co. C, 37th Tank Battalion. This tank is currently preserved at the National Museum of the United States Army at Fort Belvoir, Virginia.

The M4A3E2 assault tank was highly regarded by US tank crews. The autumn of 1944 was unusually soggy, with about 70 percent more rain than average, leading to muddy ground conditions. As a result, tank operations were often restricted to operations on the roads, leading to conditions dubbed "a front one tank wide." This was a tactical problem since the Germans could concentrate their anti-tank weapons on the roads, and US tanks could not easily outflank the German anti-tank guns without becoming bogged down in the mud. The M4A3E2 could avoid this since its armor was proof against the most common German guns, including the 75mm tanks guns and 75mm anti-tank guns. In early January 1945, Eisenhower's headquarters telegraphed Washington that the "M4A3E2 assault tank has proved itself in combat and has been most favorably received. The Theater has an immediate requirement for the maximum number that can be produced without materially reducing the flow of tanks to the Continent. These tanks must be armed with the 76mm gun and should have the best available floatation characteristics." However, the AGF concluded that by the time new production M4A3E2 tanks would be ready, the new M26 heavy tank would be available. About 100 M4A3E2 tanks were locally up-gunned with surplus 76mm guns starting in February 1945, further improving their effectiveness in the final months of the war.

ABOVE The M4 (105mm) assault gun resembled the normal Sherman but was fitted with a 105mm howitzer in the turret. Six of these were deployed in each tank battalion to provide fire support. One is seen here with the 750th Tank Battalion, supporting the 75th Division near Manhay, Belgium, during the Battle of the Bulge on December 30, 1944.

DUCK FEET

The wet weather conditions in the ETO in the autumn of 1944 led to efforts to reduce the ground pressure of tanks by using track extensions nicknamed "duck-bills" by US tankers. The normal ground pressure of the Sherman was

RIGHT The new horizontal volute spring suspension (HVSS) permitted the use of a wide 23-inch track on the Sherman to improve its floatation in soft terrain. It was introduced on the M4A3E8 that began to be distributed in the ETO starting around Christmas 1944.

The M4A3 (76mm) of 1st Lt. Arthur Sell of Co. A, 35th Tank Battalion, 4th Armored Division, confronts several German Panther tanks of Panzer-Regiment.15, 11.Panzer-Division near Guébling, France, on November 14, 1944. Sell's tank managed to knock out two of the Panthers before his own tank became bogged in the mud and was knocked out. The remaining German tanks were knocked out by other Shermans of Sell's company. Sell was awarded the Distinguished Service Cross for his actions that day. (Artwork by Steve Noon © Osprey Publishing)

about 13.7 pounds per square inch (psi). In comparison, typical human ground pressure is about 16psi, and that of the Panther tank only 12.5psi due to its wide tracks. Sherman tanks with the duck-bills reduced their ground pressure to about 12.4psi. This system had been developed by Ordnance in 1943–44 but was not available in sufficient numbers in the ETO. As a result, Bradley's 12th Army Group contracted local Belgian factories to manufacture them.

As a longer-term solution, Ordnance had been developing a new suspension system that permitted the use of wider 23-inch tracks. In comparison to the vertical volute spring suspension invented by Harry Knox in the early 1930s, the new system used horizontal volute spring suspension (HVSS). The pilot tanks were designated as M4A3E8, and the E8 suffix was applied to tanks with the experimental HVSS suspension, such as M4A2E8. This reduced ground pressure to about 10.5–11psi. Production of the first 500 M4A3 (76mm) with the new HVSS suspension was approved on March 2, 1944, and production began in August 1944. The first tanks with the new suspension began appearing in the ETO around Christmas 1944 and were first used by the 4th Armored Division in the fighting around Bastogne. Ordnance did not issue a specific designation for this new upgrade. It was first identified by the awkward designation "M4A3 (76mm) with 23-inch track" or "M4A3 (76mm) with HVSS." By 1945, the less awkward experimental designation "M4A3E8" was unofficially applied to this variant.

SPECIALIZED TANKS IN THE ETO

The US Army in the ETO used a variety of specialized tanks. These fell roughly into the categories of counter-obstacle tanks, flamethrower tanks, and rocket tanks.

Counter-obstacle tanks

The US Army was generally behind the British Army in the development of mine-clearing tanks, in part due to the greater enthusiasm of the Royal Engineers and Mechanical Engineers (REME) compared with the US Army's Corps of Engineers for the use of tanks for combat engineering tasks. The British Army had introduced mine-clearing flail tanks such as the Scorpion during the desert campaign in 1942–43. The US Army in 1943 decided to undertake limited production of a slightly modified version designated as the T3 Scorpion mine exploder, eventually totaling 41 units. The first US copies were rushed to Tunisia in April 1943. US engineers preferred mine rollers over flails due to their simplicity, and the T1 mine exploder was first tested on the M3 medium tank in early 1943. Apparently, a few of these "mine crushers" were used during the spring offensive in Tunisia in 1943. The T3 fitted on the M4 medium tank was later issued to the 16th Engineers of the 1st Armored Division, which formed a special unit for their use, the 6617th Mine Clearing Company. They saw combat use during operations in the Anzio beachhead starting in April 1944, but were not very successful.

The T3 flail mine exploder was a US copy of the British Scorpion. These were used in Tunisia in 1943 and again in Italy.

LEFT The T1E1 mine exploder consisted of three sets of armored plate discs with six discs in each set. The assembly weighed 18 tons and was propelled using an M32 tank recovery vehicle. This is a T1E1 of Co. B, 738th Tank Battalion (SMX), in Faymonville, Belgium, on January 16, 1945 at the conclusion of the Battle of the Bulge.

BELOW LEFT The T1E3 "Aunt Jemima" consisted of ten 8-foot discs each weighing 2.3 tons in two assemblies. The entire mine-exploder set weighed 30 tons. Aside from the front assembly, there was a pusher plate attached to the rear that enabled a second tank to assist in pushing the assembly through a minefield. This T1E3 was from the 25th Armored Engineer Battalion, 6th Armored Division, near Nancy, France, in October 1944.

Lacking any practical means of mine clearing, the US Army turned to the British for equipment to use during the D-Day landings in Normandy. A February 1944 request included 25 Crab Flail tanks, an improved version of the Scorpion, as well as other mine rakes and rollers. In the event, Britain was barely able to meet its own requirements for specialized equipment, so none of these arrived in US units in time for use on D-Day.

In the spring of 1944, a number of other US designed mine rollers had arrived in theater, including the T1E1 "Earthworm," pushed by a M32 TRV (tank recovery vehicle), and the T1E3 "Aunt Jemima," pushed by a modified M4 medium tank. A total of 75 T1E1 and 100 T1E3 mine exploders had been manufactured in March–May 1944. The 6th Armored Division was one of the first units equipped with T1E3 mine exploders following a May 1944 demonstration in England. Two T1E3 mine exploders were handed over to the 25th Armored Engineer Battalion and put on trials in France in the summer of 1944. In addition to the US-built T1E1 and T1E3 mine exploders, the first supply of British Crabs was finally obtained, based on the February 1944 request. A total of nine Crabs, 12 T1E1, and 27 T1E3 were used to

A handful of Crab flail tanks were supplied by Britain starting in July 1944. They served with the 739th Tank Battalion (Special Mine Exploder), and this one was photographed passing through Vicht on February 21, 1945 during the fighting on the approaches to the Roer river.

equip companies of the 702nd and 744th Tank Battalions in July 1944 for Operation *Cobra*, the Normandy breakout operation in late July. The lack of sufficient training undermined the effectiveness of these devices, which were cumbersome to use in the best of circumstances.

The problems encountered during Operation *Cobra* prompted the US Army to turn over the mine exploders to specialized units. Three former CDL units, the 738th, 739th, and 740th Tank Battalions, were reorganized as Special Mine Exploder (SMX) battalions in the fall of 1944, though the conversion of the 740th was never completed. In addition, the 6638th Mine Clearing Company, which had arrived in southern France with the Seventh US Army in August 1944 with mine scarifiers and other equipment, was again re-equipped with the newer minefield breaching equipment. These units were used for minefield clearing and saw their most extensive use in early 1945. There was other sporadic use of mine-clearing tanks by the US Army in the ETO in 1944, including the use of improvised demolition snakes to breach minefields during the attack on the Metz fortresses in October 1944.

While the T3 was being used in the Mediterranean theater, Ordnance continued to work on mine-clearing devices. Another nonexplosive means to breach a minefield was to plow the mines aside using a V-shaped dozer blade, called a mine scarifier. Ordnance developed the T5 mine scarifier, but the T5E3 did not enter production until March 1945. However, a small number of improvised mine scarifiers were built in Italy based on the M1 tank dozer, and these were used in small numbers by units of the Seventh US Army during Operation *Dragoon*, the amphibious landings in southern France on August 15, 1944.

The most widely used and successful counter-obstacle tank was the M1 dozer. Although originally developed on a 1942 engineer requirement, there was some confusion over whether it was primarily intended for mine clearing or general-purpose counter-obstacle work. In the event, the Armored Force sponsored the final development and production. On March 5, 1944, the Army standardized the LaPlant-Choate dozer as the Medium Tankdozer M1 and authorized the production of 500 kits. Production began on April 10, 1944, and they were first used on D-Day. They proved extremely popular for a wide range of combat engineer tasks and were always in high demand.

The most obscure of the counter-obstacle tanks were the bridge-laying tanks, intended to overcome German anti-tank ditches while under fire. In the Italian theater, the US Army was heavily dependent on British help. The 6617th Engineer Mine Clearing Company (EMCC) received 12 Churchill tanks with Small Box Girder bridges (SBG). The 16th Engineers of the 1st Armored Division created their own improvised bridging vehicles by developing an attachment for M2 treadway bridges on the front of an M31 TRV prior to the Anzio breakout operation in May 1944. During preparations for the Operation *Dragoon* amphibious landings in southern France on August 15, 1944, the 6617th EMCC transferred at least three British Churchill with SBG bridges to the US Seventh Army. These were used by the 6638th EMCC attached to the Gapping Team of the 3rd Infantry Division. There were a number of joint British and Canadian efforts later in Italy to explore other bridge-laying concepts, including the use of turretless Sherman Ark tanks to carry treadway and the Canadian "Plymouth" Bailey bridges to breach longer gaps. Some of the Sherman Arks were provided to the 1st Armored Division's new 1st Assault Company, a specialized unit that was formed to replace the 6617th EMCC after it was transferred to France. While the US Engineer Board continued to work on self-launched bridges, units in the field continued to improvise their own solutions. The use of tank recovery vehicles to launch treadway bridges was used in France and Germany in 1944–45. The first known conversions in France were assembled for the assault on the Metz fortifications in October 1944. Subsequently, a number of tank units made similar conversions using both M31 and M32 TRVs.

Flamethrower tanks

The US Army had experimented with flamethrower tanks since 1918. Most of the early combat efforts in flame tanks took place in the Pacific theater as is described in that chapter. On June 29, 1943, US, British, and Canadian officers held a flamethrower conference in Dumbarton Oaks, Maryland, to evaluate requirements for future mechanized operations in Europe, especially requirements for the forthcoming *Overlord* amphibious landings in France.

The most common type of tank-mounted flamethrower was the E4-5 auxiliary flamethrower, which replaced the bow machine gun. This is an example in use by the 747th Tank Battalion in Zweifall, Germany, in November 1944 during the Operation *Queen* offensive in the Roer sector. Curiously, this M4 tank is still fitted with the "Salad Fork/Green Bumper," an early type of bocage cutter from the Normandy campaign.

The conference concluded that Britain led the US in mechanized flamethrower development. US officers were shown the Churchill Crocodile in March 1943 and told of the possibility of creating a similar flame tank using the M4 Sherman tank. On August 11, 1943, the US Army informed the British War Office they would have an estimated requirement for 100 Sherman Crocodiles. A demonstration of the prototype Sherman Crocodile was held for US officers on February 3, 1944. The First US Army established a firm requirement for 65 in February 1944, later increased to 115. British factories were overwhelmed by work orders for the Churchill Crocodile and barely managed to meet earlier British Army orders. As a result, no Sherman Crocodiles were ready for US Army employment on D-Day. Four Sherman Crocodiles were delivered to the US Army in the UK in the summer of 1944, but further production was canceled on August 13, 1944.

In March 1944, the Armored Section of Eisenhower's ETOUSA headquarters requested the dispatch of an E4-5 auxiliary tank flamethrower to Britain for demonstration purposes, to be followed by 100 more at a later date. This flamethrower was fitted in the hull of the Sherman tank in place of the usual bow machine gun. This weapon had been developed by the Chemical Weapons Service (CWS) based on requests from the Pacific theater. Tank officers wanted flamethrowers available for potential use against German Siegfried Line fortifications. On July 1, 1944, Bradley's First US Army headquarters requested enough to equip each medium tank battalion with nine E4-5 flamethrowers. In the event, the first E4-5 was not shipped to Europe until June 12, 1944. In early July, an E4-5 flamethrower mounted in an M4 tank conducted a demonstration to tank and chemical warfare officers from Eisenhower's ETOUSA headquarters. Its performance was described as "positively pathetic" compared with the Churchill Crocodile. Part of the problem was that improper fuel had been used, so another demonstration followed in August 1944.

This resulted in a change of heart by Bradley's headquarters, and on September 6, 1944, 333 auxiliary flamethrowers were ordered. The overall objective was later extended to 630 flamethrowers by late 1944 and 1,012 by the end of January 1945 based on the expectation that each tank battalion would receive nine.

The combat debut in the ETO was on September 15, 1944 by the 741st Tank Battalion against a Westwall bunker with indifferent results. The lack of flamethrowers led the Ninth US Army to request British flame support during the reduction of the fortified port of Brest in Brittany in September 1944. A dozen Churchill Crocodiles arrived and were employed in the attacks against defenses around Fort Montbarey. An after-action report noted that they "contributed materially in softening unusually stubborn resistance … its demoralizing effect gives a 'shock action potential' far in excess of that possessed by the standard tank." One infantry lieutenant remarked, "I have seen the time when I would have given a million dollars for just one of those things for ten minutes. Where in the hell have the Americans been?"

The Sherman Crocodile saw its combat debut with the 739th Tank Battalion (SMX) on February 24, 1945 during the attack on the Julich citadel. The flame gun was located in the small turret on the upper lip of the hull front above the bow machine gun.

By mid-November 1944, Bradley's 12th Army Group had received 150 complete flamethrowers. The allocation was 75 to Hodges' First US Army (FUSA), 45 to Simpson's Ninth US Army (NUSA), and 30 to Patton's Third US Army (TUSA). By the time that the flamethrowers became available, the First and Ninth US Armies were heavily committed to the Operation *Queen* offensive toward the Roer river. Many tank units were reluctant to pull tanks and troops out of the line to refit with flamethrowers. A small number were used in the November 1944 fighting with inconsequential results, and progress on deploying the flamethrowers remained slow. The start of the German Ardennes offensive on December 16, 1944 also contributed to the delays in the First US Army, since it bore the brunt of the German offensive.

Of the three field armies of Bradley's 12th Army Group, Simpson's Ninth US Army showed the most enthusiasm for flamethrower tanks. They had received some of the earliest flame support from Churchill Crocodiles in the fighting at Brest, and as a result had submitted a requirement in November 1944 for Crocodile flamethrowers. This rescued the four Sherman Crocodiles from limbo in the UK, and they were sent to the 739th Tank Battalion (Special Mine Exploder) in November 1944. The Sherman Crocodile was used on only a single occasion, during the reduction of the old citadel in Jülich on February 24, 1945 during the Operation *Grenade* offensive. More Sherman Crocodiles were requested but production never resumed. In total, some 726 E4R2-4R3-5R1 auxiliary tank flamethrowers were shipped to the ETO from June 1944 to March 1945, although only a fraction of these were ever mounted in tanks.

This was a demonstration of the field expedient tank auxiliary flamethrower developed on New Caledonia in the autumn of 1943 and seen here fitted to the hull machine-gun mount of an M3A1 light tank of Co. B, 3rd Marine Tank Battalion, on October 10, 1943.

The minor role played by flame tanks in the ETO was due to a variety of factors. They were not available in time to take part in the autumn 1944 penetration of the Westwall/Siegfried Line, the one instance where they might have been most useful. The Germans had been the pioneers of flame weapons in World War I, and the Westwall bunkers were designed to resist flame attack through the effective sealing of embrasures and doors, and the use of dispersed and protected ventilation systems. Tank officers in the ETO complained that the E4-5 was too short-ranged, and the German tactic was to defend bunkers with Panzerfaust teams to prevent the approach of flame tanks. When the flamethrowers finally became available in significant numbers in early 1945, most of the Westwall defenses had been overcome except in the Saar. The E4-5 was mechanically and electrically unreliable, especially in the hands of crews with very limited training. The reliability issues could have been overcome if the troops felt that flamethrowers were badly needed, but there was little demand for mechanized flamethrowers in this theater. In contrast to the poor opinion about tank flamethrowers in the ETO, they were widely regarded as one of the most important innovations in tank armament in the Pacific theater, as will be detailed in a following chapter.

Rocket tanks

The US Navy pioneered the use of artillery rockets to supplement conventional artillery since they could be fired from landing craft and other small vessels that could not carry conventional guns. In 1943–44, the US Army began examining the use of these rockets supplement tank guns. The first efforts involved the use of 7.2-inch demolition rockets from the T40 launcher for breaching seawalls during amphibious landings. This was later standardized as the M17 Whiz-Bang launcher. This device was never very popular since its proximity to the turret roof created problems for the crew entering or escaping from the vehicle, and the rockets had a relatively short range, being intended for firing from only a hundred yards with a maximum range of barely a thousand yards. After being rejected for use on D-Day in Normandy, and after being used with little success during Operation *Dragoon* in southern France, the army decided to hand over the surviving launchers to tank battalions in the Italian theater for possible use in the artillery role. The 752nd and 760th Tank Battalions each converted a tank platoon with four Whiz-Bang launchers in mid-August 1944. These rocket platoons did not serve with their parent units, but

The T34 4.5-inch Calliope rocket launcher could fire up to sixty 4.5-inch rockets in a single salvo. This Calliope of the 6th Armored Division was moving forward through Wichte, Germany, on April 1, 1945 to provide fire support to engineers erecting a bridge over the Fulda river.

were instead transferred to the 755th and 757th Tank Battalions for operations along the Gothic line. They were used in very small numbers and had modest results. In December 1944, the 525th Ordnance Battalion converted eight T40 launchers by replacing the 7.2-inch demolition rockets with the longer-range 4.5-inch aircraft rocket launcher. They served with the 752nd and 760th Tank Battalions and saw combat starting in March 1945.

OPPOSITE A T40 7.2-inch Whiz-Bang rocket launcher on an M4A1 tank of Co. B, 752nd Tank Battalion, in Italy in August 1944. This rocket launcher could fire 20 7.2-inch rockets each weighing 61lb, including 32lb of explosive.

The US Army had already developed a launcher for the 4.5-inch rocket as the T34, better known by its nickname as the Calliope. The original plan was to use these for obstacle breaching on D-Day, but this was rejected out of hand since it was felt that the high mounting of the launcher on the M4 tank would make it unstable in landing craft. After D-Day, the 743rd Tank Battalion had 30 Calliope launchers installed for a planned attack by the 30th Infantry Division in December 1944. However, the German attack in the Ardennes pre-empted this operation and the launchers were discarded without being used. The T34 Calliope was more extensively deployed in early 1945 and was used in small numbers at various times by the 2nd, 4th, 6th, 12th, and 14th Armored Divisions and by the 702nd, 712th, 753rd, and 781st Tank Battalions. Reactions to these weapons were mixed. They were generally disliked by armored division officers who felt that they wasted tanks for tasks that should be undertaken by field artillery. Some of the separate tank battalions applauded these weapons since the massed impact of the rockets had a very demoralizing effect on German infantry.

TANK BATTLES IN THE ARDENNES

The Battle of the Bulge was the largest confrontation by German and American tanks during the campaign in the ETO in 1944–45. With Germany on a fatal spiral to military defeat, Hitler conceived of a massive counteroffensive through the Ardennes to regain the strategic initiative in the West. The final operational plan, codenamed *Herbstnebel* (*Autumn Mist*) envisioned a thrust out of the Eifel region to the Meuse river, followed by a dash for the port of Antwerp. The aim was to divide the US and British armies and force a "New Dunkirk."

The core of the *Autumn Mist* attack was a reserve of eight panzer divisions plus numerous smaller panzer formations. The *Schwerpunkt* (focal point) of the offensive was on its northern shoulder, the 6.Panzer-Armee spearheaded by the I.SS-Panzer-Korps. Once this corps reached the Meuse river, the II.SS-Panzer-Korps would be injected to propel the offensive to its main objective of Antwerp. In the center was the 5.Panzer-Armee intended to shield the left flank of 6.Panzer-Armee.

Operational panzer strength in the Ardennes sector, December 16, 1944

PzKpfw IV	Panther	Tiger	Pz IV Lg	Jagdpanther	StuG	Hetzer	Total
356	468	38	271	47	386	175	1,741

Lieutenant General Omar Bradley, commander of the 12th Army Group, felt that the Ardennes was an unlikely venue for a major German campaign. The terrain seemed completely unsuitable, especially in the winter months. Allied intelligence had detected the buildup of the panzer forces in the West but mistakenly presumed that they were intended to counterattack the Allies in a climactic battle along the Rhine river sometime in early 1945. As a result, the Ardennes was weakly defended and was dubbed the US Army's "Kindergarten and old age home." Of the four infantry divisions in the Ardennes, the 4th and 28th Divisions had suffered crippling losses during the fighting in the Hürtgen forest and were transferred to the Ardennes for reconstruction. The two other divisions, the 99th and 106th Divisions, were both inexperienced, with the 106th Division arriving only days before the German offensive.

M4 medium tanks of Gen. Bruce Clarke's Combat Command B, 7th Armored Division, conduct a rearguard action in the "fortified goose egg" of St. Vith on December 21, 1944. The prolonged defense of this key crossroads town slowed the German exploitation of the neighboring breakthroughs by obstructing key roads in the northern sector of the Ardennes battles. (Artwork by Howard Gerrard © Osprey Publishing)

An M4A3 (76mm) of Co. C, 774th Tank Battalion, passes by a knocked-out Panther tank near Bovigny on January 17, 1945 while supporting the 83rd Division during the final phase of the Ardennes campaign.

The US Army units defending in the Ardennes at the outset of the German offensive had modest numbers of tanks since an attack was not anticipated in this sector. The US Army's V Corps, the main target of the German attack, was very weak in tanks, with only three tank battalions on hand, two of which were in the northern sector away from the main German attack. Once the German offensive began, elements of nearby US armored divisions were rushed into the area, with combat commands from the 7th and 9th Armored Divisions sent to the St. Vith area, and elements of the 10th Armored Division sent to Bastogne. US armored reinforcements continued to flow into the Ardennes through December and early January, eventually totaling nine armored divisions, 17 separate tank battalions, and 25 tank destroyer battalions.

The *Autumn Mist* offensive went awry almost from the start. The *Schwerpunkt* in the northern sector facing the Elsenborn Ridge became bogged down almost immediately due to the poor road networks along the Belgian frontier, compounded by the muddy ground conditions. The infantry divisions that were supposed to overcome the initial American defenses failed to do so, causing fatal delays in the dispatch of the panzer exploitation force. Kampfgruppe Peiper of the 1.SS-Panzer-Division made a rapid thrust through the undefended Losheim Gap, but quickly lost communications with the rest of I.Panzer-Korps. It became trapped around La Gleize by newly arrived US infantry reinforcements from the 30th Infantry Division and 82nd Airborne Division. It was eventually forced to retreat out of the pocket, leaving its panzers behind. Its neighbor, the 12.SS-Panzer-Division, became caught up in the enormous traffic jams on the roads leading into the Losheim area, the only good road network toward the Meuse river. The congestion on this road

An M4A3 (76mm) of the 42nd Tank Battalion, 11th Armored Division, passes by an abandoned German PzKpfw IV tank along the Houffalize road outside Bastogne on January 15, 1945. The newly arrived 11th Armored Division had a half-and-half mixture of 75mm and 76mm Shermans at this time.

prompted the division to try to push SS-Panzer-Regiment.12 through narrow forest roads in the Krinkelterwald, leading to bruising fighting with the 2nd Infantry Division for the town of Krinkelt-Rocherath, where most of the regiment's tanks were knocked out or disabled. The infantry in this fight was ably supported by the 741st Tank Battalion, one of the units that had landed on Omaha Beach six months before. The remainder of the panzer division was frustrated in a similar fight for the Dom Bütgenbach manor farm against elements of the 1st Infantry Division, which led to heavy losses of Jagdpanthers in its attached tank destroyer battalion.

Within three days of the start of *Autumn Mist*, the I.Panzer-Korps had failed to breach the American defense line, and failed to reach the Meuse river. For all intents and purposes, the failure in this sector doomed *Autumn Mist* since it offered the quickest route to the Meuse and Antwerp. Time was not in the Wehrmacht's favor, and the US Army began rushing reinforcements into the Ardennes.

The 5.Panzer-Armee was more successful in creating breaches in the American defenses. Its commander, Hasso von Manteuffel, ignored Hitler's instructions about relying on an artillery barrage to pave the wave for the infantry. Instead, he used 1918 infiltration tactics to move special infantry assault detachments through the thin American lines "like drops of rain" before they realized an offensive was underway. In this fashion, the German infantry cut off the inexperienced 106th Infantry Division, forcing most of the unit to surrender. The badly decimated 28th Division put up a stiff fight on the approaches to Bastogne but was finally crushed by an overwhelming force. The success of the 5.Panzer-Armee led to the transfer of the II.SS-Panzer-Korps from the 6.Panzer-Armee to Manteuffel's 5.Panzer-Armee, with

An M18 76mm GMC of the 705th Tank Destroyer Battalion helps the 502nd Parachute Infantry Regiment, 101st Airborne Division, to repel an attack by Kampfgruppe Maucke of the 15.Panzergrenadier-Division outside Bastogne on December 25, 1944. (Artwork by Peter Dennis © Osprey Publishing)

a goal to propel two Panzer spearheads to the Meuse, one through the Bastogne area toward Dinant, and the other via Manhay over the Tailles plateau.

In the event, the delays in the German advance caused by the US infantry defenses ultimately doomed the 5.Panzer-Armee attack. By the time that the penetrations had been made, the US Army had rushed its two heavy tank divisions, the 2nd and 3rd Armored Divisions, to block the penetrations around Christmas. The spearheads of the Bastogne attack, the 2.Panzer-Division and 9.Panzer-Division, were surrounded and defeated in the Celles pocket northwest of Bastogne by the 2nd Armored Division. The 3rd Armored Division managed to plug the gap in the center against the 116.Panzer-Division and units of the II.SS-Panzer-Korps in a series of ferocious tank battles around Manhay and Hotton.

By Christmas, *Autumn Mist* had reached its high-water mark, and the German commander, Field Marshal Gerd von Rundstedt, asked Berlin's permission to go over to the defensive. By this time, Bradley's 12th Army Group had been reinforced by three corps from Patton's Third US Army, which made a bold winter move from the Saar region to Belgium. The first tanks from Patton's 4th Armored Division began entering the Bastogne perimeter the day after Christmas. Although the German offensive had failed, it would take another three weeks of bitter winter fighting for the US Army to recover the terrain lost in the initial German assault.

The German Operation *Nordwind* offensive in Alsace in January 1945 is not as well known as the Ardennes attack. This is a camouflaged M4A3 (76mm) of the 709th Tank Battalion supporting the 75th Division near Riedwihr during the fighting against the Colmar pocket on January 31, 1945.

Major (Dr.) P. E. Schramm, historian of the German OKW high command, concluded that "the Battle of the Bulge finally demonstrated the armored superiority of the US Army over the Wehrmacht." Schramm's comment referred to the combat capabilities of the armored units, not the technical balance.

By the time of the Ardennes offensive, the panzer divisions had lost much of their offensive capability due to shortages of armored equipment and experienced troops. The panzer divisions had shifted their organizational structure toward more infantry and fewer tanks, a configuration better suited to defensive battles. Only one of the division's six Panzergrenadier battalions received armored half-tracks, and the remaining battalions relied on trucks, often commercial types with poor cross-country capabilities. The divisional artillery had few self-propelled guns and relied on towed guns that had difficulty moving forward with the panzer regiments during offensive operations. There was a widespread shortage of experienced combat leaders due to the ferocious casualty rates in 1944.

LEFT M4 medium tank, Co. B, 68th Tank Battalion, 6th Armored Division, January 1945. (Artwork by Felipe Rodríguez © Osprey Publishing)

BELOW LEFT M4 (105mm) assault gun, Headquarters Company, 15th Tank Battalion, 6th Armored Division, January 1945. (Artwork by Felipe Rodríguez © Osprey Publishing)

By late 1944, the panzer divisions had significant tactical problems carrying out offensive missions due to the severe weakness of the associated German infantry divisions. German tactical doctrine for a breakthrough operation such as in the Ardennes was for the infantry divisions to make the initial penetration of the enemy defense line, at which point the panzer divisions were injected to carry out the exploitation phase. Even the infantry divisions assigned to I.SS-Panzer-Korps in the *Schwerpunkt* of the Ardennes campaign were rated as unsuitable for offensive action. The failure of the German infantry to penetrate the American defenses imposed costly delays which ultimately doomed the offensive.

The most significant US advantage was its stalwart infantry, backed by superior field artillery. Artillery at divisional and corps level was fully motorized, and there were ample supplies of ammunition. More importantly, the US Army had a much better fire control system than the Germans based on extensive field telephone and radio links that provided timely and accurate targeting. US field artillery, more than any other single arm, was responsible for the decimation of the German infantry divisions in the opening phase of the offensive. Artillery also played a crucial role in the defeat of the panzer divisions of I.SS-Panzer Korps in the approaches to Elsenborn Ridge, especially in the defeat of 12.SS-Panzer-Division.

In comparison to the panzer divisions, US armored divisions usually fought at near full strength. US armored infantry battalions and armored field artillery battalions were fully mechanized. Ammunition and fuel supplies were ample. The US Army units also had substantial defensive advantages.

The Wehrmacht suffered total losses of about 610 tanks and AFVs in the Ardennes fighting, with a further 770 disabled, for a total of 1,385 lost and disabled. US Army losses were of about 800 tanks and 250 tank destroyers with an additional number disabled. Although the level of tank losses were similar, the US Army could easily afford such losses while the Wehrmacht could not. In mid-January, the 6.Panzer-Armee was transferred from the Ardennes to Hungary to deal with the Red Army's winter offensives. By February 5, 1945, the Wehrmacht in the West had only 190 tanks, 533 assault guns, and 87 tank destroyers operational on the entire Western Front due to the catastrophic losses suffered in the winter campaigns in the Ardennes and Alsace.

Tanks: comparative technical characteristics

	M4A3	M4A3E8	PzKpfw IV Ausf. J	Panther Ausf. G
Crew	5	5	5	5
Dimensions: L x W x H (m)	6.27 x 2.61 x 2.74	5.89 x 2.61 x 2.74	7.02 x 2.88 x 2.68	8.86 x 3.42 x 2.98
Loaded weight (tonnes)	31.5	33.6	25.0	45.5
Main gun	75mm M3	76mm M1A1	75mm KwK40	75mm KwK 42
Main gun ammo	104	71	87	81
Engine (hp)	450	450	300	600
Max. speed (km/h)	42	42	38	46
Fuel (liters)	635	635	470	720
Range (km)	160	160	210	200
Ground pressure (kg/cm^2)	1.0	.963	0.91	.88
Armor**				
Mantlet (mm)	90*=>90	90@5=90.3	50*=>50	100*=>100
Turret front (mm)	51@30=58.9	51@30=58.9	50@5=50.2	100@5=100.4
Turret side (mm)	51@5=51.2	51@5=51.2	33@25=36.4	45@25=49.6
Upper hull front (mm)	51@45=72.1	51@45=72.1	80@8=80.8	80@55=139.4
Lower hull front (mm)	51@50=79.3	51@50=79.3	80@14=82.8	65@55=113.3
Upper hull side (mm)	38@0=38	38@0=38	30@0=30	50@30=57.7
*curved **armor data provided as: actual thickness in mm @ angle from vertical = effective thickness in mm				

Assault guns/tank destroyers: comparative technical characteristics

	StuG III Ausf. G	Pz. IV lg (V)	M10 3-inch GMC	M36 90mm GMC
Crew	4	4	5	5
Dimensions: L x W x H (m)	6.77 x 2.95 x 2.16	8.5 x 3.17 x 1.85	6.82 x 3.04 x 2.89	7.46 x 3.04 x 3.27
Loaded weight (tonnes)	23.9	25.8	29.6	28.5
Main gun	75mm StuK40	75mm KwK 42	3-in M7	90mm M3
Main gun ammo	54	55	54	47
Engine (hp)	300	300	410	500
Max. speed (km/h)	40	35	45	42
Fuel (liters)	310	470	624	726
Range (km)	155	210	320	240
Ground p ressure (kg/cm²)	0.93	0.92	0.92	0.91
Armor**				
Mantlet (mm)	80@0=80	80*	57@45=80.6	76*
Turret front (mm)	n/a	n/a	32@5=32.1	32@5=32.1
Turret side (mm)	n/a	n/a	32@5=32.1	32@5=32.1
Upper hull front (mm)	80@10=81.2	80@45=113.1	38@55=46.4	38@55=46.4
Lower hull front (mm)	80@21=85.1	80@40=104.4	51@50=79.3	51@50=79.3
Upper hull side (mm)	30@0=30	40@30=46.2	19@38=30.8	19@38=30.8
*curved **armor data provided as: actual thickness in mm @ angle from vertical = effective thickness in mm				

Ardennes lessons

For the US Army, the Ardennes campaign revealed shortcomings in US tanks that had been acknowledged since the time of the Normandy campaign, but not resolved. The technical inferiority of the M4 Sherman against the Panther tank had been clear since July 1944. But consistent US battlefield victories against the panzer force, including Operation *Cobra* in July 1944, the repulse of the Mortain panzer offensive in August 1944, and the defeat of the Lorraine panzer offensive in September 1944, had led to complacency. Many US senior officers felt that the German technical advantages were offset by US advantages in quantity and reliability, as well as even more pronounced advantages in field artillery and airpower. The relatively small scale of tank-vs.-tank fighting in the autumn of 1944 further hid the need for improvements. Observer teams sent to the ETO in the autumn of 1944 to solicit advice on future tank needs in 1945 did not encounter any strident demands for better tanks from armored division commanders.

There had been frequent complaints about the excessive height of the Sherman tank compared with its panzer opponents. This is a comparison of the Tiger II heavy tank on the left and an M4A3 (76mm) tank on the right, staged near the headquarters of Bradley's 12th Army Group to demonstrate the issue.

On January 5, 1945, Hanson Baldwin, the influential military correspondent for *The New York Times*, published an article in a series about the Ardennes campaign entitled "New German Tanks Prove Superior to Ours – Inquiry by Congress Urged." This was the first time that any public attention had been focused on the issue. This controversy would percolate on through March 1945, with Eisenhower soliciting the opinions of his subordinate commanders. In fact, the Battle of the Bulge had made this issue irrelevant. No matter how many technical advantages the Panther enjoyed over the Sherman in early 1945, it was of little consequence when there were only 96 Panthers operational on the entire Western Front on February 5, 1945, and only 24 operational on April 10, 1945, facing more than 6,000 US Army Sherman tanks. Nevertheless, a broad range of improvements were undertaken based on the lessons of the Ardennes campaign.

The lessons of the Ardennes fighting led Bradley's 12th Army Group to recommend the suspension of the shipment of any further 75mm M4 Sherman tanks to the ETO in favor of the 76mm tanks, and especially the new M4A3E8 (76mm). There had been plans to utilize about a hundred spare 76mm guns to up-gun a corresponding number of 75mm Sherman tanks. After building at least one example, the program was abandoned in favor of using the guns to improve the popular M4A3E2 assault tanks. Despite the policy favoring the new 76mm tanks, the majority of Shermans in the ETO remained the 75mm types until the final weeks of the war in the ETO.

M4A3 (76mm), Co. B, 2nd Tank Battalion, 9th Armored Division, Clervaux, December 1944. (Artwork by Felipe Rodríguez © Osprey Publishing)

M4A3 (76mm), command tank of Lt. Col. Creighton Abrams, 37th Tank Battalion, 4th Armored Division, Bastogne, December 1944. (Artwork by Felipe Rodríguez © Osprey Publishing)

12th Army Group medium tank strength 1945: (75mm gun vs. 76mm gun)*

	Jan	Feb	Mar	Apr	May
75mm	1,650	1,842	1,898	1,915	1,601
76mm	618	802	968	1,420	1,942
M4 Total	2,268	2,644	2,866	3,335	3,543
*75mm + 76mm; data as of beginning of each month					

The Ardennes campaign in December 1944 saw the tank destroyers put to their greatest test. Four US infantry divisions bore the brunt of the initial German attack, supported by several towed 3-inch tank destroyer battalions. Losses in the 3-inch towed battalions were brutally high, totaling 35 percent in December alone. The hapless 820th TD Battalion was assigned to the 14th Cavalry Group, thinly stretched across the Losheim Gap and at the center of the main German assault. The battalion was overrun in the first few days of fighting and lost 31 of its 36 guns. The neighboring 801st TD Battalion was assigned to the 99th Division and lost 15 of its guns. In an interview after the tank fighting in Krinkelt-Rocherath, a 2nd Infantry Division officer emphatically stated:

OPPOSITE TOP M4A3 (76mm) medium tank in the Ardennes, January 1945. (Artwork by Jim Laurier © Osprey Publishing)

OPPOSITE BOTTOM Combat experience comes at a price. The inexperienced 43rd Tank Battalion of the newly arrived 12th Armored Division advanced into the village of Herrlisheim on January 17, 1945 during the German *Nordwind* offensive in Alsace. Lacking sufficient infantry support, about two dozen Sherman tanks were lost in the "Herrlisheim tank graveyard" to Panzerfaust and Panzerschreck anti-tank rocket launchers of the defending 553. Volksgrenadier-Division. (Artwork by Jim Laurier © Osprey Publishing)

> I want the self-propelled guns rather than the towed 3-inch guns because the towed guns are too heavy and sluggish. You can't get them up to the front. My orders have been in almost every case to get the guns up to the front-line troops. I just couldn't do it in the daytime with the 3-inch towed gun. I can get the 57's up pretty well, but you can always get self-propelled guns up better than towed ones.

The Ardennes campaign doomed the towed battalions. The initial Ardennes fighting made it quite clear that the towed anti-tank gun battalions were extremely ineffective when fighting German armor on their own. One study concluded that the loss ratio in these circumstances was about 3:1 in favor of the attacking tanks. When integrated into an infantry defensive position, the towed anti-tank guns were barely adequate, with an exchange ratio of 1:1.3 in favor of the guns. In contrast, the self-propelled M10 3-inch tank destroyers had a favorable exchange ratio of 1:1.9 when operating on their own without infantry support, and an excellent ratio of 1:6 when integrated into an infantry defense. The study noted that the towed 3-inch guns were successful in only two out of nine defensive actions, while the M10 tank destroyer battalions were successful in 14 of 16 defensive actions against German tanks. The First US Army report noted that tank destroyer battalion losses totaled 119, of which 86 were towed guns, a remarkable disproportion that glaringly revealed the vulnerability of the towed guns. The report concluded, "It is clear that during the battle of the Ardennes, the self-propelled battalion again proved its superiority over the towed battalion for both offensive and defensive action."

Self-propelled tank destroyers in the ETO 1944–45*

	Jun 44	Jul	Aug	Sep	Oct	Nov	Dec	Jan 45	Feb	Mar	Apr	May
M10	691	743	758	763	486	573	790	760	686	684	427	427
M18	146	141	176	170	189	252	306	312	448	540	427	427
M36					170	183	236	365	826	884	1,054	1,029
Total	837	884	934	933	845	1,008	1,332	1,437	1,960	2,108	1,908	1,333

* data as of the 20th of each month

The AGF bureaucracy in Washington had been painfully slow to recognize the obvious deficiencies of the towed battalions, and so finally in January 1945, Bradley's 12th Army Group took matters into their own hands and began to convert all towed 3-inch battalions to self-propelled battalions as soon as equipment became available. The same policy was later

Aggravated by the failure of Ordnance to address the Panther threat, US tank units in ETO took measures into their own hands. The 12th Army Group offered this configuration as their solution to the problem, refitting an M4A3E8 with extra armor plate on the hull front and making a number of other changes such as a co-axial .50-cal machine gun and an additional machine gun for the commander.

adopted by Devers' 6th Army Group in Alsace after it learned similar lessons during the German *Nordwind* offensive in January 1945. Commanders especially wanted more of the M36 90mm GMC, since this was the only tank destroyer that had a reasonably good chance of success against the German Panther tank. But with shortages of M36s, and a surplus of unused M18 tank destroyers available, the M18 was used to re-equip some battalions. Lingering shortages of new tank destroyers prevented the complete reorganization, and when the war in Europe ended in May 1945, four battalions still had the towed 3-inch guns compared to 41 with self-propelled tank destroyers. Of the 41 self-propelled battalions, 13 were equipped with the M18, and the rest were equipped with the M36 or a mixture of M10 and M36 tanks destroyers.

IMPROVISED ARMOR

One of the most vexing problems facing US tanks in the ETO was the growing threat of German anti-tank rockets such as the Panzerfaust and Panzerschreck. These weapons had begun to appear in Normandy in the summer of 1944. On August 8, 1944, the ETOUSA headquarters sent a request back to Ordnance in the United States to inquire whether they had any new technologies to defeat shaped-charge warheads, especially the infantry rocket weapons. While there were programs underway, none of these Ordnance efforts reached the battlefield in World War II.

US tank units began taking matters into their own hands. As early as July 1944, some tank crews had been adding a layer of sandbags to the front hulls of their tanks. This was often discouraged by local Ordnance personnel who argued that the sandbags were not very effective, and the added weight could lead to premature transmission or suspension problems with the tanks. Regardless of these technical arguments, local unit commanders felt that the improvised protection was a morale booster.

These efforts were small scale and local until late in 1944. Anti-tank rockets were responsible for only about 4 percent of the identified tank casualties in September, rising to 12.5 percent in October and 14.6 percent in November. The growth of the Panzerfaust threat was due to the enormous increase in its manufacture. Only 40,000 were being produced monthly in October 1943, rising to 250,000 in August 1944, 1,000,000 per month by November 1944, and 1,500,000 monthly from February 1945 to the end of the war.

Allied tank casualties in ETO by Panzerfaust/Panzerschreck 1945

Jan	Feb	Mar	Apr	May
6	4	15	24	41
(% of total tank casualties)				

Patton's Third US Army banned sandbag armor and preferred to weld additional armor plate to their tanks. This is an M4A3E8 of the 11th Armored Division with armor plate added to the turret and hull front.

One of the first systematic efforts to use sandbags was undertaken by the 2nd Armored Division in November 1944 in anticipation of the Operation *Queen* offensive in the Roer sector. In January 1945, the Ninth US Army (NUSA) led another round of improvised armor in preparation for the forthcoming Operation *Grenade* advance to the Rhine. The NUSA armor was more elaborate than the simple sandbag armor. It was multilayered and consisted of an initial layer of steel track shoes welded to the hull, followed by a layer of sandbags, and finally a covering of camouflage net to help keep the sandbags in place. This system was applied to several of the separate tank battalions in NUSA as well as to many tanks of the 2nd Armored Division.

There were two other field army-wide efforts in February–March 1945 in the wake of the German winter offensives. These mainly involved Patton's Third US Army (TUSA) and Patch's Seventh US Army (SUSA).

Patton had been convinced by his Ordnance officers that sandbags were ineffective and a potential handicap to tank performance due to their weight. In lieu of sandbag armor, the Ordnance Section of TUSA recommended the use of armor plate stripped off derelict US and German tanks. This was not specifically aimed at countering the Panzerfaust, but rather as a general upgrade to the tank armor versus all anti-tank threats. The 326th Ordnance

M4A3E8 with Seventh US Army sandbag armor, Germany, 1945. (Artwork by Johnny Shumate © Osprey Publishing)

In February–March 1945, Ordnance units of the Seventh US Army in Alsace began a program to mount a sheet-metal cage on the tank hulls and turrets to contain sandbag expedient armor to defeat German anti-tank rockets. This is an example on an M4A3E8 of Co. B, 25th Tank Battalion, 14th Armored Division, near Ohlungen on March 14, 1945.

Maintenance Battalion in Esch was assigned to cannibalizing wrecked tanks for their armor. The process of attaching the armor to tanks took about 85 man-hours per tank, and eventually TUSA contracted three Belgian factories to conduct the work. Priority was given to the three armored divisions subordinate to TUSA, the 4th, 6th, and 11th Armored Divisions. Each of the divisions was issued 36 up-armored tanks, with additional tanks following once time and resources permitted.

The Seventh US Army's main concern in anti-tank rocket threat was due to heavy losses suffered by the 12th Armored Division in the fighting around Herrlisheim and losses of the 14th Armored Division around Rittershofen during the German Operation *Nordwind* offensive in January 1945. In contrast to earlier sandbag schemes, SUSA came up with a modification package that began by welding steel cages to the hull and turret of their Sherman tanks to contain the sandbags. This program also involved a much thicker layer of sandbags, generally two sandbags thick on the hull and turret sides and two to four thick on the glacis plate. The modification package added about 3 tons to the weight of the tank. In February–March 1945, virtually all of the tanks of the 12th and 14th Armored Divisions, as well as the separate tank battalions of the Seventh US Army were upgraded with this improvised armor.

On March 9, 1945, the Seventh US Army decided to test the kit using Panzerfaust launchers. The tests confirmed that the expedient sandbag armor had some defensive advantages depending on the angle and location of impact. A visiting observer team from the New Developments Division of the War Department concluded, "These tests are of course far from conclusive. The psychological value of the sandbags is the greatest value actually derived."

One of the main problems with the sandbag package was that the sandbags on the front hull were still prone to fall off when jostled during movement. As a result of these trials, the 12th Armored Division began experimenting with concrete armor on the glacis plate. Tests against the expedient concrete armor found that the Panzerfaust "could penetrate both armor plates and concrete, but the splash of the shell inside the tank was negligible." The concrete absorbed so much of the energy of the penetrating jet that by the time it bore through the armor plate, most of its energy was exhausted.

By March 1945, a significant fraction of American tanks had some form of expedient armor. Seven of the 15 armored divisions in the ETO (2nd, 3rd, 4th, 6th, 11th, 12th, and 14th) were equipped with expedient armor by 1945. The separate tank battalions in the ETO present a much more mixed picture of coverage, since these smaller units often did not have the resources to apply expedient armor in any systematic fashion. Some battalions, such as those with Seventh US Army in Alsace, tended to have more thorough coverage due to a more vigorous promotion of the effort by senior commanders. In other armies, coverage depended on time, circumstance, and the availability of resources. For example, the 3rd Armored Division managed to add additional steel armor on many of their tanks after the capture of Cologne in March 1945, where a local factory provided a source of steel plate and welding equipment.

The T26E3 Pershing entered production in November 1944, and this is serial number 12 at Aberdeen Proving Ground on December 22, 1944. This was one of 20 tanks from the first production batch of 40 tanks that was kept in the United States for further trials.

M26 Pershing tank, US Army, 1945. (Artwork by Jim Laurier © Osprey Publishing)

NEW TANKS IN 1945

Two new tanks arrived in the ETO in 1945, the much-anticipated T26E3 Pershing tank and the M24 Chafee light tank. Although there was not a great demand for a Sherman replacement after the Normandy fighting, the Ardennes campaign led to considerable pressure to field a new tank. Progress on the T26E1 tank was successful enough that on June 15, 1944, the War Department decided that the 1945 tank production program would be changed to permit production of 6,000 T26 tanks. The War Department felt that this heavy concentration on T26 tanks would satisfy the demand for better armored tanks instead of the expedient M4A3E2 assault tank. Trials of the T26E1 did not conclude until the end of 1944. The testing program uncovered a substantial number of significant modifications that would be needed before series production started. As a result, the improved production version with the 90mm gun was designated as the T26E3 heavy tank. Series production of the T26E3 began in November 1944 at the Grand Blanc tank arsenal, followed in March 1945 at the Detroit tank arsenal. The T26E3 designation was changed to M26 after the tank was standardized in March 1945.

The Ardennes fighting broke the AGF's resistance to the accelerating deployment of the T26E3 tank. Large-scale encounters with Panther and Tiger tanks led to demands for a better tank from combat units in the field. By the end of 1944, 40 T26E3 tanks had been completed. In response to the criticism of US tanks coming from Europe, the head of Ordnance research, Maj. Gen. G. M. Barnes, suggested sending half of the new tanks to Europe for impromptu combat trials, while the other 20 went to Fort Knox for the usual tests. AGF objected to the plan but finally relented when Barnes threatened to bring the issue before Gen. George C. Marshall, the Army Chief of Staff.

The first batch of 20 T26E3 were shipped to Antwerp and arrived in January 1945. This was part of a larger effort called the Zebra Mission, which included dispatch of other new weapons to deal with the German tank threat, such as new anti-tank guns. They were split into two groups, with ten each going to the 3rd and 9th Armored Divisions. Training for the 3rd Armored Division crews concluded on February 20, followed by 9th Armored Division crews at the end of the month. Training was somewhat simplified due to the fact that the T26E3 tank used the same engine as the M4A3 Sherman tank and so was already familiar to maintenance crews. The new transmission was the most complicated new maintenance challenge.

About a hundred of the M4A3E2 assault tanks were up-gunned with 76mm guns in February–March 1945. This is an example with the 37th Tank Battalion, 4th Armored Division, in Alzey, Germany, on March 20, 1945.

A total of 80 M4 and M4A3 were up-armed for the US Army by British arsenals with the 17-pdr tank gun in March and April 1945. These did not arrive in time to be deployed before the end of the war. Several are seen here at the end of the war in Britain with an M22 Locust aero tank in the foreground.

The T26E3 tanks were scattered in various companies of the 3rd Armored Division and saw their combat debut on February 25, 1945 with Task Force Lovelady during the fighting for the Roer river. The first tank was lost on February 26 when it was ambushed at night by a Tiger I tank near Elsdorf. Two crewmen were killed, but the tank was repaired and put back into action a few days later. The next day, a T26E3 of Company E, 33rd Armored Regiment, knocked out a Tiger I and two PzKpfw IV tanks near Elsdorf. The Tiger was knocked out at a range of about 900 yards with a round of the new T30E16 HVAP, followed by a round of normal T33 armor piercing, which entered the turret and set off an internal explosion. The two PzKpfw IVs were knocked out at the impressive range of 1,200 yards, beyond the normal engagement ranges for US tanks in World War II.

The T26E3 tanks with the 9th Armored Division were committed to action during the Roer fighting in late February 1945. One tank was disabled on the night of March 1, 1945, when hit twice by a 150mm field gun. This left the T26E3 tank platoon of the 14th Tank Battalion down to four tanks when it took part in one of the most famous actions of World War II. On March 7, 1945, infantry half-tracks of Combat Command B, 9th Armored Division, crested a hill overlooking the town of Remagen on the Rhine river. Amazingly, the massive Ludendorf railroad bridge was still standing even though nearly every other bridge over the Rhine had been destroyed by the Germans to prevent the Allies crossing the river. The local German commander had hesitated to drop the bridge, trying to extract a large number of his troops still on the western bank of the Rhine. Armored infantry supported by Lt. John Grimball's T26E3 platoon fought their way through the town and reached the approaches to the bridge around 1400 hours. The Germans detonated a large explosive charge, but the charge was not sufficient to drop any of the spans. The T26E3 tanks provided covering fire as the infantry moved across the bridge, with Grimball's tank knocking out a machine gun nest in one of the towers on the opposite bank.

3011

PREVIOUS PAGES On March 6, the tanks of Task Force Doan, 3rd Armored Division, entered Cologne. The Panther tank of Oberleutnant Wilhelm Bartelborth, the commander of 2.Zug, Pz.Abt.2106 of Panzerbrigade 106 "Feldherrnhalle," was lurking behind the city's famous cathedral. The Panther fired down Komödienstrasse, knocking out an advancing M4A3 tank. In the meantime, a T26E3 Pershing commanded by Sgt. Robert Early of E/32nd Armored was moving down An den Dominikanern Strasse toward the cathedral. Bartelborth's Panther tank had advanced past the front of the cathedral to control the several streets leading into the plaza. The two tanks confronted each other at point-blank range. Early's Pershing managed to fire three rounds before the Panther could respond, and the Panther erupted in flames from a catastrophic ammunition fire. (Artwork by Felipe Rodríguez © Osprey Publishing)

The only Zebra Mission T26E3 tank totally destroyed during the war was lost during the fighting near Cologne in early March when hit at point-blank range by an 88mm gun from a Nashorn self-propelled gun, which set off the turret ammunition. Fighting later on March 6, 1945 led to one of the most famous tank-vs.-tank engagements of the war. A Panther tank from Panzerbrigade.106 stationed in the courtyard in front of the cathedral in Cologne ambushed a M4 medium tank as it approached. The T26E3 tank of Sgt. Bob Early from Company E, 32nd Armored Regiment, 3rd Armored Division, was sent to deal with it and charged the Panther from the side. The Panther was still slowly turning its turret toward its opponents when the first of three rounds slammed into the tank, causing an internal fire that destroyed it. The duel was captured on film by a Signal Corps cameraman, and the footage frequently appears in documentaries about the war. The same day, other T26E3 tanks from the 3rd Armored Division knocked out a Tiger I and a PzKpfw IV near the city.

In mid-March, an additional T26 arrived in Germany, fresh from gunnery trials in the United States. This was the sole example of the so-called "Super Pershing" to see combat. The Super Pershing was the original T26E1 pilot tank that had been rearmed with a new long-barreled T15E1 90mm gun that was designed to offer performance comparable to the German 88mm KwK 43 on the King Tiger. The T15E1 gun could penetrate 220mm of armor at 1,000 yards at 30 degrees using the new T30E16 tungsten carbide HVAP round. On arrival at the 3rd Armored Division, the ordnance battalion decided to enhance the Super Pershing by adding additional armor plate to bring it closer to the armor on the King Tiger. The 5 tons of appliqué armor were designed and fabricated, using layers of 40mm boiler plate on the hull, and a plate of 80mm armor taken from a German Panther on the gun mantlet. This tank got to fire its gun in anger on only two occasions. On April 4, 1945, it engaged and destroyed a German armored vehicle, probably a Jagdpanther, at a range of 1,500 yards during the fighting along the Weser river. On April 21,

RIGHT One of the T26E1 pilots was fitted with the longer T15E1 90mm gun. It was shipped to the 3rd Armored Division, where it was fitted with additional armor, resulting in the Super Pershing. It served with Co. I, 33rd Armored Regiment, 3rd Armored Division, in the final month of the war, being credited with the destruction of at least two German tanks or tank destroyers.

1945, the Super Pershing was confronted by a "Tiger" when rounding a corner in Dessau, but the German tank missed with its first shot that flew high. A return volley by the Super Pershing ricocheted off the front armor, but when the "Tiger" attempted to climb over some rubble, the Super Pershing hit it through the belly, starting an ammunition fire. The identification of the Super Pershing's opponent has been questioned and remains a mystery unless further evidence emerges.

Armor penetration of US tank guns

Gun	Round	Type	Penetration in mm*
75mm M3	M61	APC	66
75mm M3	M72	AP	76
76mm M1	M62	APC	93
76mm M1	M79	AP	109
76mm M1	M93	HVAP	157
90mm M3	M82	APC	120
90mm M3	T33	AP	119
90mm M3	T30E16	HVAP	221
90mm T15E2	T43	AP	132
90mm T15E2	T44	HVAP	244
*@ 500 yards' range, homogenous armor plate at 30 degrees			

A second batch of T26E3 tanks arrived in Antwerp late in March. They were delivered to the Ninth US Army and were divided between the 2nd Armored Division (22 tanks) and the 5th Armored Division (18 tanks). A subsequent batch of 30 tanks was allotted to Patton's Third Army in April, all going to the 11th Armored Division. This was the last unit equipped with the T26E3 to use it in combat. In the final weeks of the war, the T26E3 tanks saw less combat due to the collapse of the German armed forces.

The T26E3 tank was received with enthusiasm by US tankers, as it offered substantially better armor and firepower than the M4 medium tank. By the end of the war, 310 T26E3 had been delivered to Europe, of which 200 had been issued to tank units. However, it was only the tanks supplied in February 1945 that saw extensive combat. The Pershing experience can best be summed up "too little, too late." A post-war report by the First US Army assessed the combat trials of the Zebra Mission. "Unfortunately for this test, the German armor had been so crippled as to present a very poor opponent and the cessation of hostilities so soon after forming these companies precluded the gaining of any real experience."

ABOVE The crew layout in the M26 Pershing. (Author)

BELOW M26 in action in Germany, March 1945. (Artwork by Jim Laurier © Osprey Publishing)

THE PANTHER PUP

The other new tank appearing in the ETO in early 1945 was the M24 Chaffee light tank. Replacement of the M5A1 light tank was long overdue but had been delayed by the cancellation of the M7 light/medium tank, one of the worst but least appreciated scandals of the Ordnance Department in the war. A 2nd Armored Division report in 1945 concluded: "The M5 light tank is obsolete in every respect as a fighting tank… The light tank is being used for working with the infantry. We subject it to direct fire just as little as we can, for it is realized that the armor will not turn the German fire or the 37mm gun damage the German tanks or SP guns."

The Armored Force's rejection of the M7 design in March 1943 prompted Ordnance to recommend the development of a new light tank, based around the powertrain of the M5A1 light tank but armed with a 75mm gun. After the M7 tank fiasco, the armor was kept light, indeed thinner than the M5A1 in some aspects, to keep the design weight under 20 tons. This was supported by the Armored Force, which had come to accept that light tanks would have a role limited to reconnaissance.

The new design was designated as the T24 light tank, and the program was approved on April 29, 1943. Development of the tank was entrusted to the Chrysler Motor Car Division of General Motors Corporation. The design effort was headed by Chrysler's chief engineer, Ed Cole, who became president of General Motors after the war. The Armored Force insisted on a change from the two-man turret on the M5A1 to a three-man turret as found in medium tanks. The vertical volute suspension used on the M5A1 was Harry Knox's old 1930s design that had outlived its potential, and the Armored Force wanted a design with wider tracks for better mobility cross-country. As a result, a new torsion bar suspension was selected. Although the design was supposed to use the powertrain from the M5A1 light tank, in fact many changes were introduced, including the substitution of a manual transfer unit for the troublesome automatic transfer of the M5A1. While Chrysler was undertaking the design of the tank, Rock Island Arsenal was developing the lightweight, short-recoil 75mm gun. The weapon selected for the T24 was a derivative of the T13E1 lightweight aircraft gun, used in the B-25 bomber. This had the same ballistics and ammunition features of the M3 75mm gun used in the M4 Sherman tank, but used a more compact T19 concentric recoil mechanism that permitted a shorter recoil.

Progress on the T24 design was so favorable that in September 1943 the Ordnance Committee recommended the production of 1,000 tanks even before the pilots were completed. The only dissenting voice was the Chief of Engineers, who complained that the weight and width of the design exceeded

Army regulations, but this complaint was ignored. The first pilot was delivered to Aberdeen Proving Ground on October 15, 1943. Trials of the new gun mount found some problems with the new recoil system, and there were many small problems with the automotive components. This was normal for a new design, and overall, the initial trials had been very satisfactory and a tribute to the experienced Chrysler design team. Tests on the second pilot began in December 1943, followed by trials by the Armored Board at Fort Knox.

Production of the T24 began at Cadillac in late April 1944 but did not begin to pick up steam until M5A1 production ended there in May. Since the procurement objective had increased from 1,000 to 1,800 tanks in December 1943, a second M5A1 manufacturer, Massey-Harris, also switched from M5A1 production in July 1944. Dissatisfaction with the M5A1 light tank in Europe was so widespread that requirements continued to increase, eventually bringing the total to more than four times the initial plans. The T24 was standardized in July 1944 as the M24 Light Tank. It was later named the Chaffee, after the first head of the Armored Force, Gen. Adna Chaffee, though the US Army seldom used this name in practice.

By the autumn of 1944, there was an urgent demand for the M24 light tank from the ETO due to the obsolescence of the M5A1 light tank. In September 1944, the Armored Section of Gen. Bradley's 12th Army Group headquarters requested that all M5A1 light tanks be replaced as soon as possible by the new M24 light tank. At the time, about a quarter of all US tanks in the ETO were the M5A1. The War Department in Washington did

M24 light tank, US Army, 1945. (Artwork by Jim Laurier © Osprey Publishing)

not concur, citing shipping and logistics problems. Following the German panzer offensives in the Ardennes and Alsace, the M5A1 had completely fallen out of favor with the tank units. Many officers wanted the light tank company abolished. An Armored Force observer from Washington who visited the 25th Tank Battalion, 12th Armored Division, in February 1945 was told that the M5A1 company was so useless that it was used as "anti-tank gun bait" for the M4 medium tank battalions. Other tank battalions used the light tank company for supply and evacuation for forward medium tank companies, refusing to expose it to close combat.

In the event, the distribution of the M24 to combat units proved to be far more erratic than planned. The original plans were to ship the first 160 tanks to the ETO by August 1944, but technical problems delayed this by four months. On November 12, 1944, a plan was established under which the two tank battalions still equipped entirely with M5A1 light tanks, the 744th and 759th Tank Battalions (Light) would be given first priority, followed by the units of the two heavy armored divisions on the old 1942 table of organization and equipment, the 2nd and 3rd Armored Divisions. As is so often the case in war, these plans were altered by circumstance.

The first batch of M24 light tanks arrived in France in early December 1944 and were loaded on tank transporters at Cherbourg on December 8 for transfer to the Ninth US Army, the northernmost of the three armies in Bradley's 12th Army Group. The 744th Tank Battalion (Light) was given priority to convert to the new M24 since the other light tank battalion, the 759th, was being used as part of the 4th Cavalry Group for reconnaissance and so less desperate for the conversion. The transport column was on the way to the front when the Battle of the Bulge broke out in the Ardennes. Two of the 20 M24s were diverted, under somewhat mysterious circumstances, to the 740th Tank Battalion of the First US Army. This battalion had arrived in Europe days before without any tanks and had been given a blank check to round up tanks from depots on an urgent basis to help stem the German attack. The two M24 tanks were unofficially "requisitioned" when they strayed into First US Army territory, much to the chagrin of the Ordnance officers managing the M24 program in the ETO. The two M24 light tanks were deployed in Company D, and they first saw combat near Remouchamps on December 20, 1944, even though their crews had received no special training. This was not a major problem, as the M24's engine was the same as in the M5A1 light tank, and the gun was operated in essentially the same fashion as that in the M4 medium tank. The two M24 tanks took part in the fighting for Stoumont and La Gleize during the skirmishes that finally stopped the advance of the spearhead of 6.SS-Panzer Army, Kampfgruppe Peiper. The M24 tanks remained in action with the battalion for most of January 1945.

A whitewashed M24 light tank with the 14th Cavalry Group in Petit-Their, Belgium, at the conclusion of the Ardennes campaign.

The arrival of the M24 in the ETO was accompanied by a program to familiarize US Army units with the new type. There was some concern that its novel shape and new suspension would lead to confusion with the German Panther tank. Indeed, the M24 soon received its popular nickname "Panther Pup" because of this effort.

The 744th Tank Battalion received the 18 remaining M24 light tanks on December 24, 1944, and was completely re-equipped with the new tanks by February 15, 1945. The unit saw its first extensive action with the new type during Operation *Grenade*, the final push over the Roer river at the end of February 1945. In general, the unit was favorably impressed with the new type. In a report after the fighting, the unit noted:

> By reason of its speed, suspension system, tracks, and power, the Light Tank M24 has been found to be very maneuverable… In snow and wet ground, the M24 has been able to walk off and leave the M5A1 and the Medium Tank M4… It had demonstrated the quality of ruggedness time and time again … and has been able to remain in the fight with minor maintenance difficulties and even when hit by anti-tank weapons… The low silhouette has been an excellent advantage in that combined with the tank's speed and maneuverability, the enemy has been provided a poor target… Ample room in the fighting compartment has resulted in increased crew efficiency and less fatigue during long periods of combat… Telescopic sights are excellent. Gunners have been able to pick up targets that tank commanders could not see… Engines are readily accessible for maintenance and can be changed in half the time of the Light Tank M5A1.

The report also highlighted the problems with the M24, many of which were inherent in any light tank design:

> Armor of the M24 is generally felt by all personnel to be incapable of preventing a penetration by any German anti-tank weapon except perhaps at the most extreme ranges. Belly armor is insufficient to protect crews from injury due to exploding mines. Knowledge of the thinness of armor did not aid morale, but most personnel have felt that the present medium tank offered no appreciable difference in protection… The 75mm gun has proven ineffective against enemy armor, even at close range… Ammunition load of all calibers is considered insufficient for normal missions. In one instance a platoon fighting in the city of Lutgen-Dortmund used two full combat loads of 75mm ammunition and three loads of .30 and .50 caliber ammunition in one day. It has been normal to expend all ammunition in almost every action.

With the 744th Tank Battalion re-equipped with the M24 light tank, the plan was to re-equip the 2nd and 3rd Armored Divisions. There was some reconsideration of this plan at the time, as in the wake of the Ardennes fighting, many officers felt that it was more important to re-equip the light tank troops in the cavalry reconnaissance squadrons which badly needed the added firepower. As a result, the first batch of 200 M24 tanks did go to the First and Ninth US Armies as planned but were divided among the cavalry reconnaissance groups. The cavalry reconnaissance units were as impressed with the M24 as were the tank battalions. The 106th Cavalry Group noted that in mid-February 1945, "The light tank companies of both squadrons turned in their 37mm gun-toting M5A1's and drew the new M24's. Armed with a 75mm cannon and nearly twice the size of their precursors, these tanks seemed beautiful to us. Our tankers itched to try them out. On 15 March, they got their chance. We were back in the line."

In a combat report from the 4th Cavalry Group, the officers noted that "The superiority of the M24 over the M5 … has greatly increased the striking power of cavalry units. We were able to employ them as assault guns and use our [M8 HMC] assault guns as supporting artillery." A March 1945 report from the 28th Cavalry Reconnaissance Squadron, 6th Cavalry Group, echoed these sentiments: "This tank is one of the best combat vehicles ever furnished our army: it is the answer to a lot of our problems. We have fought with them for over a month now and there are few improvements that can be made." The 6th Cavalry Reconnaissance Squadron chimed in, "This tank is a wonderful improvement over the M5 light tank. It will go places that the M5 light tank and the M4 medium tank cannot negotiate." The 6th Cavalry Group commander commented, "I would rather have the M24 light tank than the M4 medium. The former can do everything that the M4 can do and the heavier armor of the latter is of no value. We have M4s and M5s operating in conjunction with the M24s, and they could not go where the M24 tanks went. Mobility of the M24 tank is outstanding."

While the M24 was not designed to fight enemy tanks, such incidents did occur on occasion. In early March 1945, a pair of M24s of F Troop, 4th Cavalry Recon Squadron, stumbled into a pair of German tanks which they identified as Tigers on the outskirts of Dormagen, Germany. More likely they were Panthers, but in either case, it was a considerable mismatch. But the German crews were as surprised as their American opponents, and the M24 had the advantage of faster turret traverse. Before the panzers could swing their clumsy turrets at their smaller foe, the M24s slammed several high-explosive rounds against the thinner side and rear turret armor. These were enough to set off an internal fire which destroyed both panzers. While such incidents were flukes, they reaffirm that the outcome of tank-vs.-tank battles cannot be predicted with any certainty by paper calculations of tank characteristics. Circumstance, luck, and crew performance sometimes overcome disparities in equipment.

By the end of the fighting in the ETO in May 1945, the M24 constituted 34 percent of the light tanks deployed with the US Army. Shipments to US units in Italy had a much lower priority, and the only unit to receive any significant number of these tanks was the 1st Armored Division, especially its 81st Cavalry Reconnaissance Squadron, beginning in January 1945. These were first deployed in significant numbers in March 1945 and saw action in the final months of the campaign. The M24 was not deployed in time to see combat in the Pacific. The US Marine Corps obtained ten in 1945 and were used to test fording trunk designs. The Marine Corps rejected the type for standard use, mainly due to their thin armor.

US ARMY TANK ORGANIZATION IN THE ETO

Of the 16 armored divisions raised by the US Army in World War II, all but one were deployed to the ETO; 1st Armored Division remained in Italy until the end of the war. With two exceptions, the armored divisions in the ETO were in the "light" 1943 TO&E (table of organization and equipment). These divisions contained a balanced mix of three tank battalions, three armored infantry battalions, and three armored field artillery battalions.

The other two divisions, the 2nd and 3rd Armored Divisions, retained the earlier "heavy" 1942 TO&E. This configuration had two armored regiments with three tank battalions each but only a single armored infantry regiment with three battalions. This resulted in a tank-heavy configuration, with six tank battalions and three armored infantry battalions. The reasons for this exception were bureaucratic rather than doctrinal. During the conversion of the divisions from the 1942 to 1943 pattern, Lt. Jacob Devers was head of the US Army in the ETO. Devers had previously led the Armored Force, and he did not agree with the Army Ground Forces rationale for the new 1943 organization. He argued that it was too disruptive to convert the two divisions already in Britain, the 2nd and 3rd Armored Divisions, into the 1943 pattern. As a result, the 2nd and 3rd Armored Divisions retained a modified version of the 1942 pattern.

In practice, the unbalanced configuration of the heavy armored divisions proved to be a problem since there was too few infantry for many operations. The solution was to attach an infantry regiment from a neighboring infantry division for significant operations. This essentially created a mini armored corps.

These two divisions played a vital role in two of the most consequential operations of the war during the Ardennes offensive and the encirclement of the Ruhr. In the Ardennes, the 2nd Armored Division encircled the lead elements of 5.Panzer-Armee in the Celles pocket outside Bastogne, ending the German advance. The 3rd Armored Division counterattacked the II.SS-Panzer-Korps on the approaches to the Tailles plateau, preventing a breakthrough in that sector. During the Ruhr encirclement, these two divisions were the pincers of Bradley's 12th Army Group envelopment of Heeresgruppe B. The 2nd Armored Division was the spearhead of the Ninth US Army on the northern side of the Ruhr pocket, and the 3rd Armored Division was the spearhead of the First US Army on the southern side.

The core tenet of US Army armored doctrine was the combined-arms team, a practice borrowed from study of the German blitzkrieg-era panzer division. Each 1943-pattern armored division had three combat command headquarters (CCA, CCB, CCR/Reserve). The combat command was a temporary brigade, tailored to the mission. Typically, each combat command would have a tank battalion, armored infantry battalion, and armored field artillery battalion, plus companies from other elements such as armored engineer, tank destroyers, and anti-aircraft artillery. The combat commands could have other compositions for specific missions – for example, two armored infantry battalions for some missions such as fighting in urban areas or forests. The combined-arms composition of the combat commands was carried a step further at company level with the temporary organization of task forces within the combat command. These consisted of several mixed companies from the combat command's attached battalions.

Of the 88 US Army tank battalions deployed to the ETO, 51 were organic to the armored divisions, while 37 were separate tank battalions. The separate tank battalions were primarily used for support of the infantry divisions. The original pattern in the summer of 1944 was to deploy an armored group headquarters with each corps. These had two or three separate tank battalions attached. The armored group headquarters could then deploy its tank battalions en masse as a concentrated armored force or dole out the tank battalions to the infantry battalions for support. This doctrine was largely ignored in the ETO, as the corps commanders had recognized since the 1943 Tunisian campaign that infantry divisions regularly needed tank support in the conduct of offensive operations. There were never enough separate tank battalions to permanently incorporate a tank battalion in each infantry division. Instead, tank battalions were assigned to infantry divisions on a temporary basis depending on their mission. Since their tactical role had almost entirely evaporated, in late October 1944 the armored group staffs were gradually reassigned as CCR headquarters in the armored divisions.

Two separate tank battalions, the 744th and 759th, were configured in the unusual light tank configuration, equipped only with M5A1 light tanks. Three tank battalions were nominally under the special mine exploder configuration, the 738th, 739th and 740th Tank Battalions (SMX). The plan was to deploy one SMX battalion per field army as an equivalent of the "Armoured Funnies" of the British 79th Armoured Division. In the event, the 738th Tank Battalion (SMX) became part of the First US Army, and the 739th Tank Battalion (SMX) was attached to the Ninth US Army. The 740th Tank

By D-Day, the M5A1 was obsolete, though still useful for reconnaissance. It remained in service due to the late arrival of its replacement, the M24, in December 1944. This is an M5A1 of the 17th Cavalry Reconnaissance Squadron (Mecz) of the Ninth US Army in the German frontier on January 11, 1945. It is still fitted with a T2 Richardson bocage cutter from the Normandy campaign.

Battalion was still awaiting equipment at the time of the Ardennes campaign and was hastily rushed to Belgium as part of the reinforcement effort. It never received specialized equipment, and so reverted back to the standard 1943 tank battalion TO&E.

A total of 55 tank destroyer battalions were deployed to the ETO. Of these, 15 were attached to the armored divisions. The remainder were deployed at corps level under a tank destroyer group headquarters. As in the case of the separate tank battalions, the tank destroyer battalions were generally attached to infantry divisions for fire support. There were two different configurations of these battalions – self-propelled and towed. The Army Ground Forces had begun converting 15 self-propelled battalions to towed battalions in 1943 based on a mistaken interpretation of the combat lessons of the Tunisian campaign. They were equipped with the M5 3-inch gun, a towed version of the 3-inch gun used on the M10 3-inch tank destroyer. During the fighting in France in 1944, the towed battalions had demonstrated inferior combat effectiveness compared with the self-propelled battalions. The continued poor performance of the towed battalions in the Ardennes campaign was the last straw, and the towed battalions were largely converted to self-propelled during 1945.

Of the various armored formations of the US Army, the tank destroyer battalions were the most problematic. They had been designed to counter massed panzer attacks of the 1940–41 blitzkrieg era and so were primarily defensive in orientation. This doctrinal orientation was ill-suited to the offensive posture of the US Army in the ETO. Facing so few panzers in 1945, tank destroyers ended up being used as surrogate tanks for direct fire support of the infantry.

The US Army's cavalry regiments were reorganized in late 1943 and 1944 as CRSM (Cavalry Reconnaissance Squadrons – Mechanized). The CRSM were mixed armored car/tank units with 40 M8 light armored cars, 17 M5A1 light tanks, six M8 75mm howitzer motor carriages, and 30 half-tracks. The CRSM in the ETO were deployed as organic elements of the armored divisions or subordinated to cavalry group headquarters. They conducted the traditional cavalry roles of scouting and flank security. A total of 13 cavalry groups served in the ETO in 1944–45.

Besides the 15 US armored divisions, the French Army deployed three armored divisions that had been raised and trained by the US Army. For political reasons, the 2e Division Blindée usually served under US command, while the 1er and 5e Divisions Blindées served in the 1er Armée Française (First French Army), part of Gen. Jacob Devers' 6th Army Group. The French divisions were all organized under the standard US Army 1943 TO&E, although the battalions retained traditional French regimental designations.

US TANKS IN THE BATTLE FOR GERMANY 1945

By the time the Allies initiated new offensives in February 1945, the tank balance in the West was skewed heavily against the Wehrmacht. Only about 900 panzers and AFVs faced 4,400 British/Canadian tanks and AFVs plus 12,200 US tanks and AFVs, an imbalance of 1 to 18. The imbalance continued to worsen through the spring of 1945, reaching its nadir in April–May 1945 at less than 1 to 60.

Compared with the Normandy campaign in 1944 or the Ardennes campaign in 1944–45, the diminished strength of the Wehrmacht made panzers a much less potent threat in 1945 than in previous campaigns. The proportion of Allied tank losses caused by German tanks and AFVs was not recorded in any detail, and other types of weapons were presumably responsible for the majority of tank casualties.

M24 light tank, Co. D, 36th Tank Battalion, 8th Armored Division, Germany, 1945. (Artwork by Jim Laurier © Osprey Publishing)

T26E3 Pershing, 18th Tank Battalion, 8th Armored Division, Plzeň, Czechoslovakia, May 1945. (Artwork by Felipe Rodríguez © Osprey Publishing)

M24 light tank, F Troop, 2nd Cavalry Reconnaissance Squadron (Mecz), Bavaria, Germany, April 1945. (Artwork by Felipe Rodríguez © Osprey Publishing)

From the Allied perspective, towed and stationary German anti-tank guns posed a far greater threat than German tanks and AFVs. In February 1945, there were about 775 towed 75mm PaK 40 anti-tank guns and 130 towed 88mm PaK anti-tank guns assigned to German infantry divisions and supporting units of OB West. A total of 1,400 fixed 50mm, 75mm, and 88mm anti-tank guns had been assigned to the West-Stellung defense lines along the Rhine of which about 550 were emplaced by February 1945. As a result, there were about 1,455 anti-tank guns along the Westfront in February 1945 compared with fewer than 900 operational German tanks and AFVs. In addition, many German cities in the Ruhr and Saar industrial zones were ringed with 88mm, 105mm, and 128mm Flak guns that were used as improvised anti-tank guns in the final battles. While the number of towed and static anti-tank guns continued to increase in March–April 1945, there was a steady decline in operational German panzer and AFV strength.

A combined-arms team based around Lt. Col. Derrill Daniel's 2/26th Infantry, 1st Infantry Division, advances through the streets of Aachen on October 15, 1944 supported by an M10 3-inch GMC of the 684th Tank Destroyer Battalion (to the left) and M4 Sherman tanks of the 745th Tank Battalion (to the right). Artwork by Steve Noon © Osprey Publishing

The second batch of T26E3 tanks was issued to the 9th Armored Division. Here, one of their Pershing tanks passes through Euskirchen, Germany, on March 5, 1945.

As mentioned earlier, German infantry anti-tank rocket weapons became a growing threat in 1945. German infantry and Volksgrenadier regiments had a nominal allotment of 36 crew-served 8.8cm Panzerschreck launchers, compared with a dozen towed 75mm PaK 40 anti-tank guns. The smaller Panzerfaust rocket-propelled anti-tank grenade was far more numerous, typically with more than 500 issued to each regiment. By 1945, OB West's 56 infantry and Volksgrenadier divisions had only about a third of the authorized towed 75mm PaK 40 anti-tank guns, and anti-tank rocket launchers often served as a substitute.

The Rhine river was Germany's last major strategic barrier to the Allied advance in the West. On February 8, Montgomery's 21st Army Group initiated Operation *Veritable*. This British/Canadian offensive pushed across the Dutch frontier into the Reichswald, a heavily forested area southwest of Kleve. Panzer formations in this sector were very weak; the 116.Panzer-Division had only six operational PzKpfw IV and ten Panthers. *Veritable* was followed on February 20 with Operation *Blockbuster*, which pushed to the southeast, reaching the Rhine near Xanten. On March 9, Berlin gave 1.Fallschirm-Armee permission to withdraw over the Rhine.

M4A3E2 assault tank, 69th Tank Battalion, 6th Armored Division, Germany, March 1945. (Artwork by Felipe Rodríguez © Osprey Publishing)

Eisenhower had planned to deploy the Ninth US Army to assist Operation *Veritable* on February 10. However, the Germans opened up the Roer river dams, flooding the Roer plains. As a result, Operation *Grenade* was delayed until February 23 to allow the plains to dry out enough for mechanized operations. Once started, these attacks progressed well enough that on March 1, Lt. Gen. William Simpson, commander of the Ninth US Army, suggested a hasty Rhine river crossing near Düsseldorf. Montgomery refused, favoring an intricately planned river crossing operation three weeks later, codenamed *Varsity/Plunder*.

Early March saw the two US army groups closing on the Rhine. The First US Army began Operation *Lumberjack*, clearing the west bank of the Rhine from Cologne southward, while the 6th Army Group launched Operation *Undertone* from the Wissembourg Gap up along the Rhine. The March campaign was based on the premise that the American Rhine crossings would wait until after Montgomery's forces jumped the Rhine with Operation *Varsity/Plunder*. The main American objective was to trap and destroy as many German units as possible along the western bank of the Rhine, before they could escape over the river. Hitler's adamant refusal to permit withdrawals only hastened the demise of the Wehrmacht in the West. By this stage of the war, nearly all of the major Rhine bridges had been knocked down by Allied air attack or demolished by German units after they withdrew over the Rhine.

German panzer strength continued to deteriorate through early 1945 due to the lack of replacement vehicles. By mid-March, OB West had only 316 tanks, of which only 107 (34 percent) were operational and the rest battle-damaged or in repair. The British/Canadian 21st Army Group was facing only two major panzer formations, 15.Panzergrenadier-Division and 116.Panzer-Division, with only 26 operational tanks combined. The bulk of the German panzer force was in Heeresgruppe B, facing Bradley's 12th Army Group, but with only 79 operational tanks. Heeresgruppe G, facing the US/French 6th

Even with the arrival of the new M24 Chaffee light tank, most US separate tank battalions still had the old M5A1 light tank. This is an M5A1 of Co. D, 761st Tank Battalion, one of two segregated African American tank battalions that fought in the battle of Germany. It is seen here in front of the statue of Prince Albert in the market square of Coburg on April 11, 1945.

Army Group in the Saar region had only the 17.SS-Panzergrenadier-Division, equipped mainly with assault guns and only two tanks.

On March 7, the US 9th Armored Division arrived near Remagen to discover the Ludendorff railroad bridge still standing. The bridge was quickly seized, giving the First US Army a toehold on the east bank of the Rhine. Eisenhower ordered the bridgehead to be reinforced but still waited for *Varsity*/*Plunder* as the main Rhine crossing effort. On March 12, Patton's Third US Army launched its local offensive in the Saar-Palatinate. Opposing German forces had already been crushed to the north and south by *Lumberjack* and *Undertone*, and the German defense quickly disintegrated. This led to the so-called "Rhine Rat Race" as Patton's armored divisions charged ahead against retreating German units. On reaching the Rhine, Patton staged a hasty crossing on March 22 near Oppenheim, followed by additional Rhine crossings over the following week. By month's end, Patton had reached Frankfurt.

Montgomery's 21st Army Group launched Operation *Varsity*/*Plunder* on March 23–24 north of Wesel, against very weak opposition Korps. This enormous airborne-amphibious-ground operation included one of the few uses of airborne tanks, when a handful of M22 Locust light tanks were landed by Hamilcar gliders as part of Operation *Varsity*. The Ninth US Army launched a subsidiary mission codenamed Operation *Flashpoint* to push over the Rhine south of the British attack.

Although Eisenhower had originally supported the scheme to concentrate on the British Operation *Varsity*/*Plunder* as the focus for the Rhine campaign, the success of the various US field armies, and especially the Remagen bridgehead, led him to reconsider. He reverted to his preferred strategic approach of a broad, multi-army advance.

On March 25, Bradley's 12th Army Group launched Operation *Voyage*. The northern prong of the attack was a drive by Simpson's Ninth US Army along the northern side of the Ruhr industrial belt while the First US Army attacked out of the Remagen bridgehead, aiming for the southern side of the Ruhr. Patton's Third US Army began an even deeper envelopment from further south. The rapid progress of these spearheads in the final days of March led Bradley to propose enveloping the Ruhr between the Ninth and First US Armies.

Sherman Crocodile flame tank, 739th Tank Battalion (SMX), Germany, 1945. (Artwork by Richard Chasemore © Osprey Publishing)

The remaining strength of Heeresgruppe B was concentrated in the Ruhr sector, including most of the panzer force. By this stage, panzer strength in the West was meager – only 47 operational tanks on April 10, 1945. Indeed, there was greater panzer strength in peripheral theaters such as Italy and Norway.

By the spring of 1945, the German panzer force had been largely eliminated. An M4A1 of Co. F, 33rd Armored Regiment, Combat Command B, 3rd Armored Division, passes by a knocked-out PzKpfw IV Ausf. G, probably from the 11. Panzer-Division, in Bad Marienburg on March 28, 1945 during the breakout from the Remagen bridgehead.

In 1943, work began on the T28 super-heavy tank armed with the powerful new T5E1 105mm tank gun and protected by 12-inch (305mm) frontal armor. Since it was designed for attacking fixed fortifications such as the German Siegfried Line, its configuration was based on a fixed casemate rather than a turret. Due to its 95-ton weight, it used two parallel sets of tracks on both sides to provide adequate ground floatation. The first pilot was not completed until late 1945, so it never saw combat service during the war.

One of the few tank battles of the 1945 spring campaigns took place in the final days of March when Gen. Fritz Bayerlein's 53.Armee-Korps staged a counterattack against the US Army's VII Corps around the panzer training grounds at Paderborn, attempting to prevent the encirclement of the Ruhr. These attacks were crushed, and elements of the 2nd Armored Division (Ninth US Army) and 3rd Armored Division (First US Army) met on April 1, 1945 near Lippstadt, closing the trap around the Ruhr.

Bradley assumed that the Wehrmacht had evacuated the Ruhr and anticipated that only about 70,000 troops remained. In fact, Hitler had refused Field Marshal Walter Model's plea to withdraw Heeresgruppe B from the Ruhr. The Ruhr pocket held out until April 18 with the surrender of about 317,000 German troops; this was a larger bag of prisoners than Stalingrad or Tunisia. Model committed suicide rather than surrender.

The destruction of Heeresgruppe B ended any coordinated German defense in the West for the last three weeks of the war. The new OB West commander, Field Marshal Albert Kesselring, referred to the final battles as the "makeshift campaign." Berlin ordered numerous preposterous counterattacks based on fantasy paper formations. There were scattered encounters between Allied and German armored vehicles, but usually involving only a handful of German AFVs.

Although Montgomery proposed a lightning armored thrust to reach Berlin, Eisenhower refused on the grounds that the Roosevelt, Churchill, and Stalin had already agreed at the Yalta Conference to place Berlin in the Soviet occupation zone.

The final campaigns in late April involved four major operations. The First Canadian Army was assigned to liberate the Netherlands as quickly as possible due to widespread civilian suffering from severe winter food shortages. The British Second Army was directed northeast to seize the German North Sea ports. The final phase of the British advance, codenamed Operation *Enterprise*, had the strategic objective to race to the Baltic Sea, thereby preempting the Soviet occupation of Denmark.

In the center, the First and Ninth US Armies were instructed to advance to the Elbe river to meet the Red Army. This objective was reached first on April 25 by the 69th Infantry Division, followed by other US and Soviet units through early May. The fourth major operation to the south involved Patton's Third US Army and Devers' 6th Army Group. These formations cleared southern Germany with an aim to prevent the formation of an "Alpine Redoubt" by diehard Nazis. This threat proved to be ephemeral. In the event, the southern drive linked up 6th Army Group along the Italian border with Gen. Mark Clark's 15th Army Group coming north out of Italy though the Alpine passes. Patton's Third US Army advanced the deepest of all of Eisenhower's formations, reaching into Austria and Czechoslovakia. With the collapse of the Third Reich, these were the last major actions by the Allies in the West.

A number of heavy tanks were in development at the end of the war but were not completed in time to see combat. The T30 heavy tank was armed with the 155mm T7 gun, the largest caliber gun ever deployed on a US tank. Construction began in April 1945, but the pilots were not ready until 1947.

CHAPTER FOUR

US TANKS IN THE PACIFIC THEATER

"The enemy's power lies in their tanks. It has become obvious that our overall battle against the American forces is a battle against their M3 and M4 tanks." This statement was written by Gen. Mitsuru Ushijima, the commander of the Japanese 32nd Army on Okinawa when preparing his troops for the final battle in spring 1945. His statement may come as a surprise to many military historians who seldom associate the Pacific battles with tank warfare. Yet tanks played a vital role in many of the major campaigns of the Pacific War from 1941 to 1945, and indeed a decisive tactical role in some battles. The general lack of appreciation of the importance of tanks in the Pacific campaign is due to the misconception that tank warfare in World War II was primarily tank-vs.-tank warfare. This was not the case in Europe, and even less so in the Pacific. Most tank actions in the Pacific involved the fire support of infantry in overcoming fortified enemy positions. Although there were no epic tank-vs.-tank battles in the Pacific, nonetheless the United States committed a third of its separate Army tank battalions to this theater, as well as all six Marine tank battalions.

Aside from the initial battles of 1942, the technological balance in the Pacific favored the United States. The most common Japanese tank in the theater was the Type 95 Ha-Go, a 1935 design intended for the China theater. It was thinly armored and weakly armed with a 37mm gun. It was overmatched even by the US M3 light tank. When the US began introducing the M4 Sherman medium tank in 1943, the technological contest was over. The Japanese Type 97 Chi-Ha was armed with a short 57mm gun with poor

The sole combat use of the M2A4 in US hands was by the US Marines' 1st Tank Battalion on Guadalcanal in the summer of 1942.

anti-tank performance. The improved Type 97 kai Shinhoto Chi-Ha had the much superior 47mm gun, but it was completely outclassed by the M4 medium tank. The Japanese Type 97 medium tanks did not begin to appear in significant numbers until the Marianas campaign of 1944. More modern types such as the Type 1 tank were never deployed outside Japan since they were reserved for the final apocalyptic battle in the Home Islands, a battle that never took place.

EARLY BATTLES

In September 1941, the United States Army reinforced the US garrison in the Philippines with the Provisional Tank Group, including 108 new M3 light tanks. Several National Guard tank companies were combined to form the new 192nd and 194th Tank Battalions assigned to the group. The Japanese invasion force likewise included two tank regiments. The first

"Colorado" – an M4A2 of the 3rd Platoon, Co. C, IMAC Tank Battalion – is seen on Tarawa a few days after the end of the fighting with a couple of M3A1 light tanks of the 2nd Marine Tank Battalion evident behind.

ABOVE LEFT M3 light tank, Co. B, 192nd Tank Battalion, Philippines, December 1941. (Artwork by Jim Laurier © Osprey Publishing)

ABOVE RIGHT M2A4 light tank, Co. A, 1st Marine Tank Battalion, Guadalcanal, September 1942. (Artwork by Jim Laurier © Osprey Publishing)

tank-vs.-tank engagement took place on December 22, 1941 against Japanese Type 95 Ha-Go light tanks of the 4th Tank Regiment. The Provisional Tank Group often formed the rearguard of US and Philippine forces as they withdrew into the Bataan Peninsula where they were eventually overwhelmed. This was one of the few campaigns where the Japanese tank force enjoyed technical parity with the US Army.

It is hard to imagine terrain less suited to tank warfare than the muddy and tropical islands of the Southwest Pacific. Yet US tanks were used in most of the battles there, usually in small numbers. In August 1942, Company A, 1st Marine Tank Battalion, landed on Guadalcanal with its M2A4 and M3 light tanks, followed in November by Company B, 2nd Marine Tank Battalion. They were used to support Marine attacks against Japanese defenses. Guadalcanal was densely jungled, which hampered tank support. Most actions involved a few tanks supporting Marines by routing out Japanese bunkers and breaking up Japanese infantry counterattacks with machine-gun and canister fire. The Japanese infantry was very poorly equipped with anti-tank weapons and resorted to heroic but suicidal

The only combat use of the M3A5 medium tank by the US Army in the Pacific theater was by the 193rd Tank Battalion on Butaritari island in the Makin Atoll in the Gilberts on November 20, 1943 in support of the 165th Infantry Regiment.

An M3A1 light tank of Co. C, 191st Tank Battalion, pushing through brush near Red Beach on Butaritari during the Makin operation on November 10, 1943. This was one of the first uses of the Project Blue Freeze deep-wading trunks in the Pacific theater.

close-range attacks on the tanks using improvised means such as satchel charges. This pattern was repeated again on New Georgia in July 1943, Bougainville in November 1943, and many other small tank actions.

The flamethrower tank became a hallmark of US tank operations in the Pacific. The first combat use of American flamethrower tanks took place during the fighting on Bougainville in the northern Solomons on January 30, 1944. Subsequent use of these improvised flamethrowers by the 1st Marine Tank Battalion on New Britain in February 1944 and by the US Army on M5A1 light tanks during the February 1944 Kwajalein attack were unsuccessful due to waterlogged electrical circuits.

M3A1 light tank with M1A1 flamethrower, Co. A, 754th Tank Battalion, Bougainville, January 1944. (Artwork by Richard Chasemore © Osprey Publishing)

Probably no image better exemplifies the popular perception of the jungle fighting on the Pacific islands than this one taken on Bougainville on March 16, 1944. "Lucky Legs II" – an M4 medium tank of the 754th Tank Battalion – is supporting riflemen of Co. F, 129th Infantry, 34th Division.

AMPHIBIOUS TANKS

The US Navy had pioneered the use of amphibious tractors (amtracs) in 1941 to help move troops and supplies ashore. The first of these, the LVT-1 (Landing Vehicle Tracked) was used to transport supplies on Guadalcanal in 1942, during Operation *Torch* in North Africa, and in the Aleutians campaign. This type was followed by the more durable LVT-2 in 1942. The Marine Corps began to consider using the amtracs in the assault phase of amphibious landings, starting with the Tarawa landings, since the amtracs could surmount coral reefs that would have stopped conventional landing craft.

Some consideration was given to producing an armed version of the amtrac as early as 1941. On June 27, 1941, the Marine commandant made a formal request for an armed amphibian. Having won Navy approval, in August 1941 the project was handed off to FMC Corporation and Borg-Warner, two companies that were designing the first amtracs. Borg-Warner's Model A was fitted with the turret from an M3 light tank. FMC used its new LVT-2 as the basis for an armed version. The original plan was to use the machine-gun turret from a Marmon-Herrington light tank or the 37mm gun turret from the T9E1/M22 aero tank. These options were dropped in September 1942 when the Army suggested the use of the turret from the M3A3 and M5A1 tanks with the rear radio bustle eliminated to save weight. The FMC LVT(A)1

LEFT The first of the amphibious tanks was the LVT(A)1 that was based on the LVT-2 amphibious tractor with a new superstructure, including a 37mm gun turret and two ring-mounted .30-cal light machine guns.

BELOW LEFT A column of LVT(A)4 amphibious tanks of the Marine 1st Armored Amphibian Battalion on Guam during the Marianas campaign in July 1944.

was selected in the summer of 1942, but due to a lack of priority, production didn't begin until August 1943, with first deliveries in November 1943.

The Marine Corps deployed the new amtanks in armored amphibian battalions. The first was formed in August 1943, followed by two more in 1943–44. The Army had been following this program closely and joined in procurement of the LVT(A)1, with 328 going to the Army and 182 to the Marine Corps by the time that production ceased in February 1944. The Army raised its first amphibian tank battalion in October 1943.

The combat debut of the LVT(A)1 in the Marshalls in February 1944 made it clear that the 37mm gun on the LVT(A)1 was inadequate to deal with typical Japanese fortified bunkers. In the meantime, the main Army amtrac training unit, the 18th Armored Group in Monterey, California, suggested the substitution of the turret of the M8 75mm howitzer motor carriage. This took minimal development effort beyond extending the superstructure to accommodate its wider turret race. The only downside to this change was that the two .30-cal machine guns behind the turret had to be eliminated. Production of the LVT(A)4 began in March 1944, and they were available for the campaign in the Marianas. The LVT(A)4 was used by both the Army and Marines in the Pacific theater. No amtanks were ever deployed to the European theater.

THE CENTRAL PACIFIC: 1944

The jungle terrain of the Southwest Pacific conforms to popular stereotypes of warfare in the Pacific. The battles on the Central Pacific islands took place in very different terrain, which made it possible to use tanks on a larger scale and in a more effective manner.

The first of these battles, Tarawa, took place on the coral atolls in the Gilbert Islands on November 20, 1943. Tarawa saw the first use of amtracs in a contested landing. The tanks assigned to support the 2nd Marine Division landings were M4A2 medium tanks of Company C, I Marine Amphibious Corps (IMAC) Tank Battalion, followed by M3A1 light tanks of the 2nd Marine Tank Battalion in the days after the initial landings. The new

LVT(A)4 amphibious tank, US Army, 1945. (Artwork by Mike Badrocke © Osprey Publishing)

M4A2 medium tank, Co. C, I Marine Amphibious Corps Tank Battalion, Tarawa, November 1943. (Artwork by Richard Chasemore © Osprey Publishing)

deep-wading trunks developed under Project Blue Freeze had not yet arrived in the Pacific, and many Marine tanks drowned out before reaching the shore. The M4A2 medium tanks proved very effective in attacking Japanese bunkers, but the 37mm guns on the M3A1 light tanks were not powerful enough for this role. The Marine Corps tank battalions began shifting to the Sherman as their main type became more available. The Army attack on neighboring Makin Island was swift and less costly compared with Tarawa. The Army landed elements of the 193rd Tank Battalion, the only unit to use obsolete M3 medium tanks in combat in the Pacific.

The next objective for US amphibious forces was Kwajalein, the largest atoll in the world. The Marshalls campaign saw the combat debut of the LVT(A)1 with the Army's 708th Amphibian Tank Battalion and the Marines' 1st Armored Amphibian Battalion. These new amtanks spearheaded the amtracs during the amphibious landings on February 1, 1944. The US Army's 7th Division landed on the main islands in the Kwajalein Atoll, supported by

The crew of D-21 "Dusty," an M3A1 light tank fitted with a Satan flamethrower of Co. D, 2nd Marine Tank Battalion, on Saipan in June 1944, displaying captured Japanese weapons.

RIGHT M4A2 medium tank, Co. C, 4th Marine Tank Battalion. (Artwork by Richard Chasemore © Osprey Publishing)

BELOW RIGHT LVT(A)1 amphibious tank, US Army 708th Amphibious Tank Battalion, Saipan, July 1944. (Artwork by Terry Hadler © Osprey Publishing)

the 767th Tank Battalion. The 4th Marine Division landed on the neighboring Roi-Namur Islands, supported by ten M4A2 medium tanks and 13 M5A1 light tanks of the 4th Marine Tank Battalion. There were a handful of Japanese tanks on the islands, and the role of both the Army and Marine tanks was close-fire support of the infantry. The next objective was Eniwetok, another atoll. On February 18, 1944, the Marine 22nd Regiment landed at outlying Engebi, supported by the 2nd Separate Tank Company. The Army landing on Eniwetok was supported by light tanks of Company C, 766th Battalion.

The Marianas were the first large islands in Japan's inner defense belt to be attacked by the US. The initial waves of the landings were made by the amtanks, followed by three or four waves of amtracs. There were two amtank battalions used on Saipan, the Army's 708th Amphibious Tank Battalion and the Marine's 2nd Armored Amphibian Battalion. Army doctrine rejected the use of the amtanks beyond the beachhead except for indirect fire support. The Marine battalion was not yet experienced enough to appreciate the problems and took heavy amtank losses when advancing beyond the beachhead due to the thin armor of the amtanks.

The Japanese garrison on Saipan was reinforced by the 9th Tank Regiment, equipped with some of the new Type 97 kai Shinhoto Chi-Ha medium tanks. The Japanese infantry in the Marianas were better armed than those on the Marshalls, having finally begun to receive the new Type 1 47mm anti-tank gun, a towed relative of the weapon that armed the Shinhoto Chi-ha tank. Most of the Japanese tanks on Saipan were destroyed in a nighttime banzai charge on June 16–17, 1944.

Saipan was a complete change from previous Pacific campaigns since the open terrain permitted freer use of tanks. But tank losses were quite heavy due to Japanese artillery and hand-emplaced magnetic mines. The Marines soon learned that there had to be close cooperation between the tanks and infantry to defeat these tactics. By now, the Marines had found that telephones mounted on the rear of the tanks were essential to coordinate their actions with the accompanying infantry.

On July 24, nearby Tinian was assaulted by Marines supported by the 2nd and 4th Marine Tank Battalions. Tinian was taken by early July. The 3rd Marine Division assaulted Guam while the Tinian operation was taking place, supported by the 2nd and 4th Marine Separate Tank Companies, the 3rd Marine Tank Battalion, and the Army's 706th Tank Battalion. The Marianas campaign made it quite clear that tanks were invaluable in the Central Pacific fighting. Both the Marines and the US Army concluded that further work was needed to improve tank-infantry cooperation, and the Marines began a program to reinforce their tanks against the threat of close-in Japanese suicide anti-tank tactics, by layering wooden planks on the side of their tanks to prevent the attachment of magnetic mines.

One of the most controversial campaigns was the decision to assault Peleliu in the Palau Islands, another fortified crag grimly reminiscent of Tarawa. The 1st Marine Division landed on September 15, 1944. Every one of the first tanks which the 1st Marine Tank Battalion put ashore was hit by Japanese gunfire. The fighting involved the usual pattern of tank fire support for the Marine riflemen.

THE PHILIPPINES: 1944–45

The campaign in the Philippines involved the largest tank operations by either side in the Pacific War. It marked the first time that the Japanese Army committed one of its few armored divisions against US forces, the 2nd Tank Division on Luzon. The Japanese commander, Gen. Tomoyuki Yamashita, forbade the massed use of Japanese tanks. As was evident from the one-sided encounter on Saipan, Japanese tanks were not well enough armored to

"Tokyo or Bust" – an M4 of the 44th Tank Battalion – during the fighting in the hills east of Manila on March 10, 1945. This is a late production M4 with the hybrid hull that had a cast front section and a welded rear section.

survive even the smallest US anti-tank weapons. Nor did the terrain encourage such tactics. Instead, Yamashita decided to disperse the 2nd Tank Division on Luzon to form the nucleus of a series of village strongpoints, intended to slow the US Army advance while his other units withdrew north.

The US Army landings began on Leyte in October 1944. There were few Japanese tanks on this island, and US Army tank battalions were mainly used to provide infantry support. The US Army landed on Luzon beginning on December 15, 1944. The first significant tank fighting took place on January 24, 1945, at San Manuel. Through February, US Army infantry units supported by tanks gradually ground down the scattered garrisons of the Japanese 2nd Armored Division.

Not only did the Philippines campaign see the most extensive use of tanks by both sides, but it also included the largest and costliest urban fighting of the Pacific campaign – the liberation of Manila. This bloody battle began on February 3, 1945 and resulted in the death of over 100,000 civilians and the complete devastation of the city. The US Army's 37th Infantry Division was supported by the 44th Tank Battalion, and additional tank units later joined the fighting due to the tenacious Japanese defense.

M4A3 medium tank of 716th Tank Battalion in Action on Luzon, Philippines, February 1945. (Artwork by Richard Chasemore © Osprey Publishing)

The largest tank-vs.-tank battles of the Pacific War were fought in the Philippines in January–February 1945, pitting the Japanese 2nd Armored Division against several US Army tank companies and infantry units. Here, an M4A3 tank named "Classy Peg" of Co. C, 716th Tank Battalion, passes a smoldering Type 97 kai Shinhoto Chi-Ha of the Takaki Detachment of the 4th Company, 7th Tank Regiment, which had been knocked out during the fighting around Binalonan on January 17, 1945.

Technical comparison: M4A3 Sherman vs. Type 97 kai Shinhoto Chi-Ha

	M4A3(W)	Type 97 kai
Combat weight ton/tonne	34.8/31.5	17.4/15.8
Main gun	75mm	47mm
Gun penetration @500 yards	74–86mm*	67mm
Gun penetration @1,000 yards	66–79mm*	55mm
Engine	Ford GAA	Mitsubishi SA 12200VD
Horsepower	450	170
Horsepower/weight ratio (hp/ton)	12.9	9.7
Road speed (mph/kmh)	26/42	24/38
Range (miles/km)	100/160	130/210
Ground pressure (psi)	14.3	8.7
Armor thickness		
Turret front	89mm curved	33mm @ 0°
Turret sides	51mm @ 5°	26mm @ 11°
Hull glacis	64mm @ 47°	25mm @ 11°
Lower hull	51–114mm curved	20mm @ 30°
Hull side	38mm @ 0°	26mm @ 25°
*difference due to homogenous vs. face-hardened plate		

An M4A3 medium tank of the Co. C, 716th Tank Battalion, confronts a Japanese Type 97 kai Shinhoto Chi-Ha tank of the Shigemi Detachment, Japanese 2nd Armored Division, in the outskirts of San Manuel, Leyte, Philippines, on January 24, 1945. The 47mm gun on the Japanese tank had considerable difficulty in penetrating the frontal armor of the Sherman tank, while the Sherman's 75mm gun could penetrate the Chi-Ha's armor from any angle. (Artwork by Richard Chasemore © Osprey Publishing)

IWO JIMA

Like Tarawa, Iwo Jima would go down in Marine legend as one of their most bitter battles of the Pacific War. Iwo Jima was Tarawa writ large, a sulfuric volcanic island laced with natural caves and extensive Japanese fortifications. Japanese defenses on Iwo Jima were based on a honeycomb of caves and bunkers built into the volcanic island. The only Japanese armor on the island was the understrength 26th Tank Regiment entrenched as pillboxes. Marine amtanks formed the initial wave of the attack, followed by wave after wave of amtracs, totaling 68 amtanks and 380 amtracs. The Marines avoided the problems discovered at Saipan when using amtanks inland.

In anticipation of the Japanese defenses, the Marines accelerated their acquisition of flamethrower tanks. Three Marine tanks battalions were deployed on Iwo Jima, the 3rd, 4th, and 5th Marine Tank Battalions. Each Marine tank battalion in 1945 included 67 M4A2/M4A3 tanks, of which nine were armed with E4-5 auxiliary flamethrowers. By now, standard tactics had been developed to attack the well-fortified Japanese bunkers, called "corkscrew and blowtorch" tactics. The bunkers were suppressed with tank fire or satchel charges, and then burned out with flamethrowers. The main threats to Marine tanks on Iwo Jima were mines. Close cooperation between tanks and infantry and the relatively open nature of the terrain limited the Japanese from using their normal close-attack tactics against tanks.

M4A3 "Comet" (38) of Co. C, 4th Tank Battalion, seen near the landing beaches on Iwo Jima displays many of the modifications introduced by the battalion prior to the February 1945 landings. A special appliqué armor was added to the hull side consisting of an outer layer of wood to prevent the Japanese infantry from attaching magnetic anti-tank mines; supplemented with an inner layer of steel reinforcing mesh and concrete to offer added protection against the new Japanese 47mm anti-tank gun. "Birdcages" of steel reinforcing mesh have been added over the hatches and sandbags over the sponsons to defeat satchel charges.

Once again, the flamethrower tanks proved to be invaluable, especially the small numbers of POA-CWS-H1 flame tank that had a long-range flamethrower mounted as its main armament. A Marine after-action report concluded, "The flame-tank performed splendidly, and constantly overcame resistance which all other weapons had failed to silence." The commander of the 28th Marines called the flame tanks the "best single weapon of the operation." The 9th Marines described the mechanized flamethrower as the most powerful weapon at their disposal. Their after-action report attributed its effectiveness to the ability of the flame stream to enter small pillbox apertures

The M4A3 tank named "Co-Ed" (40) of Co. C, 4th Tank Battalion, was one of four tanks in the battalion on Iwo Jima equipped with the POA-CWS-H1 flamethrower mounted in place of the main gun. This was by far the most successful of the flamethrowers adopted by the Marine Corps during the Pacific fighting and was in great demand when Japanese bunkers were encountered.

RIGHT M4 flame tank with POA-CWS-H1 flamethrower. (Artwork by Richard Chasemore © Osprey Publishing)

BELOW RIGHT M4A3 medium tank, Co. B, US Marine 4th Tank Battalion, Iwo Jima, 1945. (Artwork by Richard Chasemore © Osprey Publishing)

and cave openings, engulfing all contours and folds with fire. Defenses that had withstood constant artillery, naval gunfire, and close-range 75mm tank gun succumbed to the POA-CWS-H1. The V Corps commander identified the mechanized flamethrower as "the only effective means" of attacking the numerous pillboxes, bunkers, and fortified caves. In contrast to the POA-CWS-H1, the E4-5 auxiliary flamethrower was not well liked. "The short range of the small (E4-5) flame thrower rendered it next to useless… The E4-5 flame thrower has too little range, takes too long to refuel, and does not have sufficient duration of fire."

M4A3, Co. C, US Marine 4th Tank Battalion, Iwo Jima, 1945. (Artwork by Richard Chasemore © Osprey Publishing)

OKINAWA

The largest combined amphibious operation of the war took place at Okinawa in April 1945 on the heels of the Iwo Jima campaign. The Okinawa fighting was the first battle on Japanese soil, and it was a brutal foretaste of the expected invasion of the Japanese Home Islands. After the fruitless experience of the 2nd Armored Division in the Philippines, the Japanese Army decided to retain its best armor for the defense of the Home Islands. The only major Japanese tank unit on Okinawa was the understrength 27th Tank Regiment that was mostly dug-in as static strongpoints.

ABOVE T6 device, US Army 711th Tank Battalion, Okinawa, April 1945. (Artwork by Henry Morshead © Osprey Publishing)

RIGHT The LVT(A)4 underwent several upgrades after the Marianas campaign. These Marine LVT(A)4 along the seawall on Okinawa on May 10, 1945 have added armor around the turret opening as well as an added .50-cal machine gun for vehicle defense.

The amphibious landings involved a combined Army/Marine total of 290 amtanks and 872 amtracs. Four divisions were put ashore on the main beaches, and additional units were used to attack neighboring islands. The critical role played by US tanks in the Marianas, on the Philippines, and on Iwo Jima led to the decision to commit the heaviest US tank force ever in the Pacific theater, totaling eight Army and two USMC tank battalions, and two USMC separate tank companies, totaling over 800 tanks. In addition, there were hundreds of Marine amphibious tanks, Army SP guns, half-tracks, and other armored vehicles. General Lemuel Shepherd of the 6th Marine Division later commented that "if any one supporting arm can be singled out as having contributed more than any other during the progress of the campaign, the tank would certainly have to be selected."

The success of flamethrower tanks in previous campaigns led to great demand for more of these weapons. Due to shortages, a decision was made that the prized POA-CWS-H1 flamethrower tanks would be concentrated in the Army's 713th Flame Tank Battalion to support both Army and Marine units.

The 1st Marine Tank Battalion after-action report summarized the tactics on Okinawa:

> Tanks fought at all times as infantry tanks and functioned as a major direct fire close-support weapon. At no time did tanks operate beyond the observation and cover of the infantry. Terrain and density as well as the type of enemy underground defenses precluded successful panzer attack and none was attempted by this battalion. Such tactics at times attempted by the Tenth Army tank units met with disaster in each case… A highly effective, battle-proven Tank-Infantry SOP [standard operating procedure] had been used in training and numerous refinements in the technique of employment had been developed to a high degree prior to this operation. Of particular importance and inestimable value was the prior establishment between infantry and tank units of mutual trust and pride in each other and a realization of the power of the combined team.

The Japanese defenders viewed the American tank-infantry team with alarm. Following his capture, the commander of the Japanese 22nd Separate Automatic Gun Battalion – a corps-level 47mm anti-tank gun unit – remarked that "the tank-infantry team on this operation was so successful that he did not see how any defense line, however protected, could not be penetrated… He was astounded with the volume of fire laid down by the tanks and the speed with which the American tank can traverse and bring fire to bear upon Japanese anti-tank guns after the anti-tank gun opens fire."

There was universal praise for the valuable contribution by the 713th Army Flamethrower Tank Battalion. An Army observer group reported that "the consensus of opinion … is that the armored flamethrower is a most valuable weapon, as it will kill the enemy or cause him to leave positions that no other weapon can reach. It is quite a morale builder to our own infantry. This was proven on numerous occasions as our infantry would move forward with the flame tank but not with standard tanks." The 17th Infantry, 7th Division, reported that the flame tanks "were invaluable against enemy entrenched in coral formations, heavy undergrowth and in caves, driving them from these positions when all other means had failed … in some cases flame tanks were the only weapons which could drive the enemy from positions." The 7th Division reported that the flame tanks "were outstandingly successful and of the greatest value" and recommended that in the future one company in each tank battalion attached to infantry divisions be equipped with flame tanks.

US plans for the final invasion of the Japanese Home Islands placed considerable emphasis on tanks due to their demonstrated value in the Okinawa operation. One of the few demands from the Army commanders in the Pacific was for a better flame-throwing tank, preferably with a longer-range flame gun and better armor. Ordnance obliged by redesigning the M4A3E2 assault tanks with a flame gun, and there were plans to rebuild the surviving assault tanks in Europe in this configuration. This apocalyptic final battle never took place.

An M4 tank with a POA-CWS-H5 main armament flamethrower of the US Army's 713th Tank Battalion attacking a cave defense on Okinawa on June 25, 1945.

CONCLUSION

Until World War II, American tank development was unremarkable. Nevertheless, design work at Rock Island Arsenal in the 1930s established a sound technical basis for the enormous expansion of American tank production in 1940–41.

At the outset of World War II, American tank policy contrasted from that of its allies and adversaries in several respects. The most important difference was the enormous distances from America's tank factories in the industrial Midwest to the battlefields in Europe and the Pacific. This constrained tank designs in weight and size due to the difficulties of shipping such heavy weapons over long distances. As a result, the US Army was reluctant to procure heavy tanks such as the German Tiger and Panther. The distance between the manufacturing plants and the battlefields also encouraged the US Army to place particularly high emphasis on reliability. It was impractical to send tanks back to industrial facilities in the United States for rebuilding due to premature mechanical exhaustion or technical failings. American tanks earned a well-deserved reputation for reliability and ease of maintenance compared with many European designs.

American tank development during World War II suffered from a number of problems, both tactical and technical. The Ordnance Department was not yet accustomed to the dynamics of machine-vs.-machine warfare. Its traditional products such as small arms and artillery did not require rapid evolution. Their principal targets were enemy soldiers, and this mission did not change greatly through time. Improvements were always desired but tended to be incremental and slow. A Springfield rifle from 1903 may have been outdated by 1941 but was still a viable weapon. Likewise, a 155mm gun from 1918 could still perform its mission in 1941. In contrast, a 6-Ton tank from 1918 was useless by 1941 in all critical respects: armor protection, armament, and mobility. Machine-vs.-machine combat demanded a more robust developmental perspective since the opposing weapons, such as enemy tanks, anti-tank guns, and other weapons, determined the viability of the American tank on the battlefield.

Neither Ordnance nor the Army Ground Forces were organizationally prepared to assess the future threat in a timely fashion. Traditionally, Ordnance relied on the combat arms to establish the requirements for future weapons. The AGF policy of "battle-need" depended on feedback from the combat theater to determine future weapons requirements. In the European theater, the evolution of tank and anti-tank technology was very rapid in 1941–43. Much of this was invisible to American observers since the Russian Front dominated German weapons development. Britain showed greater perception of these dynamics, but Anglo-American cooperation in tank development was not synchronized enough to accelerate American technological improvements in the critical years of 1942–43.

Of the key benchmarks of tank design – armor, firepower, and mobility – the most serious deficit of US tanks and tank destroyers in 1944 was in firepower. Ordnance failed to develop a dedicated tank gun capable of defeating the 1944 threat. The 76mm gun had mediocre armor penetration compared with German tank guns, largely due to a failure to anticipate the 1944 threat. Part of the problem was that Ordnance policy limited the use of high-pressure propellant loads in order to reduce barrel erosion and extend gun-tube life. This was part of the broader effort to increase the reliability and durability of US guns. But at the same time, it reduced the velocity of tank gun projectiles and their armor penetration. In an assessment after the war, the Equipment Board of the Army Ground Force, ETOUSA, specifically recommended that "long [tank] gun tube life should be reduced in favor of higher velocities."

The tank gun problem was not the fault of Ordnance alone, but of the combat arms as well. The AGF, Armored Force, and Tank Destroyer Center failed to establish the need for better anti-armor weapons until it was too late. The outcry over the shortcomings in US tanks after the Battle of the Bulge occurred too late for Ordnance to respond beyond modest extemporizations, such as the dispatch of small numbers of Pershing tanks. In the event, this didn't really matter a great deal since the German panzer force had been gutted in the Ardennes and no longer played a major role in the European theater after January 1945.

Although the armor protection of the Sherman has been widely criticized, it should be recalled that it had frontal hull armor of 51mm angled at 56 degrees, which provided it an effective thickness of 91mm. By contrast, the vaunted Tiger I had effective frontal hull armor of 101mm. The problem with the Sherman in tank-vs.-tank combat was not so much its armor, which was not so different from typical German tanks, but rather its inability to penetrate German tanks in frontal engagements due to its mediocre guns.

While the Sherman was technically inferior to the Panther in 1944, it should be noted that the Panther represented only a fraction of German tank and AFV strength. For example, at the start of the Normandy campaign, the Panther constituted about a third of German tanks strength and only a quarter of overall German tank and AFV strength. "AFV" here refers to tank surrogates such as Sturmgeschütz assault guns and Panzerjäger tank destroyers.

Even during the Battle of the Bulge, the Panther constituted less than 40 percent of German tank strength, and only about a quarter of total German tank and AFV strength. The Tiger was never more than a tiny fraction of German panzer strength in the ETO.

Not only were the vaunted Tiger and Panther only a fraction of German panzer strength, but the Wehrmacht was significantly outnumbered through the ETO campaign largely due to America's prodigious tank output. In Normandy in June 1944, about 1,800 panzers and AFVs faced about 4,700 British tanks and 1,100 American tanks. By the beginning of August 1944, panzer strength had been reduced to only about 590 operational tanks compared with about 2,100 American and 4,500 British/Canadian tanks, or an 11-to-1 imbalance. The start of the Battle of the Bulge in December 1944 was one of the few times that the Wehrmacht had a larger tank and AFV force than opposing US units. Due to German losses and the American transfer of tanks to the Ardennes, by the end of the campaign in mid-January 1945 the Wehrmacht again suffered its usual imbalance, with about 865 panzers and AFVs facing 3,040 US tanks and AFVs. The German panzer force in the West declined precipitously after the Battle of the Bulge, numbering only about 920 operational tanks and AFVs in early February 1945, falling to about 195 in mid-March 1945. US tank and AFV strength climbed from 12,220 in February 1945 to 13,560 by war's end. British/Canadian/Polish strength went from 7,745 to about 8,870 at war's end. In other words, the Wehrmacht was outnumbered in tank and AFV strength about 20-to-1 in February 1945 and about 100-to-1 by March 1945.

The relative importance of tank-vs.-tank fighting in World War II is usually exaggerated. This has especially been the case in recent years due to the advent of popular online games such as "World of Tanks" and "War Thunder." These games unrealistically portray tank combat exclusively as a tank-vs.-tank contest. In reality, US tanks in World War II mainly engaged other types of targets. Enemy tanks and armored vehicles represented only 14 percent of targets, anti-tank guns another 13 percent, while troops, strongpoints, and other targets represented the remaining 73 percent. In terms of US tank casualties, about half of US tank losses were due to enemy gunfire, with mines being the next largest threat at about 17 percent of US tank losses. Patton's Third US Army estimated that of their tanks' gunfire casualties, only about 30 percent were due to German tanks or assault guns while about 70 percent were due to towed anti-tank guns. So, roughly 15 percent of US tank casualties in the ETO in 1944–45 were due to German tanks and other armored vehicles.

Wartime American tank production increased a hundredfold from about 300 tanks in 1940 to about 30,000 tanks in 1943. This remarkable industrial achievement occurred even though other production programs including aircraft and warships had higher priority. The scale of American tank production was strongly shaped by Roosevelt's decision to support Allied armies via Lend-Lease. More than 40 percent of American tank and tank destroyer production was exported via Lend-Lease. The United States supplied Britain with more tanks and tank destroyers than total British production in 1941–45. American supplies to the Soviet Union were about 13 percent of the Red Army wartime supply, but this was largely due to Soviet preference for American trucks over American tanks.

The US Army conducted a number of studies after the war to examine combat lessons. There was an almost universal rejection of the tank destroyer concept in favor of the tank taking over this mission. For example, the Equipment Review Board of Army Ground Forces, ETOUSA, concluded that "The characteristics required in tanks and in self-propelled tank destroyers for fighting tanks are so alike that there is no justification for a separate line of tank destroyers." This largely ended the development of tank destroyers in the United States. The trend toward the integration of tanks as an organic element of infantry divisions continued during post-war reorganization, accompanied by considerable development of heavy tanks after the war, based on the wartime encounters with the German Tiger and Tiger II heavy tanks. However, US Army actually produced very few heavy tanks, preferring instead to design medium tanks with better guns that were capable of defeating most enemy tanks.

APPENDIX

AMERICAN TANKS BY THE NUMBERS

US tank production 1940–45

	1940	1941	1942	1943	1944	1945	Total
M2A4 light	325	40	10				375
M3 light		2,551	7,841	3,425			13,817
M5 light			2,858	4,063	1,963		8,884
M22 light				680	150		830
MH (T14/T16)*			240				240
MH (KNIL)**		65	363	125			553
LVT(A) amtank			3	288	1,708	670	2,669
M24 light					1,930	2,801	4,731
M3 medium		1,342	4,916				6,258
M4 (75mm)			8,017	21,245	3,504	651	33,417
M4 (76mm)					7,135	3,748	10,883
M4 (105mm)					2,286	2,394	4,680
M26***				1	339	2,374	2,714
Other med, heavy	6	88	4	39			137
Total	331	4,086	24,252	29,866	19,015	12,638	90,188

*Marmon-Herrington light tanks for China **Marmon-Herrington tanks for Dutch East Indies
***includes T23 and T25

US armored vehicle production 1940–45

	1940	1941	1942	1943	1944	1945	Total
Tanks	331	4,086	24,252	29,866	19,015	12,638	90,188
Tank destroyers			639	6,879	1,882		9,400
SP Arty (tracked)			2,461	2,156	1,239	1,315	7,171
SP Arty (half-track)		87	2,880	9,356	1,974		14,297
Armored car	825	1,908	7,205	19,023	6,450	1,671	37,082
Half-track APC		5,424	9,846	21,585	3,394	920	41,169
LVT(A) amtrac				277	1,265	295	1,837
Other (armored tracked)		4	4,083	6,455	8,493	1,407	20,442
Total	1,156	11,509	51,366	95,597	43,712	18,246	221,586

Sherman: manufacture and distribution 1942–45

Type	Manufactured	Issued to US Army overseas	Issued to US Army Stateside	Issued to USMC	In depots 1945	Tests, other	US Sub-total	Lend-Lease
M4 (75mm)	6,748	3,573	372	0	240	414	4,599	2,149
M4A1 (75mm)	6,281	2,932	374	0	249	1,780	5,335	946
M4A2 (75mm)	8,053	48	1	493	62	36	640	7,413
M4A3 (75mm)	4,761	2,765	580	330	579	500	4,754	7
M4A3E2	254	250	0	0	1	3	254	0
M4A4	7,499	0	6	1	37	11	55	7,443
M4A6	75	0	62	0	13	0	75	0
M4A1/A3 (76mm)	7,968	5,174	545	1	837	81	6,638	1,330
M4A2 (76mm)	2,915	0	0	0	704	133	837	2,078
M4/-A3 (105mm)	4,680	2,009	556	289	1,119	114	4,087	593
Total	49,234	16,751	2,496	1,114	3,841	3,072	27,274	21,959

US tank production by factory 1941–45

Facility	Tank production 1940–45	% of Total
Detroit Tank Arsenal	22,234	25.2
American Car & Foundry	15,224	17.2
Fisher Tank Arsenal	13,137	14.9
Cadillac Motor Company	10,142	11.5
Pressed Steel	8,648	9.8
Pullman Standard	3,926	4.4
American Locomotive Works	2,985	3.4
Baldwin Locomotive Works	2,515	2.9
Massey Harris Company	2,473	2.8
Ford Motor Company	1,690	1.9
Lima Locomotive	1,655	1.9
Montreal Locomotive Works	1,144	1.3
Marmon-Herrington	1,070	1.2
Pacific Car and Foundry	926	1.0
Federal Machine	540	0.6
Rock Island Arsenal	94	*
International Harvester	7	*

US tank prices ($)

Type	Base price	with GFE*	Lend-Lease
M3A1 (gas) light tank	32,195	32,915	42,236
M5A1 light tank	25,949	27,057	37,661
M24 light tank	36,439	39,653	n/a
M3 medium tank	53,250	55,244	64,814
M4, M4A1 (75mm) medium tank	44,699	47,725	60,534
M4A1 (76mm) medium tank	47,569	51,509	69,288
M4 (105mm) assault gun	41,961	45,766	64,873
M4A2 (75mm) medium tank	42,788	45,814	60,214
M4A2 (76mm) medium tank	41,923	45,863	66,987
M4A3 (75mm) medium tank	41,530	44,556	60,214
M6A1 heavy tank	167,792	171,615	n/a
M26 heavy tank	76,266	81,324	83,273

*government-furnished equipment

US tank and tank destroyer strength in the ETO 1944–45*

	M5A1	M24	M4 (75, 76mm)	M4 (105mm)	M26	M10	M18	M36	Total
Jun 1944	1,489	0	2,202	114	0	691	146	0	4,642
Jul	1,545	0	2,093	132	0	743	141	0	4,654
Aug	1,693	0	2,557	156	0	758	176	0	5,340
Sep	1,695	0	2,423	163	0	763	170	0	5,214
Oct	1,643	0	2,464	238	0	486	189	170	5,190
Nov	1,800	0	2,832	312	0	573	252	183	5,952
Dec	2,206	0	4,076	459	0	790	306	236	8,073
Jan 1945	2,950	20	4,561	620	0	768	312	365	9,596
Feb	3,351	128	5,297	804	0	686	448	826	11,540
Mar	2,617	364	6,249	612	20	684	540	684	11,770
Apr	2,691	736	5,727	612	75	427	427	1,054	11,749
May	2,956	1,163	6,336	636	108	427	427	1,029	13,082

*as of the 20th of each month; US Seventh Army (6th Army Group) figures included starting in November

US tank and tank destroyer losses in the ETO 1944–45

	M5A1, M24	M4 (75, 76mm)	M4 (105mm)	M26	M10	M18	M36	Total
Jun 1944	52	167	4	0	1	0	0	224
Jul	26	121	3	0	17	0	0	167
Aug	201	557	2	0	28	6	0	794
Sep	116	436	11	0	40	6	0	609
Oct	156	237	10	0	71	14	2	490
Nov	83	257	11	0	45	7	5	408
Dec	134	495	28	0	62	44	21	784
Jan 1945	208	585	29	0	69	27	26	944
Feb	93	320	62	0	106	16	18	615
Mar	136	463	0	1	27	21	21	669
Apr	190	554	13	0	37	55	34	883
May	112	207	5	0	37	21	25	407
Total	1,507	4,399	178	1	540	217	152	6,994

GLOSSARY

AEF	American Expeditionary Force (in France, 1917–18)
AFV	Armor fighting vehicle
AGF	Army Ground Forces
ALCO	American Locomotive Company, Schenectady, NY
APC	Armor-piercing-capped
APCBC	Armor-piercing-capped ballistic-cap
APG	Aberdeen Proving Ground, Maryland
ASF	Army Service Forces
CCA	Combat Command A
CCB	Combat Command B
CCR	Combat Command R (reserve)
COSSAC	Chief of Staff to Supreme Allied Commander
CRSM	Cavalry Reconnaissance Squadrons – Mechanized
CWS	Chemical Warfare Service
EMCC	Engineer Mine Clearing Company
ETO	European Theater of Operations
ETOUSA	US Army in the ETO
FUSA	First US Army
GMC	Gun motor carriage
HMC	Howitzer motor carriage
HVAP	High-velocity armor-piercing
LVT	Landing Vehicle, Tracked
MTO	Mediterranean Theater of Operations
NARA	National Archives and Records Administration
NATO	North African Theater of Operations
NUSA	Ninth US Army
pdr	Pounder
PTO	Pacific Theater of Operations
RIA	Rock Island Arsenal, Iowa
SBG	Small Box Girder
SUSA	Seventh US Army
TUSA	Third US Army
Ton	short ton (2,000lb)
Tonne	Metric ton (1,000kg)

FURTHER READING

This book was compiled by the author from many of his previous Osprey Publishing titles. Rather than provide a lengthy bibliography, a list of these many books is provided below. For readers interested in specific US tanks, these volumes provide additional detail beyond that contained in this short survey. In addition, these books contain further bibliographic references. These Osprey titles have been heavily based on archival records, especially those at the National Archives and Records Administration (NARA II) in College Park, MD. The main record groups used by the author are listed below.

ARCHIVAL RECORDS

RG 156 (Entry 649A) Office of Chief of Ordnance, Technical Division
RG 156 (Entry 894) Records of Armored Force Board, Fort Knox
RG 160 Records of the Headquarters, Army Service Forces
RG 165 US Army Military Intelligence Division
RG 331 6th Army Group, G-3 Records
RG 331 Records of Headquarters, Supreme Headquarters Allied Expeditionary Force
RG 331 Headquarters, 12th Army Group Special Staff, Ordnance Section
RG 331 Headquarters, 12th Army Group Special Staff, Armored (AFV&W) Section
RG 337 Headquarters, Army Ground Forces
RG 337 Headquarters, Army Ground Forces, Requirements Division
RG 337 Records of Tank Destroyer Board, Fort Hood
RG 337 Records of Armored School
RG 337 Records of Cavalry School
RG 338 Records of US Third Army 1945–47
RG 338 Records of US 12th Army Group 1945–47
RG 338 Headquarters, ETO US Army, Armored Vehicles Section
RG 338 Headquarters, ETO US Army, Ordnance Section
RG 338 AFV&W Section, Headquarters, European Theatre of Operations US Army
RG 338 Headquarters, G-3, First US Army Group
RG 338 Headquarters, 12th Army Group
RG 338 Headquarters, Armored Force
RG 407, Headquarters, 12th Army Group, Armored Section
RG 407, US Army ETO, US Armored Division, Armored Group, Tank Battalion, Tank Destroyer Battalion after-action reports

BOOKS BY THE AUTHOR

Osprey Battle Orders Series

US Armored Divisions: The European Theater of Operations, 1944–45 (2004)
US Tank and Tank Destroyer Battalions in the ETO 1944–45 (2005)
US Armored Units in the North African and Italian Campaigns 1942–45 (2006)

Osprey Campaign Series

Lorraine 1944: Patton vs Manteuffel (2000)
Operation Cobra 1944: Breakout from Normandy (2001)
Battle of the Bulge 1944 (1): St Vith and the Northern Shoulder (2003)
D-Day 1944 (1): Omaha Beach (2003)
D-Day 1944 (2): Utah Beach and the UA Airborne Landings (2004)
Battle of the Bulge 1944 (2): Bastogne (2004)
Kasserine Pass 1943: Rommel's Last Victory (2005)
Anzio 1944: The Beleaguered Beachhead (2005)
Remagen 1945: Endgame Against the Third Reich (2006)
The Siegfried Line 1944–45: Battles on the German Frontier (2007)
Liberation of Paris 1944: Patton's Race for the Seine (2008)
Operation Dragoon 1944: France's Other D-Day (2009)
Operation Nordwind 1945: Hitler's Last Offensive in the West (2010)
Operation Pointblank: Defeating the Luftwaffe 1944 (2011)
Metz 1944: Patton's Fortified Nemesis (2012)
Sicily 1943: The Debut of Allied Joint Operations (2013)
Operation Market-Garden 1944 (1): The American Airborne Missions (2014)
Cherbourg 1944: The First Allied Victory in Normandy (2015)
Downfall 1945: The Fall of Hitler's Third Reich (2016)
St Lô 1944: The Battle of the Hedgerows (2017)
Brittany 1944: Hitler's Final Defenses in France (2018)
Mortain 1944: Hitler's Normandy Panzer Offensive (2019)

Osprey Duel Series

Panther vs Sherman: Battle of the Bulge 1944 (2008)
M4 Sherman vs Type 97 Chi-Ha: The Pacific 1945 (2012)
M10 Tank Destroyer vs StuG III Assault Gun: Germany 1944 (2013)
Panzer IV vs Sherman: France 1944 (2015)
Bazooka vs Panzer: Battle of the Bulge (2016)
Pershing vs Tiger: Germany 1945 (2017)
Panzerfaust vs Sherman: European Theater 1944–45 (2019)

Osprey New Vanguard Series

M3 & M5 Stuart Light Tank 1940–45 (1999)

M26/M46 Pershing Tank 1943–53 (2000)
M10 and M36 Tank Destroyers 1942–53 (2002)
M8 Greyhound Light Armored Car 1941–91 (2002)
M4 (76mm) Sherman Medium Tank 1943–65 (2003)
M24 Chaffee Light Tank 1943–85 (2003)
M18 Hellcat Tank Destroyer 1943–97 (2004)
US Anti-tank Artillery 1941–45 (2005)
M3 Grant/Lee Medium Tank 1941–45 (2005)
M551 Sheridan: US Airmobile Tanks 1941–2001 (2009)
US Marine Corps Tanks of World War II (2012)
US Amphibious Tanks of World War II (2012)
M7 Priest 105mm Howitzer Motor Carriage (2013)
US Flamethrower Tanks of World War II (2013)
Early US Armor: Tanks 1916–40 (2017)
Soviet Lend-Lease Tanks of World War II (2017)
Early US Army: Armored Cars 1915–40 (2018)
Tanks in the Battle of the Bulge (2020)
Tanks of D-Day 1944 (2021)
Allied Tanks in Normandy 1944 (2021)
Tanks in the Battle of Germany 1945: Western Front (2022)

Osprey Vanguard Series

The Sherman Tank in US and Allied Service (1981)
Armour of the Pacific War 1937–45 (1983)
US Armour Camouflage and Markings 1917–45 (1984)
US Light Tanks 1944–84 (1984)
Amtracs: American Amphibious Assault Vehicles (1987)
The Renault FT Tank (1988)

Osprey Warrior Series

US Army Tank Crewman 1941–45: European Theater of Operations (ETO) 1944–45 (2004)

Other Publishers

Armored Thunderbolt: The U.S. Army Sherman in World War II (Stackpole, 2008)
Armored Attack 1944: U.S. Army Tank Combat in the European Theater from D-Day to the Battle of Bulge (Stackpole, 2011)
Armored Victory 1945: U.S. Army Tank Combat in the European Theater from D-Day to the Battle of Bulge (Stackpole, 2012)

INDEX

Page numbers in **bold** refer to illustrations and their captions.